W9-CDY-114

EMPOWERMENT EVALUATION PRINCIPLES IN PRACTICE

Empowerment Evaluation Principles in Practice

edited by **David M. Fetterman**
and **Abraham Wandersman**

FOREWORD BY RICARDO A. MILLETT

THE GUILFORD PRESS
New York   London

© 2005 The Guilford Press
A Division of Guilford Publications, Inc.
72 Spring Street, New York, NY 10012
www.guilford.com

All rights reserved

No part of this book may be reproduced, translated, stored in a retrieval system, or transmitted, in any form or by any means, electronic, mechanical, photocopying, microfilming, recording, or otherwise, without written permission from the Publisher.

Printed in the United States of America

This book is printed on acid-free paper.

Last digit is print number: 9 8 7 6 5 4 3 2

Library of Congress Cataloging-in-Publication Data

Empowerment evaluation principles in practice / edited by David M. Fetterman, Abraham Wandersman.
    p. cm.
    Includes bibliographical references and indexes.
    ISBN 1-59385-114-6 (pbk.: alk. paper)—ISBN 1-59385-115-4 (hardcover: alk. paper)
    1. Evaluation research (Social action programs). 2. Organization.
3. Industrial organization. 4. Social systems. 5. Employee empowerment.
6. Human services—Evaluation. I. Fetterman, David M. II. Wandersman, Abraham.
    H62.E574 2005
    361'.0068'3—dc22

                                                              2004021022

Foreword

*E*mpowerment Evaluation Principles in Practice represents a significant leap forward in defining and operationalizing empowerment evaluation. The book sets its subject apart from participatory, collaborative, and emancipatory evaluation and makes the road to empowerment evaluation clear and compelling. With this volume, David M. Fetterman, Abraham Wandersman, and their fellow contributors draw a line in the sand. Their evaluation approach is authentically controlled "by the people and for the people." The book clearly delineates a set of principles that define the practice of empowerment evaluation and firmly posits the utility and purpose of this approach in the realm of a community-owned and -defined methodology. The evaluator's role is described as coach, teacher, friendly critic, and even expert. However, the evaluator does not establish the goals or strategies. As a partnership, the participants determine credible forms of evidence.

Empowerment evaluation is a seminal, critical, and welcome evaluation approach, particularly for all of us who lament the failure of the evaluation profession to shape and frame an approach that is as useful to practitioners working on the ground as it is to policymakers and others making decisions at the highest levels. Empowerment evaluation does not compromise on science or rigor—or on achieving results. It is an invaluable tool for those of us convinced that community residents have collective insights, wisdom, and experiences that can and should be mined to inform programs and policies.

As a foundation president, I embrace empowerment evaluation. I am also a contributor to its continual development and want to join the family of practitioners who assist in the growth and refinement of this authentic approach to program evaluation. I am convinced that our democratic society needs to hone tools and develop the capacity of its people to better define and address our increasing inequalities. Empowerment evaluation has a prominent role to play in the community and the nation. This is a challenge that cannot be left to the current experts alone.

RICARDO A. MILLETT, PhD
President, Woods Fund of Chicago

Contents

CHAPTER 1

A Window into the Heart and Soul of Empowerment Evaluation

LOOKING THROUGH THE LENS OF EMPOWERMENT EVALUATION PRINCIPLES

David M. Fetterman

Empowerment evaluation has become a global phenomenon, reaching the four corners of the Earth in less than a decade. It is a change process that has supported people and communities in improving their lives in places ranging from the corporate offices of Hewlett-Packard to townships in South Africa. Empowerment evaluation can also be found in the U.S. Department of Education's Office of Special Education and Rehabilitation Services as well as on Native American reservations. Empowerment evaluation has been used in higher education in accreditation self-studies as well as state department of education partnerships with local school districts to build local capacity (see *http://homepage.mac.com/profdavidf*). Empowerment evaluation has been applied to night ministries[1] as well as rabbinical colleges. Youths are conducting their own empowerment evaluations. It can be found operating in child abuse prevention programs as well as after school program collaborations. Empowerment evaluation projects are operating in countries ranging from Brazil[2] to Finland.[3] Empowerment evaluation has been used in reaching for the stars, contributing to the NASA/Jet Propulsion Laboratory's prototype Mars Rover (Fetterman & Bowman, 2002). Much has been written and discussed about empowerment evaluation, ranging from its methods to the characterization of empowerment evaluation as a movement (Scriven, 1997; Sechrest, 1997). However, empowerment evaluation is first and foremost about principles, theories, ideas, and values. This collection serves as a window into the heart and soul of empowerment evaluation, viewed through the lens of its principles. The principles of empowerment evaluation highlighted in this book are:

1. Improvement
2. Community ownership
3. Inclusion
4. Democratic participation
5. Social justice
6. Community knowledge
7. Evidence-based strategies
8. Capacity building
9. Organizational learning
10. Accountability

These principles guide every part of empowerment evaluation, from conceptualization to implementation. The principles of empowerment evaluation serve as a lens to focus an evaluation. The principle of inclusion, for example, recommends erring on the side of including rather then excluding members of the community, even though fiscal and scheduling constraints might suggest otherwise. The capacity building principle reminds the evaluator to provide community members with an opportunity to collect their own data, even though it might initially be faster and easier for the evaluator to collect the same information. The accountability principle guides community members to hold one another accountable. It also situates the evaluation within the context of external requirements. The community is accountable for reaching specific standards or delivering specific results, products, and/or outcomes.

Empowerment evaluation is secondarily about methods and specific activities. Some methods are more empowering in their orientation than others. Communities may adopt a three-step approach (Fetterman, 2001) or a 10-step approach, such as the Getting to Outcomes model (Wandersman, Kaftarian, Imm, & Chinman, 1999; Wandersman, Imm, Chinman, & Kaftarian, 2000; Chinman, Imm, & Wandersman, 2004). In addition, there are many specific tools and methods that can be used to conduct empowerment evaluations, ranging from online survey software to video storytelling. However, these are only tools to accomplish specific objectives. Empowerment evaluation practice is a reflection or manifestation of empowerment evaluation principles and values.

The principles chapter (Chapter 2) is the heart of the collection and the product of a collaborative endeavor by a group of experienced empowerment evaluators. Numerous animated discussions transpired and multiple drafts were generated. These were followed by additional conference calls as well as individual telephone conversations. Principles were added and subtracted. Although there wasn't 100% agreement about every principle, the group came to a consensus about the 10 principles discussed in this collection.[4] The collaborative approach used to write the principles chapter spilled over into the rest of the collection, encouraging a critical friend spirit that influenced the other chapters, resulting in higher-quality exchange of ideas and product.

OVERVIEW

This introductory chapter is designed to prepare the reader for our presentation of the principles, as well as the remaining chapters in the volume. This chapter begins with a brief sketch of our past, since it provides insight into the present and informs our future. It highlights the similarities and differences among collaborative, participatory, and empowerment evaluations. This historical contextualization represents a foundation of understanding about empowerment evaluation.

It is followed by a discussion about process use and quality. The power of having people conduct their own evaluation cannot be overstated. In addition, the quality of the evaluation is influenced by the number of people involved in the evaluation, the types of individuals who participate in the evaluation, and the configuration of principles applied to the effort. The discussion about process use makes more sense when grounded in empowerment evaluation's historical context, particularly given the influence of collaborative and participatory approaches.

Such terms as empowerment, empowerment evaluation, participatory democracy, community, and self-determination are fundamental to the discourse about empowerment evaluation. There are definitions for each of these terms in various evaluation texts; however, the terms are like a Rorschach test for many, generating multiple meanings for the same term. A brief discussion about these pivotal terms allows us to speak the same language before engaging in our discussion about principles and practices throughout this collection. In the same way that it is useful to speak the same language about common terms, it is also important to speak the same language about how we define the role of the empowerment evaluator.

The role of the empowerment evaluator entails many assumptions. Empowerment evaluators are critical friends. They ensure that community members remain in charge of the evaluation. However, it is important to dig a little deeper into that role since it shapes how the principles are applied in practice. The role of the empowerment evaluator is characterized more by facilitation and influence than by outright authority.

An introduction to these principles would not be complete without discussing a few underlying theories that help explain what a community of learners does in practice. The theories of action and use help communities reduce the gap between the espoused theory of what a program is designed to do and what people actually accomplished in practice. It is important to have this theoretical model in mind when examining the principles and case studies. The theories presented in this chapter are not the only theories used in empowerment evaluation, but they are instructive. (See Fetterman, 2001, pp. 12–14; Zimmerman, 2000; Mithaug, 1991, 1993, for a discussion about additional theories used in empowerment evaluation.) The discussion also demonstrates how there is nothing as practical as a good theory.

One final section pertains to the order of the principles. There is no absolute rank or order that can be applied to every situation and context. However, there is a logical flow of the principles in practice. This exploration into order and sequencing sheds light on the interdependence of the principles with one another.

These introductory comments, ranging from terminology to theory as well as roles and relationships, are all baseline understandings. They serve to prepare the reader for an in-depth discussion about the specific principles and the case examples throughout the collection. The remainder of this chapter provides a summary of each chapter included in this book. It is an intellectual road map for the rest of the journey.

RECENT HISTORY: SPEAKING TO THE HEART OF EVALUATION

The roots of empowerment evaluation influence its practice (see Alkin, 2004). Empowerment evaluation was introduced in a presidential address at the American Evaluation Association (Fetterman, 1994). The empowerment evaluation approach was painted with broad strokes focusing on the definition, conceptual roots, and facets—including facilitation, advocacy, illumination, and liberation. In addition, caveats and concerns were raised. The new approach created a tremendous amount of intellectual and emotional excitement and commentary. It was an idea "whose time had come." The approach was embraced by evaluators from around the world. It also touched a nerve among traditional evaluators, resulting in highly charged exchanges in *Evaluation Practice* (Fetterman, 1995; Stufflebeam, 1994). Proponents of the approach made it clear that "empowerment evaluation is not a panacea" (p. 10). Nevertheless, evaluators seized the moment and applied the approach to a wide-variety of programs and diverse populations. Empowerment evaluation spoke to issues at the very heart of evaluation: Who is in control? What is the purpose of evaluation? Who am I (as an evaluator)?

The introduction of empowerment evaluation to the American Evaluation Association and the resulting dialogues led to the first collection of works about this approach, titled *Empowerment Evaluation: Knowledge and Tools for Self-Assessment and Accountability* (Fetterman, Kaftarian, & Wandersman, 1996). The collection highlighted the work of the W. K. Kellogg Foundation, a well-recognized philanthropic organization, and the Accelerated Schools Project, a national educational reform movement, both of which adopted empowerment evaluation. Demonstrating the breadth and depth of empowerment evaluation, this book presented case examples that ranged from battered women's shelters to HIV prevention initiatives. The volume, which launched a new approach to evaluation, also represented a fundamental developmental stage in empowerment evaluation.

A second book, *Foundations of Empowerment Evaluation* (Fetterman, 2001), raised the bar in empowerment evaluation. While respecting other models, it provided a clear three-step approach to empowerment evaluation. In utilizing case examples, including a high-stakes higher education accreditation self-study, the book also applied particular standards to empowerment evaluation, including utility, feasibility, propriety, and accuracy standards (see Joint Committee on Standards for Educational Evaluation, 1994). *Foundations of Empowerment Evaluation* made several additional contributions, including:

1. Explaining the role of process use (as people conduct their own evaluations).
2. Comparing collaborative, participatory, and empowerment evaluation.
3. Discussing similarities with utilization-focused evaluation.
4. Discussing the multiple purposes of evaluation, including program development, accountability, and knowledge.

This collection was followed by a number of articles and contributions to encyclopedia and leading texts in the field (e.g., Fetterman, 2004a, 2004b;

Wandersman et al., 2004). Empowerment evaluation, at that stage of development, had become a part of the intellectual landscape of evaluation. However, the roots of empowerment evaluation grow much deeper.

DIGGING A LITTLE DEEPER: SIMILARITIES AND DIFFERENCES

One of the best ways to see the future is to look to one's past. Empowerment evaluation owes a debt to many evaluation traditions that influenced its formation and development. It did not emerge from a vacuum. The similarities to other approaches are not accidental. Empowerment evaluation has much in common with collaborative and participatory forms of evaluation. For example, participatory research and participatory evaluation, close relatives (or cousins) of empowerment evaluation, created an environment conductive to the development of empowerment evaluation (Brunner & Guzman, 1989; Cousins & Earl, 1995; Green, 2003; Green & Mercer, 2004; King, 2004; Minkler & Wallerstein, 2002; Whitmore, 1998). Participatory evaluation's focus on participation and active engagement are features central to empowerment evaluation. Similarly, its commitment to local control and capacity building are aligned with empowerment evaluation values. Participatory evaluation laid much of the philosophic and political groundwork for empowerment evaluation.

Collaborative approaches to evaluation also shaped the tone and tenor of empowerment evaluation (Oja & Smulyan, 1989; O'Sullivan, 2004; Stull & Schensul, 1987). Collaborative approaches compel the evaluator to listen, share the evaluative endeavor, and work together with other participants.[5] Collaborative forms of evaluation also demonstrate a respect for participants' views. Valuing community knowledge is a basic theme, or leitmotif, in empowerment evaluation.

Utilization-focused evaluation's emphasis on use (Alkin, Daillak, & White, 1979; Patton, 1996) is a central tenet in empowerment evaluation. Empowerment evaluation is designed to be constructive, helpful, and useful at every stage of the evaluation. The pragmatic and utilitarian interplay between theories of use and action discussed later in this chapter reinforces this characterization about empowerment evaluation. Democratic evaluation (Greene, 1996; House & Howe, 1999; MacDonald, 1977; Papineau & Kiely, 1994) shares the same commitment to underrepresented stakeholders as empowerment evaluation. Both democratic and empowerment evaluation approaches engage stakeholders in a dialogue about program and policy change. The list of additional influences is enormous, ranging from the organizational development and transformation literature (Argyris & Schön, 1978; Preskill & Torres, 1999; Mezirow, 1991) to that relating to the reflective practitioner (Schön, 1987). These acknowledgments, although incomplete, are an appreciation of the work conducted before and alongside empowerment evaluation. This work continues to inform empowerment evaluation theory and practice.

The similarities among these closely aligned approaches provide some insight into the history and culture of empowerment evaluation. The differences are also useful in defining what empowerment evaluation is and is not. There are real differences between empowerment evaluation and closely related approaches. There have been significant contributions to differentiating among collaborative, participatory, and empowerment evaluation (Alkin, 2004; Christie, 2003; Cousins, 2003; Cousins & Whitmore, 1998; Fetterman, 2001). For example, Cousins, Donohue and Bloom (1996) have highlighted the high degree of stakeholder participation and control that distinguishes empowerment evaluation from participatory (Brunner & Guzman, 1989), stakeholder-based (Bryk, 1983), and objectivist evaluation (Stufflebeam, 1994). Alkin and Christie (2004) note that "Although these approaches [participatory and empowerment evaluation] employ similar practices, to consider them synonymous would be a fundamental misunderstanding of the theories" (p. 56). They discuss distinguishing features of empowerment evaluation such as social justice ideals and process use. In addition they focus on goals: "Since participatory evaluation emerges from a utilization framework, the goal of the participatory process is increased utilization through these activities [design, implementation, analysis, and interpretation], as opposed to empowering those that have been oppressed, which is political or emancipatory in nature" (p. 56). Christie has taken the discussion one step further distinguishing how social justice ideals are practiced in empowerment evaluation as compared with other social justice-oriented approaches such as House's deliberative democratic evaluation (Christie, 2003, pp. 18–19). According to Christie, in empowerment evaluation stakeholders have "*a role in all aspects of the evaluation*, from inception to conclusion"; however in deliberative democratic evaluation, stakeholders have "a role in limited aspects of the evaluation" (pp. 18–19).

O'Sullivan (2004) also contrasts collaborative, participatory, and empowerment evaluation. O'Sullivan begins by presenting Cousins's definition of collaborative evaluation, which is "any evaluation in which there is a significant degree of collaboration or cooperation between evaluators and stakeholders in planning and/or conducting the evaluation" (Cousins, Donohue, & Bloom, 1996, p. 210). She also presents their definition of participatory evaluation, which is "applied social research wherein evaluators train key program staff to work with them in the evaluation" (O'Sullivan, 2004, p. 24). O'Sullivan draws the line between her own collaborative work and empowerment evaluation, which helps to further define empowerment and distinguish it from collaborative forms of evaluation. "The participation of program staff in the evaluation, however, does not allow the evaluator to abrogate fundamental responsibility for the evaluation" (p. 26). In addition, according to O'Sullivan, "Collaborative evaluation is often empowering to participants. It enhances their understanding of evaluation so that they gain new skills. As such, it is a valuable positive outcome of the process, but not an intended one as described by Fetterman et al. (1996) or Burke (1998)" (O'Sullivan, 2004, p. 26). In other words, empowerment is a desirable side benefit of collaborative work but not required, whereas it is one of the primary goals of empowerment evaluation. Another distinguishing feature of empowerment evaluation is its commitment to evidence-based strategies, including the development of systems that incorporate evidence-based strategies (Wandersman et al., 2000). Empowerment evaluation's respect extends beyond the local community to the community of scholars who have worked hard to establish credible results concerning specific programs and interventions. Evidence-based strategies need to be adapted to the local context, but they can save the community precious time and resources and merit consideration before reinventing the wheel. Typically, evidence-based strategies are not part of collaborative or participatory evaluation approaches.

The dialogue about these similarities and differences in the literature has been useful and necessary. It has provided greater insight into the intellectual roots of empowerment evaluation. In addition, the distinctions make it easier to determine when to use one approach over another. When one steps back from the detailed comparisons and characterizations, however, one theme remains constant: the community's being in charge of its own evaluation remains the driving force behind empowerment evaluation.

GETTING INVOLVED: PROCESS USE

Ideally, members of the community, organization, or program conducting their own evaluation are engaged in various aspects of the evaluation, ranging from the conceptual direction to specific data collection, analysis, and reporting responsibilities. This is at the heart of process use and knowledge utilization (Fetterman, 2001; Patton, 1977). The more community members participate in and control the evaluation, the more likely they are to embrace the findings and recommendations, because they own them. However, not every community member engaged in the evaluation has to conduct a survey or write a report. The group may elect or appoint representatives. They (the individuals, groups, or representatives) must be involved in a substantive component of the evaluation and take control of the direction of the effort, but there are no absolute mandates concerning specific rules of engagement or the percentage of time on task.

QUALITY: CONFIGURATION OF PRINCIPLES ADOPTED

The quality of an empowerment evaluation will vary, depending on the configuration of principles adopted and applied to the effort. As a general rule, the quality increases as the number of principles are applied, because they are synergistic. Ideally, each of the principles should be in force at some level. However, specific principles will be more dominant than others in each empowerment evaluation. The principles that dominate will be related to the local context and purpose of the evaluation. Not all principles will be adopted equally at any given time or for any given project. However, the whole is greater than the sum of its parts. The presence or absence of any specific principle will have an impact that far exceeds the influence of that principle alone. In addition, the quality of an empowerment evaluation is enhanced as each member of the evaluation plays a prominent role in the evaluation, including the community member, evaluator, and funder.

QUALITY: LEVELS OF INVOLVEMENT

There are minimal and optimal levels of involvement in an empowerment evaluation. For example, if the evaluator is in complete control of the evaluation, then it is not an empowerment evaluation. Similarly, if the approach is top-down and decision making is dictated from outside of the program or by decree, then it is not an empowerment evaluation. If the group does not adopt an inclusive and capacity-building orientation with some form of democratic participation, then it is not an empowerment evaluation. However, if the community takes charge of the goals of the evaluation, is emotionally and intellectually linked to the effort, but is not actively engaged in the various data collection and analysis steps, then it probably is either at the early developmental stages of empowerment evaluation or it represents a minimal level of commitment. Similarly, if the group is inclusive and aimed at improvement, but does not adopt the principles of capacity building, democratic participation, or evidence-based strategies, then the evaluation may be only minimally empowerment-oriented. In contrast, a group that adopts principles such as social justice, improvement, inclusion, participatory democracy, community ownership, evidence-based strategies, and accountability is probably conducting an empowerment evaluation. In line with this picture, a group that is involved in the design, data collection, analysis, and reporting processes (and is guided by these principles) is probably conducting an empowerment evaluation. Levels of involvement are discussed in more detail in Chapter 3, "Empowerment Evaluation Principles in Practice: Assessing Levels of Commitment."

SPEAKING THE SAME LANGUAGE: TERMS AND CONCEPTS

The terms empowerment, empowerment evaluation, participatory democracy, community, and self-determination represent focal points for this collection and the field. A brief discussion about these terms serves to clarify and lay bare the evolving nature of empowerment evaluation terminology and practice. It also helps to ensure that we are all speaking the same language.

Empowerment is a pivotal concept in empowerment evaluation. It is an enabling and emancipatory concept (Fetterman, 1996, p. 16). Coombe (2002) expands on this idea: "Central to the empowerment concept is the importance of individuals and communities having influence and control over decisions that affect them (Israel et al., 1994, p. 3)." Empowerment is the process by which people take charge of their environment (physical, economic, social, cultural, and psychological) with the resources available to them (Zimmerman, 2000). Empowerment is most commonly associated with political or decision-making power. Empowerment evaluation is designed to share decision-making power. More precisely, empowerment evaluation places decision making in the hands of community members. However, there is another level that is important. It is psychological power. The ability of a group to achieve their goals as members of a learning community, improving their lives and the lives of those around them, produces an extraordinary sense of well-being and positive growth. People empower themselves as they become more independent and group problem solvers and decision makers. It is a liberating or emancipatory experience (Vanderplaat, 1995, 1997). Empowerment evaluation is about helping people help themselves.

"*Empowerment evaluation* is the use of evaluation concepts, techniques, and findings to foster improvement and self-determination" (Fetterman 1994). The definition has remained stable for over a decade—from Fetterman's 1993 presidential address to the American Evaluation Association, through two books (Fetterman et al., 1996; Fetterman, 2001), to the present. This book provides the evaluation community with an opportunity to unpack that definition in terms of principles and values that shape empowerment evaluation in practice. In that spirit, some of the chapters build on this foundational definition by highlighting more specifically the organizational learning and program improvement implications. For example, one definition that builds on this base is presented in the principles chapter (Wandersman et al., Chapter 2, this volume): "Empowerment evaluation is an evaluation approach that aims to increase the likelihood that programs will achieve results by increasing the capacity of program stakeholders to plan, implement, and evaluate their own programs" (p. 27). This carefully crafted sentence highlights the commitment to results or accountability as well as capacity building. It also emphasizes the concept of process use. This definition makes many of the implicit values of empowerment evaluation explicit. Similarly, Lentz et al., in Chapter 7 of this volume, on organizational learning, write:

> We continue to develop the definition of empowerment evaluation by discussing the use of cycles of reflection and action . . ., and knowledge creation to foster the development of the Collaborative as a learning organization with the capacity to use empowerment evaluation to inform the planning, implementation, and improvement of its initiatives. (p. 156)

This is perfectly consonant with the original definition. However, it brings the cycles of reflection and action to the forefront. In addition, it explicitly presents one of the central goals of empowerment evaluation: to create a learning organization. This evolution, expansion, and unpacking of the original definition is knowledge creation in action.

Participatory democracy is another foundational concept or principle that merits attention. The principle of inclusion focuses on bringing groups, often disenfranchised groups, to the table. Ethnic groups, religious groups, and individuals with disabilities are often left out of the conversation, simply because they were not invited when decisions were being made. Participatory democracy builds on this concept but focuses on the democratic nature of the participation or inclusion. There are two levels of participatory democracy. The first focuses on the mechanical means, such as voting or coming to a group consensus. The second emphasizes the environment created that is conducive to intelligent and shared decision making. It rests on the assumption that people can make intelligent and well-informed decisions and the actions when the proper environment is cultivated. Empowerment evaluation has the capacity to create this kind of environment.

Community is a simple term used to refer to the members of the group, nonprofit agency, or organization that conducts its own evaluation. A more precise but cumbersome term is community of evaluation use or practice. The term community does not refer to anyone on the street who is not aware of or engaged in the empowerment evaluation. A community of evaluation practice is the community of learners who apply evaluation concepts and techniques to assess their performance and plan for the future. They are the engine of a learning organization. Communities of evaluation use are groups of individuals who use evaluation to improve, first, their decision making and, second, their organizational behavior or performance. The first focuses on the application of evaluation concepts and techniques to their organization, to better understand how the organization is working. The second focuses on the use of the evaluation findings to improve performance.

Self-determination is the ability to govern oneself or chart one's own course in life (Fetterman, 2001). It involves numerous skills, including the ability to identify needs, establish goals, create a plan of action, identify resources, make rational choices, take appropriate steps or action, and evaluate short- and long-term results. Self-determination is similar to self-efficacy (Bandura, 1982). It is part of the theoretical foundation of empowerment evaluation. It is also a desired outcome.

This brief discussion is designed to help ensure that we are using the same terms in the same way, thus enhancing our ability to speak accurately and meaningfully as this dialogue continues. A brief discussion of the role of the empowerment evaluator will also help ensure that everyone is "on the same page" before launching into a detailed discussion about the principles.

THE ROLE OF THE EMPOWERMENT EVALUATOR: INFLUENCE VERSUS CONTROL

"People are demanding much more of evaluation and becoming intolerant of the limited role of the outside expert who has no knowledge or vested interest in their community (Green & Frankish, 1995)" (Coombe, 2002). Empowerment evaluators are critical minded friends. They support the purpose of the program. They have a vested interest in the program. For example, they may see the need for programs in their communities that serve high school dropouts, help prevent teenage pregnancy, or promote recovery from drug addiction. They may also want these programs to succeed because they care about their communities. When evaluators have a vested interest in programs, it enhances their value as critics and evaluators. They will be more constructively critical and supportive of the program because they want the program *to work*, that is, to succeed.

The empowerment evaluator facilitates and coaches community members engaged in evaluation. However, community members are in charge of the evaluation. The empowerment evaluator helps community members develop a rigorous and organized approach. Critical friends help community members clarify their theory of change. They also help the community establish a baseline, monitor specific interventions, and document change over time.

"Evaluation approaches that maintain the separate and hierarchical relationship between evaluator and community foster dependence and powerlessness and thereby mitigate against empowerment as an outcome" (Coombe, 2002; see also Wallerstein, 1992). The empowerment evaluator is not superior or inferior to any member of the community. However, as a facilitator, he or she does not dominate the dialogue. The evaluator can remove the "facilitator hat" occasionally to provide insights and expertise. This is a role of influence, not control over the evaluation process. The community remains in charge of the evaluation, from beginning to end. Typically, the evaluator would not cast a vote along with the community members as they make critical decisions. However, there are exceptions. In situations where the empowerment evaluator is a legitimate and ongoing community member (before and after the evaluation), he or she has a citizen's responsibility to cast a vote in the community decision-making process. For example, I served as a critical friend and facilitator at an institute undergoing an accreditation review. I was also a professor and research director at the institute. Thus, I had a responsibility to participate (with an actual vote) in each of the group's decisions. I did not dominate any discussion I facilitated and I asked a colleague to facilitate for me when I wanted to speak in my role as a research director. The role of facilitator precludes significant authority and minimizes contributions associated with that person's role. The group's voice comes first.

Overall, the role of an empowerment evaluator is complex and different from the traditional evaluator. It involves assessment, trust, facilitation, friendship, systematic inquiry, ethical and methodological standards, and a combination of traditional evaluation expertise with a commitment to (and expertise in) capacity building. The challenge is great, because "We've got a bunch of evaluators who do program evaluation; we've got a very small number of evaluators who do capacity-building evaluation" (Light, 2002). An accurate and shared understanding of empowerment evaluation terminology and the role of the empowerment evaluator is critical to be effective in helping people accomplish their goals and "close the gap" in practice.

CLOSING THE GAP: THEORIES OF USE AND ACTION

One of the primary tasks in an empowerment evaluation is the reduction in the gap between what people say they want to do and what they are actually doing in practice. The aim is to reduce "the gap" between what is intended and what actually happens. In order to accomplish this objective, empowerment evaluation relies on the reciprocal relationship between theories of action and use. A *theory of action* is usually the espoused operating theory about how a program or organization works. It is a useful tool, generally based on program personnel views. The theory of action is often compared with a theory of use.[6] The theory of use is the actual program reality, the observable behavior of stakeholders (see Argyris & Schön, 1978; Patton, 1997; Senge, 1994). People engaged in empowerment evaluations create a theory of action at one stage and test it against the existing theory of use during a later stage. Similarly, they create a new theory of action as they plan for the future. Because empowerment evaluation is an ongoing and iterative process, stakeholders test their theories of action against theories of use during various microcycles in order to determine whether their strategies are being implemented as recommended or designed. The theories go hand in hand in empowerment evaluation.

These theories are used to identify gross differences between the ideal and the real. For example, communities of empowerment evaluation practice compare their theory of action with their theory of use in order to determine if they are even pointing in the same direction. Three common patterns that emerge from this comparison include: in alignment, out of alignment, and alignment in conflict (see Figure 1.1). "In alignment" is when they are parallel or pointed in the same direction. They may be distant or close levels of alignment, but they are on the same general track. "Out of alignment" occurs when actual practice is divergent from the espoused theory of how things are supposed to work. The theory of use is not simply distant or closely aligned but actually off target or at least pointed in another direction. "Alignment in conflict" occurs when the theory of action and use are pointed in diametrically opposite directions. This signals a group or organization in serious trouble or in self-denial.

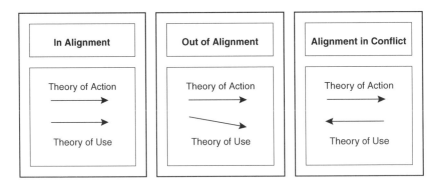

FIGURE 1.1. Contrasting patterns of alignment.

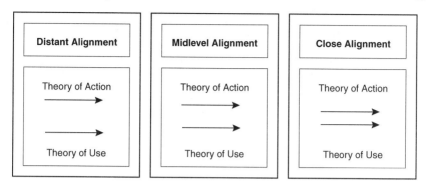

FIGURE 1.2. Aligning theories of action and use to reduce the gap.

After making the first-level comparison, a gross indicator, to determine if the theories of action and use are even remotely related to each other, communities of empowerment evaluation practice compare their theory of action with their theory of use in an effort to reduce the gap between them. This assumes they are at least pointed in the same direction. The ideal progression is from distant alignment to close alignment between the two theories. This is the conceptual space where most communities of empowerment evaluation strive to accomplish their goals as they close the gap between the theories (see Figure 1.2).

The process of empowerment embraces the tension between the two types of theories and offers a means for reconciling incongruities. This dialectic in which theories of action and use are routinely juxtaposed in daily practice creates a culture of learning and evaluation.

A SEQUENCE OR LOGICAL ORDER TO THE PRINCIPLES

Every community of learners has rules. The discourse is more manageable and efficient when terms and concepts are held in common. This chapter represents a conscientious effort to build a common foundation of understanding and shared meanings. One final point is explored before outlining the remainder of this book. Are these all the principles, and is there a logical sequence or order to the principles?

The answer is simple: the list of principles is not meant to be exhaustive, and the sequencing is not absolute. It would be difficult to argue that there is only one sequence or order to the principles that can be applied to every situation. However, a logical sequence or order can be identified or at least recommended. The 10 empowerment evaluation principles and the sequence or logical flow presented in this book is the product of a collaborative and deliberate endeavor by a team of empowerment evaluators.[7] The list and the relative order of the list have also benefited from the advice of colleagues on the Empowerment Evaluation listserv. The sequencing of the principles is discussed in detail in the conclusion, because it logically flows after a discussion about the principles and practice in the remainder of this collection.

SUMMARY

This chapter began by outlining the principles of empowerment evaluation. These principles represent the heart and soul of empowerment evaluation. In order to ensure a common set of understandings about empowerment evaluation, a few conceptual points were presented and discussed. This sets the stage for an engaging discussion about the principles and practices of empowerment evaluation in the remaining chapters in the book. A list of the key points made in the chapter is presented below:

1. *Principles shape practice.* Methods matter, but they are an extension of the values associated with the principles of empowerment evaluation.
2. *The past informs the present.* The theoretical and philosophical roots of empowerment evaluation shape practice. The similarities among collaborative, participatory, and empowerment evaluations are not an accident. The similarities should be recognized and embraced. They are reinforcing approaches to evaluation. However, there are differences between the approaches that should be acknowledged and examined to better understand empowerment evaluation's unique contribution.
3. *Process use is fundamental.* One of the constant underlying themes in empowerment evaluation is community involvement and engagement. Community members actively engaged in conducting their own evaluations remain the sign post for empowerment evaluation.
4. *The configuration of principles adopted will determine the quality of the empowerment evaluation.*
5. *The quality of the empowerment evaluation will increase as the level of community involvement in the evaluation increases.* Conversely, the quality will diminish if any one of the partners (community member, evaluator, or funder) decreases its investment and involvement in the effort.
6. *Terms and definitions matter.* Not all terms have to be operational-

ized. However, common understandings enhance communication about empowerment evaluation.

7. *The role of the empowerment evaluator is important.* The empowerment evaluator has authority in terms of expertise. Decision-making authority, however, remains in the hands of the community, as does control of the evaluation.

8. *Closing the gap between espoused theory and actual practice is the dialectic, or tension, that drives much of empowerment evaluation in practice.*

9. *There is no absolute sequence concerning these principles.* However, a logical order has been presented and can be helpful in building a meaningful and cohesive empowerment evaluation.

This summary crystallizes the most significant points in this chapter. It is like a scaffold, preparing readers for the next steps outlined in this book. A common understanding enables readers to have a more meaningful engagement with the principles and practice of empowerment evaluation.

OUTLINE OF THE BOOK

Empowerment Evaluation Principles in Practice represents the next logical step in the evolution of empowerment evaluation, making explicit the key values of empowerment evaluation. Chapter 2, collaboratively written and titled "The Principles of Empowerment Evaluation," represents the consensus of a group of empowerment evaluators concerning the principles underlying and guiding empowerment evaluation. The principles, as discussed earlier, include improvement, community ownership, inclusion, democratic participation, social justice, community knowledge, evidence-based strategies, capacity building, organizational learning, and accountability. Wandersman, Snell-Johns, Lentz, Fetterman, Keener, Livet, Imm, and Flaspohler unpack the terms used to express empowerment evaluation principles. These are the principles that make empowerment and self-determination possible. They are also the principles that guide program planning, implementation, and evaluation.

Chapter 3, "Empowerment Evaluation Principles in Practice: Assessing Levels of Commitment," is designed to provide scholars and practitioners with additional guidance in empowerment evaluation. Fetterman explains how the principles are applied to real world circumstances and conditions. For example, the inclusion principle reminds empowerment evaluators to include rather than exclude even when it is more expeditious and less expensive to leave hard-to-reach constituencies out of decision-making deliberations. This chapter also clarifies the distinctions between inclusion and democratic participation. The chapter makes a unique contribution by highlighting the roles and responsibilities of the three distinct groups affiliated with an empowerment evaluation: the evaluator, the community, and the funder. It concludes with a detailed discussion of the levels of empowerment evaluation by role in an easily accessible table format.

Chapter 4, "Lessons That Influenced the Current Conceptualization of Empowerment Evaluation: Reflections from Two Evaluation Projects," presents the first set of case studies in the collection. Case studies breathe life into discussions about principles and practice. The two case studies presented in this chapter are based on the same community health foundation initiative. Keener, Snell-Johns, Livet, and Wandersman reflect on the role of the empowerment evaluator, particularly concerning capacity building, improvement, and accountability. The chapter addresses the question of how much of the work and responsibilities are in the hands of the community as compared with the empowerment evaluator. It also addresses the issue of how to balance program improvement efforts with accountability requirements. Keener and colleagues highlight strategies for increasing evaluation capacity. The contributors also adumbrate later chapters in this collection by discussing the role of organizational structures and contexts in shaping empowerment evaluations. The tensions associated with overemphasizing one principle over another are also explored. The chapter concludes with a summary of lessons learned.

Chapter 5, "Empowerment Evaluation: From the Digital Divide to Academic Distress," highlights two specific empowerment evaluations. The first is a $15-million Hewlett-Packard Digital Village project, the purpose of which was to help disenfranchised communities across the United States bridge the digital divide. Empowerment evaluation was the tool to help them accomplish their goals. The accomplishments range from 18 American Indian tribes building the largest unlicensed wireless system in the country to the distribution of laptops to teachers and students in urban school systems. The second case example focuses on academically distressed schools in Arkansas Delta school districts. Using empowerment evaluation, these school districts emerged from academic distress. The results are significant because they demonstrate how useful empowerment evaluation is to guide standards-based work and produce results in terms of higher test scores. In addition, results included greater parental involvement, reduction of violence, and educational and administrative capacity building. Fetterman uses the principles to organize the presentation of each study. This approach demonstrates how each principle guides these projects. It also demonstrates that some principles apply more than others to specific projects or programs. Both projects received significant media attention, including television coverage.

Chapter 6, "Organizational Functioning: Facilitating Effective Interventions and Increasing the Odds of Programming Success," focuses on organizational contexts and conditions. It explores the relationship be-tween organizational characteristics and the successful implementation of effective interventions. Empowerment evaluators have become increas-ingly sensitive to the role of organizational contexts and conditions. They are significant factors determining the relative success of an empowerment evaluation. Livet and Wandersman view specific organizational character-istics as facilitators and inhibitors of the use of empowerment evaluation and the implementation of effective interventions. For example, some organizations are more receptive to empowerment evaluation or in align-ment with empowerment evaluation principles and practices. Other orga-nizations are more prepared to implement an empowerment evaluation than others, based on staffing, leadership, communication patterns or practices, tenure of staff members in the agency, expertise, organizational complexity, and philosophy. One of the key features of this chapter, as in Chapter 4, is that it is written for evaluators, practitioners, and funders. In addition it highlights a specific form of empowerment evaluation labeled "Getting to Outcomes." This chapter about organizational features and attributes sets the stage for the next chapter, which is also organizationally related.

Chapter 7 is the last case study presented in this collection. In "Empowerment Evaluation and Organizational Learning," Lentz, Imm, Yost, Johnson, Barron, Simone, and Treistman focus on a community coali-tion designed to prevent child abuse and neglect. This chapter demon-strates the role of empowerment evaluation in facilitating organizational learning while emphasizing the role of evidence-based strategies and accountability. In discussing the transformative nature of the dialogue and learning process that exists in a learning organization, these contributors elaborate the role of a dynamic community of learners in creating a learn-ing organization. For Lentz et al., empowerment evaluation is a "trans-formative process that aims to supply concepts, tools, and techniques to help individuals develop their capacity for intelligent judgment and action within the context of a dynamic community of learners" (p. 163). This chapter also highlights the significance of engaging the community, initiat-ing a conversation about evidence-based strategies, capacity building, and leadership. The chapter reinforces the earlier chapters in terms of viewing empowerment evaluation as a partnership encompassing the evaluator, the community member, and the funder.

Brad Cousins's Chapter 8 shares the insights of a critical friend. Titled "Will the Real Empowerment Evaluation Please Stand Up?: A Critical Friend Perspective," it is a critique, a comparison, and a reflection. It is designed to improve and refine our work. Cousins provides additional conceptual clarity regarding empowerment, collaborative, and participa-tory evaluations. His differentiation between practical and transformative participatory evaluations is instructive and sheds light on two similar streams in empowerment evaluation. Cousins posits two streams in empowerment evaluation: practical empowerment evaluation (P-EE) and transformative empowerment evaluation (T-EE). By differentiating these contrasting streams in empowerment evaluation, he helps users perceive the two different empowerment evaluation purposes and paths rather than viewing them as contradictions in practice. Most empowerment evaluations are pragmatic. However, many are also committed to transformative change in organizations, agencies, and people. Understanding the different purposes helps users select the most appropriate approach for the desired outcome. Identifying and acknowledging these distinctions within empowerment evaluation also allows for a more accurate and fair assessment of each type of empowerment evaluation in practice. For example, judging a practical empowerment evaluation using transformative empowerment evaluation criteria would be inappropriate and not particularly useful. This distinction also helps colleagues visualize a continuum of empowerment evaluation approaches. Cousins concludes with a few recommendations. He would like to see additional discussion about how the 10 principles of empowerment evaluation might be applied differently in practical and transformative streams. He would also like to see more detail about the problems and conflicts associated with many of these projects. Additional detail about the routine problems encountered in empowerment evaluations would be reassuring to other colleagues. They would be able to see the daily difficulties and have a more realistic expectation of what it is like to facilitate an empowerment evaluation. These are useful suggestions and recommendations posed by a critically minded friend. They are not met with defensive protestations but instead are embraced in the spirit in which they were intended, namely, to foster improvement.

Although we value these insights and comments, we recognize there is room for disagreement as well. One of the differences of opinion with our colleague is the focus on results. Cousins classifies empowerment evaluation primarily within the process-oriented domain; however, as discussed in Chapters 2, 3, and 5, empowerment evaluation is committed to *both* process and outcome accountability. The outcomes may range from building the largest unlicensed wireless system in the country to increases in Stanford 9 test scores. The bottom line is that empowerment evaluation has been and always will be committed to outcomes, or results.

This collection concludes with a reflection on the art and science of empowerment evaluation within two dimensions, time and space. Empowerment evaluation, as portrayed in textbooks, appears simple, linear, and easy. This chapter provides a logical sequence or order to the application of empowerment evaluation principles. There is a synergistic logic associated with this sequence of principles through time. However, the reality is that empowerment evaluations are difficult, periodically conflictual, and rarely a simple linear process. There are many false steps, obstacles, personalities, and renegotiated deadlines. Ironically, the difficulties associated with pursuing empowerment evaluations are typically the reason they are successful and sustainable. They engage large numbers of stakeholders. They invite diverse views, cultures, and ways of knowing. In addition, they are democratic. The principles guiding empowerment evaluation invite dialogue, which makes the conversation richer and the decisions stronger and more long-lasting. The process of accomplishing objectives as a group is fraught with difficulties. However, this process also providing the most rewarding moments in many people's lives, pushing people into the proximal zone of development—into a space beyond their comfort and perceived level of competence. The experience stretches people. The suggested sequence simply provides a community with a road map—one possible path among many others.

The conclusion builds on the discussion about the logical sequence of principles through time by focusing on another dimension: space. A three-dimensional view of empowerment evaluation is presented and discussed in terms of the space in which community capacity expands (or contracts). The level of human capital, empowerment, and self-determination is similar to water rising and falling—in this case in a social container—depending on the degree of participation and the degree to which the principles of empowerment evaluation are applied. The more (appropriate) people are engaged and the more complete the selection and application of the principles, the greater the level of empowerment and self-determination. These conceptualizations of empowerment evaluation are designed to help communities visualize both the goals and the process of empowerment and self-determination.

The contributors to this collection practice what they preach. They are an active and engaged community of learners. The list of principles was a product of much deliberation and dialogue. We have each grappled with our evolving knowledge of empowerment evaluation. The experience and "learnings" we share in this book are designed to help scholars and practitioners alike as we move empowerment evaluation one step forward.

ACKNOWLEDGMENTS

Abraham Wandersman deserves much of the credit for the collaborative process adopted to compose this work. He organized many of the discussions using email attachments with track changes to facilitate our dialogue online. He also arranged many of the conference calls. His insistence on quality, even in the face of harsh deadlines, helped produce a product we could all live with for some time to come. Using written comments and conference calls with senior authors, Abe's program evaluation students Jen Duffy, Laura Gambone, Alice Fields, and Annie Wright helped us grapple with challenging issues, as well as clarity, in several chapters. Jessica Snell-Johns provided valuable exchanges in each of our dialogues. Her attention to detail as well as the larger picture was invaluable. Dana Keener and Melanie Livet's commitment to produce the most accurate portrayal possible was commendable. Barry Lentz was an intellectual and theoretical powerhouse, reminding us of the Deweyian roots of our work. His instance on considering and reconsidering the sequence of the principles proved to be a critical contribution. Pamela Imm brought her practical experience to the discussion at every turn. Her unflagging commitment to discourse and advocacy concerning the representation of specific principles shaped the course of the book. Paul Flaspohler highlighted connections between the principles that might otherwise have gone unnoticed. Brad Cousins deserves much credit for serving in the difficult role of critical friend to a band of committed scholars and practitioners. His insights helped us grow and refine our thinking. A special thanks is extended to our colleagues on the Empowerment Evaluation listserv who generously provided comments and commentary about our work. William Shadish is a special colleague. He served as a sounding board for specific ideas including an effort to apply empowerment evaluation to the guiding principles. Denis Phillips and Eamonn Callan, colleagues at Stanford University, provided useful insights and clarifications about standards and guidelines from a philosophical perspective.

NOTES

1. The Night Ministry, which used an empowerment evaluation approach, is a nondenominational church-based organization that reaches out to Chicago's nighttime street communities (e.g., male and female prostitutes, chronically mentally ill individuals) through a street and health outreach program (see Wandersman et al., 2004).
2. Dr. Thereza Penna Firme (2003) at the Federal University of Rio de Janeiro and the Cesgrandio Foundation in Brazil is applying empowerment evaluation to educational programs in Amazonian Brazil.
3. Riitta Haverinen from Stakes National Research and Development Centre for Welfare and Health; Liisa Horelli, Research Fellow at the University of Helsinki; and Juha Siitonen (1998) from the University of Oulu and Heljä Antola Robinson from Bradley University are applying empowerment evaluation.
4. The process took longer than anticipated, paralleling empowerment evaluation practices in general. This is because it takes more time to consult with multiple stakeholders and engage in a dialogue about process and decisions. However, the quality is always much improved and more closely represents the values of the group.
5. Collaborative approaches are typified by attempts to "work together" with staff members and participants, with the understanding that the evaluator remains the "expert in charge."
6. Logic models are often used to determine the logic of linkages in a program theory. Theoretically there should be logical connections among resources, activi-

ties, and outputs. Data can then be collected to determine whether the described program matches the implemented program. If the connections are not clear, the logic model represents an excellent tool to initiate an inquiry about fundamental program assumptions (see Dugan, 1996).

7. The team includes Abraham Wandersman, Jessica Snell-Johns, Dana C. Keener, Melanie Livet, David Fetterman, Barry Lentz, Pam Imm, and Paul Flaspohler.

REFERENCES

Alkin, M. (2004). *Evaluation roots: Tracing theorists' views and influences.* Thousand Oaks, CA: Sage.

Alkin, M., & Christie, C. (2004). An evaluation theory tree. In M. Alkin (Ed.), *Evaluation roots: Tracing theorists' views and influences.* Thousand Oaks, CA: Sage.

Alkin, M., Daillak, R., & White, P. (1979). *Using evaluation: Does evaluation make a difference?* (Sage Library of Social Research, Vol. 7a6). Beverley Hills, CA: Sage.

Argyris, C., & Schön, D. (1978). *Organizational learning: A theory of action.* London: Perspective.

Bandura, A. (1982). Self-efficacy mechanism in human agency. *American Psychologist, 37,* 122–147.

Brunner, I., & Guzman, A. (1989). Participatory evaluation: A tool to assess projects and empower people. In R. F. Connor & M. H. Hendricks (Eds.), *International innovations in evaluation methodology: New directions for program evaluation* (No. 42, pp. 9–17). San Francisco: Jossey-Bass.

Bryk, A. (Ed.). (1983). *Stakeholder-based evaluation* (New Directions for Program Evaluation, No. 17). San Francisco: Jossey-Bass.

Burke, B. (1998). Evaluation for a change: Reflections on participatory methodology. *New Directions for Program Evaluation, 80,* 43–56.

Chinman, M., Imm, P., & Wandersman, A. (2004). *Getting to outcomes 2004: Promoting accountability through methods and tools for planning, implementation, and evaluation.* Santa Monica, CA: RAND.

Christie, C. (2003). What guides evaluation?: A study of how evaluation practice maps onto evaluation theory. *New Directions for Evaluation,* No. 97, 7–35.

Coombe, C. (2002). Participatory evaluation: Building community while assessing change. In M. Minkler & N. Wallerstein (Eds.), *Community-based participatory research for health.* San Francisco: Jossey-Bass.

Cousins, J. B. (2003, November). *Will the real empowerment evaluation please stand up?: A critical friend perspective.* Paper presented at the annual meeting of the American Evaluation Association, Reno, NV.

Cousins, J. B., & Whitmore, E. (1998). Framing participatory evaluation. *New Directions for Evaluation, 80,* 5–23.

Cousins, J. B., Donohue, J. J., & Bloom, G. A. (1996). Collaborative evaluation in North America: Evaluators' self-reported opinions, practices, and consequences. *Evaluation Practice, 17*(3), 207–226.

Cousins, J. B., & Earl, L. M. (Eds.). (1995). *Participatory evaluation in education: Studies of evaluation use and organizational learning.* London: Falmer.

Dugan, M. (1996). Participatory and empowerment evaluation: Lessons learned in training and technical assistance. In D. M. Fetterman, S. Kaftarian, & A. Wandersman (Eds.), *Empowerment evaluation: Knowledge and tools for self-assessment and accountability*. Thousand Oaks, CA: Sage.

Fetterman, D. M. (1994). Empowerment evaluation. *Evaluation Practice, 15*(1), 1–15.

Fetterman, D. M. (1995). In response to Dr. Daniel Stufflebeam's "Empowerment evaluation, objectivist evaluation, and evaluation standards: Where the future of evaluation should not go and where it needs to go." *Evaluation Practice, 16*(2), 177–197.

Fetterman, D. M. (1996). Empowerment evaluation: An introduction to theory and practice. In D. M. Fetterman, S. Kaftarian, & A. Wandersman (Eds.), *Empowerment evaluation: Knowledge and tools for self-assessment and accountability*. Thousand Oaks, CA: Sage.

Fetterman, D. M. (2001). *Foundations of empowerment evaluation*. Thousand Oaks, CA: Sage.

Fetterman, D. M. (2004a). Empowerment evaluation. In S. Mathison (Ed.), *Encyclopedia of evaluation*. Thousand Oaks, CA: Sage.

Fetterman, D. M. (2004b). Empowerment evaluation. In A. R. Roberts & K. R. Yeager (Eds.), *Evidence-based practice manual: Research outcome measures in health and human services*. Oxford, UK: Oxford University Press.

Fetterman, D. M., & Bowman, C. (2002). Experiential education and empowerment evaluation: Mars rover educational program case example. *Journal of Experiential Education, 25*(2), 286–295. Available online at http://www.stanford.edu/~davidf/mars.pdf.

Fetterman, D. M., Kaftarian, S., & Wandersman, A. (1996). *Empowerment evaluation: Knowledge and tools for self-assessment and accountability*. Thousand Oaks, CA: Sage.

Firme, T. (2003, November 5–8). *Designing evaluation in international contexts: Lessons from the external evaluation of the educational program in Amazonian Brazil*. Paper presented at the annual meeting of the American Evaluation Association, Reno, NV.

Green, L. W. (2003). Tracing federal support for participatory research in public health. In M. Minkler & N. Wallerstein (Eds.), *Community-based participatory research* (pp. 410–418). San Francisco: Jossey-Bass.

Green, L. W., & Frankish, C. J. (1995). Finding the right mix of personal, organizational, decentralized, and centralized planning for health promotion. In B. Beery, E. Wagner, & A. Cheadle (Eds.), *Community health promotion*. Seattle: University of Washington Press.

Green, L. W., & Mercer, S. M. (2004). Participatory research. In N. Anderson (Ed.), *Encyclopedia of health and behavior.* (Vol. 2, pp. 650–653). Thousand Oaks, CA: Sage.

Greene, J. C. (1996). Qualitative evaluation and scientific citizenship: Reflections and refractions. *Evaluation, 2*, 277–289.

House, E. R., & Howe, K. R. (1999). *Values in education and social research*. Newbury Park, CA: Sage.

Israel, B. A., Checkoway, B. Schultz, A., & Zimmerman, M. (1994). Health education and community empowerment: Conceptualizing and measuring perceptions of individual, organizational, and community control. *Health Education Quarterly, 21*(2), 149–170.

Joint Committee on Standards for Educational Evaluation. (1994). *The program evaluation standards.* Thousand Oaks, CA: Sage. Available online at *http://www.eval.org/Evaluation/Documents/progeval.html.*

King, J. A. (2004). Tikkun Olam: The roots of participatory evaluation. In M. C. Alkin (Ed.), *Evaluation roots: Tracing theorists' views and influences.* Thousand Oaks, CA: Sage.

Light, P. (2002). A conversation with Paul Light. *The Evaluation Exchange, Harvard Family Research Project, 8*(2), 10–11.

MacDonald, B. (1977). A political classification of evaluation studies. In D. Hamilton, D. Jenkins, C. King, B. MacDonald, & M. Parlett (Eds.), *Beyond the numbers game.* London: Macmillan

Mezirow, J. (1991). *Transformative dimensions of adult learning.* San Francisco: Jossey-Bass.

Minkler, M., & Wallerstein, N. (Eds.). (2002). *Community-based participatory research for health.* San Francisco: Jossey-Bass.

Mithaug, D. E. (1991). *Self-determined kids: Raising satisfied and successful children.* New York: Macmillan.

Mithaug, D. E. (1993). *Self-regulation theory: How optimal adjustment maximizes gain.* New York: Praeger.

Oja, S. N., & Smulyan, L. (1989). *Collaborative action research.* London: Falmer.

O'Sullivan, R. (2004). *Practicing evaluation: A collaborative approach.* Thousand Oaks, CA: Sage.

Papineau, D., & Kiely, M. C. (1994). Participatory evaluation: Empowering stakeholders in a community economic development organization. *Community Psychologist, 27*(2), 56–57.

Patton, M. Q. (1996). *Utilization-focused evaluation.* Newbury Park, CA: Sage.

Patton, M. Q. (1997). *Utilization-focused evaluation: The new century text* (3rd ed.). Thousand Oaks, CA: Sage.

Preskill, H., & Torres, R. T. (1999). *Evaluative inquiry for learning in organizations.* Thousand Oaks, CA: Sage.

Schön, D. A. (1987). *Educating the reflective practitioner.* San Francisco: Jossey-Bass.

Scriven, M. (1997). Empowerment evaluation examined. *Evaluation Practice, 18*(2), 165–175. Available online at *http://www.stanford.edu/~davidf/scriven.html.*

Sechrest, L. (1997). Review of the book *Empowerment evaluation: Knowledge and tools for self-assessment and accountability.* Thousand Oaks, CA: Sage. Available online at *http://www.stanford.edu/~davidf/sechrest.html.*

Senge, P. (1994). *The fifth discipline: The art and practice of the learning organization.* New York: Doubleday.

Siitonen, J., & Robinson, H. A. (1998). Empowerment: Links to teachers' professional growth. In R. Erkkilä, A. Willman, & L. Syrjälä (Eds.), *Promoting teachers' personal and professional growth.* University of Oulu, Department of Teacher Education. *Acta Universitatis Ouluensis, E, 32,* 165–191.

Stufflebeam, D. L. (1994). Empowerment evaluation, objectivist evaluation, and evaluation standards: Where the future of evaluation should not go and where it needs to go. *Evaluation Practice, 15*(3), 321–338.

Stull, D., & Schensul, J. (1987). *Collaborative research and social change: Applied anthropology in action.* Boulder, CO: Westview.

Vanderplaat, M. (1995). Beyond technique: Issues in evaluating for empowerment. *Evaluation, 1*(1), 81–96.

Vanderplaat, M. (1997). Emancipatory politics, critical evaluation, and government policy. *Canadian Journal of Program Evaluation, 12*(2), 143–162.

Wallerstein, N. (1992). Powerlessness, empowerment, and health: Implications for health promotion programs. *American Journal of Health Promotion, 6*(3), 197–205.

Wandersman, A., Imm, P., Chinman, M., & Kaftarian, S. (2000). Getting to outcomes: A results based approach to accountability. *Evaluation and Program Planning, 23*(3), 389–395.

Wandersman, A., Kaftarian, S. J., Imm, P., & Chinman, M. (1999). *Getting to outcomes: Methods and tools for planning, evaluation, and accountability.* Rockville, MD: Center for Substance Abuse Prevention.

Wandersman, A., Keener, D. C., Snell-Johns, J., Miller, R., Flaspohler, P., Dye, M., Mendez, J., Behrens, T., Bolson, B., & Robinson, L. (2004). Empowerment evaluation: Principles and action. In L. A. Jason, C. B. Keys, Y. Suarez-Balcazar, R. R. Taylor, M. Davis, J. Durlak, & D. Isenberg (Eds.), *Participatory community research: Theories and methods in action.* Washington, DC: American Psychological Association.

Whitmore, E. (Ed.). (1998). *Understanding and practicing participatory evaluation: New Directions for Evaluation* (No. 80). San Francisco: Jossey-Bass.

Zimmerman, M. A. (2000). Empowerment theory: Psychological, organizational, and community levels of analysis. In J. Rappaport & E. Seidman (Eds.), *Handbook of community psychology.* New York: Kluwer Academic/Plenum.

CHAPTER **2**

The Principles of Empowerment Evaluation

Abraham Wandersman, Jessica Snell-Johns, Barry E. Lentz, David M. Fetterman,
Dana C. Keener, Melanie Livet, Pamela S. Imm, and Paul Flaspohler

Empowerment evaluation is an evaluation approach that aims to increase the likelihood that programs will achieve results by increasing the capacity of program stakeholders to plan, implement, and evaluate their own programs. This chapter identifies and defines the set of principles that guide our decision making and practice as empowerment evaluators. Developing the set of principles that guides empowerment evaluation involved consideration of the traditions and values of other approaches to evaluation, including traditional forms of evaluation (e.g., Rossi, Lipsey, & Freeman, 2004) and empowerment evaluation's close relatives—participatory evaluation (e.g., Cousins & Whitmore, 1998) and utilization-focused evaluation (e.g., Patton, 1997). The process also involved a series of dialogues and exchanges intended to ensure that the set of empowerment evaluation principles reflects our most current thinking as a team of authors and colleagues in the field. Empowerment evaluation's distinct contribution to the field can best be understood when viewing it in its entirety and by understanding its principles of empowerment evaluation, as a whole, as well as the tools and evaluator, funder, and stakeholder practices that are unique to empowerment evaluation.

This chapter evolved from a chapter originally titled "Empowerment Evaluation: Principles and Action" (Wandersman et al., 2004). The original list of empowerment evaluation principles proposed by Wandersman et al. (2004) combined the principles and practices that were considered descriptive of the empowerment evaluation approach. In an effort to further clarify this approach, we have teased out the principles from the corresponding practices and are presenting them in separate chapters in this book. Additional chapters (see Chapters 3–7) illustrate the evaluator, funder, and stakeholder practices that are likely to result from an evaluation guided by these principles.

DEFINITIONS AND PURPOSES OF EMPOWERMENT EVALUATION

While the overall purpose of empowerment evaluation has remained consistent since the origin of this approach, the definition, theory, methods, and values have continued to evolve and become more refined over time (Wandersman et al., 2004). Fetterman defined empowerment evaluation as "the use of evaluation concepts, techniques, and findings to foster improvement and self-determination" (2001, p. 3). In 1999, Wandersman built on this definition by emphasizing that the goal of empowerment evaluation is to improve program success. Wandersman proposed that "by providing program developers with tools for assessing the planning, implementation, and evaluation of programs, program practitioners have the opportunity to improve planning, implement with quality, evaluate outcomes, and develop a continuous quality improvement system, thereby increasing the probability of achieving results" (1999, p. 96). Fetterman and Wandersman's theories and definitions of empowerment evaluation are unified in the following definition to be used throughout this chapter and the remainder of the book:

> *Empowerment evaluation: An evaluation approach that aims to increase the probability of achieving program success by (1) providing program stakeholders with tools for assessing the planning, implementation, and self-evaluation of their program, and (2) mainstreaming evaluation as part of the planning and management of the program/organization.*

Empowerment evaluation expands the purpose, roles, and potential settings of evaluation beyond that of traditional evaluation approaches (Wandersman et al., 2004). However, this does not preclude the need for or importance of more traditional evaluation approaches (Fetterman, 2001). Neither empowerment evaluation nor traditional evaluation is inherently a "better" approach. Instead, the value of each evaluation approach depends upon the purpose of the evaluation (Chelimsky, 1997; Patton, 1997).

Chelimsky (1997) describes three purposes of evaluation, including: (1) evaluation for development (e.g., information collected to strengthen programs or institutions); (2) evaluation for accountability (e.g., measurement of results or efficiency); and (3) evaluation for knowledge (e.g., increasing understanding about factors underlying public problems). Empowerment evaluation is especially appropriate for the purpose of development. It actively seeks to develop people, programs, and institutions (Wandersman, 2003). In addition, it can be used effectively for the purpose of demonstrating accountability. The frameworks and methodology (e.g., Prevention Plus III, Getting to Outcomes) developed by Wandersman and colleagues (e.g., Chinman, Imm, & Wandersman, 2004; Linney & Wandersman, 1991; Wandersman, Imm, Chinman, & Kaftarian, 2000) are designed not only to improve programs but also to measure the results of programs (results-based accountability). Empowerment evaluation is also committed to contributing to knowledge creation (Lentz et al., Chapter 7, this volume; Nonaka & Takeuchi, 1995). This form of knowledge development can be more fully realized once more empowerment evaluation-based cases are available for review.

THE PRINCIPLES OF EMPOWERMENT EVALUATION

Empowerment evaluation shares some values and methods with other approaches to evaluation, including traditional evaluation and empowerment evaluation's close relatives—collaborative, participatory, and utilization-focused evaluation. However, it is the set of empowerment evaluation principles (see Table 2.1) considered in their entirety that distinguishes it from other evaluation approaches. Below, we present each principle on its own terms, recognizing that our work becomes more complex as we integrate these principles in our practice. The numbering of the principles does not reflect any type of hierarchy or prioritization of one principle over another. Instead, the principles are to be considered as a set of core beliefs that, as a whole, communicate the underlying values of empowerment evaluation and guide our work as empowerment evaluators.

PRINCIPLE 1: IMPROVEMENT

Empowerment evaluation theory and practice are guided by the fundamental assumption that the vast majority of programs desire to achieve positive results (e.g., education, health, social welfare) in the lives of those affected by the program. Empowerment evaluators want programs to suc-

TABLE 2.1. The Principles of Empowerment Evaluation

- Principle 1: Improvement
- Principle 2: Community ownership
- Principle 3: Inclusion
- Principle 4: Democratic participation
- Principle 5: Social justice
- Principle 6: Community knowledge
- Principle 7: Evidence-based strategies
- Principle 8: Capacity building
- Principle 9: Organizational learning
- Principle 10: Accountability

ceed. Toward that end, empowerment evaluation values improvement in people, programs, organizations, and communities. Empowerment evaluators use the methods and tools of empowerment evaluation to help programs, organizations, and communities achieve results. This is in contrast to traditional evaluation, which values neutrality and objectivity and wants to examine programs in their "natural state" in order to determine a program's effect without the influence of the evaluator. Many funders are interested in empowerment evaluation because they are tired of receiving evaluations that show no results and would like evaluation to be helpful to grantees in achieving results (e.g., W. K. Kellogg Foundation, 1999).

Some argue that because empowerment evaluators are not neutral, evaluation findings are more likely to be biased, self-congratulatory, or press relations (Stufflebeam, 2001). Empowerment evaluation provides three important responses to this concern. First, the integrity of an evaluation can be compromised in any evaluation approach. Practitioners working within an empowerment evaluation system may actually be less likely to misrepresent data than practitioners who feel threatened by evaluation. Some empowerment evaluators have found that because these evaluators and practitioners are striving for program improvement, they are actually more honest (Fetterman, 2001). Increased honesty means giving voice to the program limitations that must be addressed before desired outcomes can be achieved, and because empowerment evaluators value improvement and take the time to build relationships with stakeholders, these limitations are likely to be known and documented by the evaluators and the other stakeholders. Second, empowerment evaluation has a "bottom-line" orientation. This means that empowerment evaluation, like other evaluation approaches, uses quantitative (e.g., school achievement, rates of AIDS cases) and qualitative data sources to evaluate program implementation processes and short- and long-term outcomes. Finally, empowerment evaluation adheres to the standards of evaluation (utility, feasibility, propriety, and accuracy) set forth by the Joint Committee of Education Evaluation (1994; Fetterman, 2001, pp. 87–99), which serve to provide a common language and set of values for the field and strive to ensure quality across all evaluation philosophies and methodologies.

PRINCIPLE 2: COMMUNITY OWNERSHIP

Empowerment evaluators believe that the community has the right to make decisions about actions that affect their lives. Empowerment evaluators also believe that evaluation is most likely to lead to program improvement when the community is empowered to exercise its legitimate authority to make decisions that direct the evaluation process. In empowerment evaluation, the stakeholders, with the assistance of the empowerment evaluators, conduct the evaluation and put the evaluation findings to use. Program stakeholders have the responsibility of making critical decisions about the program and the evaluation. This commitment to community ownership is in contrast to typical traditional evaluation approaches, where decision-making power regarding the purpose, design, and use of evaluation results is held by the evaluator and the funder.

Empowerment evaluation's commitment to community ownership is also distinct from practical participatory evaluation designs, where decision-making power is shared by both evaluators and practitioners (Cousins & Whitmore, 1998). Specifically, in practical participatory evaluation, there are certain roles for evaluators (e.g., technical evaluation roles) and for stakeholders (e.g., problem definition). In empowerment evaluation, there is not joint ownership and control of evaluation decision making, rather, the ownership is by the community or program. In empowerment evaluation, all of the evaluation roles are eventually to be assumed by program personnel. The reason that practitioners do not take all of these roles initially is because it is often a developmental process, and they may not have the initial capacity to do so. In summary, practitioners should take charge of the content of the evaluation as soon as is practicable, ranging from stating their mission to prioritizing and evaluating key activities. A major assignment for empowerment evaluators is to promote a developmental approach to capacity building and community ownership that enables program personnel and participants to perform empowerment evaluation—starting from "where they are at" and working to higher levels of evaluation capacity.

Empowerment evaluators have influence in the process as consultants, facilitators, coaches, teachers, and critical friends, but they do not have decision-making power. Sociologists and social psychologists have made distinctions between power and influence (e.g., Bruins, 1999). In empowerment evaluation, power involves control, ownership, and decision making, while influence involves shaping the direction of programming and providing insight and information regarding the decision-making process. Program personnel and other stakeholders have the power to choose whether to incorporate this influence into their decision making.

Community ownership does not mean that empowerment evaluators do not strongly state their opinions. The empowerment evaluation value of community ownership means that the voice of the evaluator is just one voice at the table, and through democratic participation the community decides what to do or not to do with opinions expressed by the empowerment evaluators. In other words, empowerment evaluators do not relinquish their authority as experts in the area of evaluation, but this authority does not extend to the point of usurping the decision-making authority of the community. The use of evidence-based strategies and results-based accountability are also woven into empowerment evaluation (principles 7 and 10). Therefore, communities use knowledge provided by all parties to inform their decision making and are expected to be accountable by considering relevant information when making their decisions. Empowerment evaluation embraces the value of community ownership because putting evaluation in the hands of program staff and participants is thought to foster self-determination and responsibility instead of dependency. In addition, empowerment evaluation is guided by the theory that people are more likely to believe and use findings and follow recommendations if they were responsible for creating them.

PRINCIPLE 3: INCLUSION

Empowerment evaluation is committed to community ownership that is inclusive and that involves direct participation of key stakeholders in decision making whenever possible. Empowerment evaluators believe the evaluation of a program or organization benefits from having stakeholders and staff from a variety of levels involved in planning and decision making. Being inclusive is distinct from how people make their decisions as a group, such as democratic forms of participation (see Principle 4). (A group can adopt a democratic form of government or decision making, but this does not mean that everyone was invited to participate.) First, a broad representation of participants should be recruited and asked to participate in a meaningful way. Not being inclusive can be counterproductive to empowerment evaluation and often results in poor communication, undermining behavior, and a lack of human resources for stakeholders to help one another in improving practices. Empowerment evaluators find that better solutions emerge as a result of inclusive consultation with program staff, program/community members, funders, and participants. Furthermore, inclusion is thought to be an important way of facilitating ownership of the evaluation processes and use of evaluation results by all stakeholders to guide practice and program improvement.

PRINCIPLE 4: DEMOCRATIC PARTICIPATION

The definition of empowerment evaluation assumes that stakeholders have the capacity for intelligent judgment and action when supplied with appropriate information and conditions. This assumption echoes John Dewey's characterization of participatory democracy as a "way of personal life controlled, not merely by faith in human nature in general, but by faith in the capacity of human beings for intelligent judgment and action if proper conditions are furnished" (Dewey, 1940, p. 224). As with the principles of community ownership and inclusion, democratic participation is a principle that is seen as critical for establishing stakeholder buy-in. Democratic participation also (1) underscores the importance of deliberation and authentic collaboration as a critical process for maximizing use of the skills and knowledge that exist in the community and (2) emphasizes that fairness and due process are fundamental parts of the empowerment evaluation process.

Connected to the value of democratic participation is the emphasis on transparency. Empowerment evaluators should strive to make evaluation plans and methods clear and straightforward. Clarity and openness increase trust, which is critical to stakeholders being willing to share negative findings and to modify programs based on evaluation results. The use of democratic participation is also based on the belief that when stakeholders are involved in decision making, programs are more likely to fit the needs and values of participants. Furthermore, participation has been shown to increase feelings of control (Wandersman, 1979; Wandersman & Florin, 2000) and should increase ownership and use of evaluation tools and findings (Jason et al., 2004).

PRINCIPLE 5: SOCIAL JUSTICE

Empowerment evaluators believe in and have a working commitment to social justice—a fair, equitable allocation of resources, opportunities, obligations, and bargaining power (Dalton, Elias, & Wandersman, 2001;

Prilleltensky, 1999). This means that empowerment evaluators recognize that there are basic social inequities in society and strive to ameliorate these conditions by helping people use evaluation to improve their programs so that social conditions and communities are positively impacted in the process. As people become more confident, self-determined, and ready to take control of their lives, they are better able to confront inequities in their lives. The aim of empowerment evaluation is to make a difference with an eye toward the larger social good.

Empowerment evaluation is well suited for most programs and populations that are interested in improving their performance. Not all programs identify directly with social justice as part of their mission. However, we believe that almost any program that is designed to help people and communities at any level (individuals, families, neighborhoods) and domain (e.g., education, health, economic), ultimately contributes to the larger goal of social justice. The image of the just society that is being invoked here requires no great leap beyond a commitment to the principles already discussed. A commitment to social justice naturally follows from the commitment of empowerment evaluation to help individuals develop their capacity for intelligent judgment and action by supplying them with the methods, tools, techniques, and training to improve their programs through the use of evaluation.

PRINCIPLE 6: COMMUNITY KNOWLEDGE

Several participatory and collaborative evaluation approaches view community members as experts on their community. In transformative participatory evaluation, popular knowledge is as valid and useful as scientific knowledge (Cousins & Whitmore, 1998). In empowerment evaluation, community-based knowledge and wisdom are also valued and promoted. Empowerment evaluation embraces local community knowledge and posits that people typically know their own problems and are in a good position to generate their own solutions. For the empowerment evaluator, respect of community knowledge often involves recognizing the tacit ("know-how") knowledge of stakeholders and making this knowledge explicit so that it can be shared through communicative action and synthesized to create new knowledge (see Chapter 7 for a more detailed discussion of this issue).

In empowerment evaluation, there is an emphasis on developing tools that can be used to help reinforce, test, or modify local community knowledge. The experience of the community is seen as an essential resource for contextualizing science and "best practices." Science and "best practices" are valued complements to local knowledge (see principle 7). Various collaborative and participatory approaches value local community knowledge but are silent or skeptical about science and "evidence-based strategies." Empowerment evaluators recognize the limitations of externally exported solutions derived from varying contexts. However, empowerment evaluation, in contrast to some other evaluation approaches, embraces evidence-based strategies to enhance local thinking and practice.

PRINCIPLE 7: EVIDENCE-BASED STRATEGIES

Empowerment evaluation values the role of science and evidence-based strategies and holds that a review of relevant evidence-based or "best-practice" interventions is important to consider early in the process of designing and/or selecting a program to address a community need. Just as empowerment evaluation respects the work of the community and its knowledge base, it also respects the knowledge base of scholars and practitioners who have provided empirical information about what works in particular areas (e.g., prevention, treatment). This value of using existing knowledge is part of the commitment to avoid reinventing the wheel and to build from existing literature or practice. However, evidence-based strategies should not be adopted blindly and without regard for the local context (Fetterman, 1998; Green, 2001; Wandersman, 2003).

The empowerment evaluation value placed on community knowledge is an essential counterbalance to the respect for evidence-based, best-practices strategies. In most instances, adaptations (informed by community knowledge) are necessary before the practices can be useful in a community setting. Empowerment evaluators believe that part of their role is to assist stakeholders in combining evidence-based knowledge—regarding what works—and the community's knowledge of context and participants when planning and implementing interventions.

PRINCIPLE 8: CAPACITY BUILDING

We view capacity building in Patton's (1997) description of process use—namely, individual changes in thinking and behavior, and program or organizational changes in procedures and culture that result from the learning that occurs during the evaluation process (p. 90). Empowerment evaluators believe that when stakeholders learn the basic steps and skills involved in conducting program evaluation, they are in a better position to shape and improve their lives and the lives of those who participate in their programs. Empowerment evaluation is designed to simultaneously enhance the stakeholders' capacity to conduct evaluation (often called evaluation capacity) and to improve program planning and implementation (often called program capacity).

Increasing stakeholder capacity to plan, implement, and monitor program activities supports the mainstreaming of evaluation (Barnette & Sanders, 2003) and organizational learning. As already discussed, empowerment evaluators believe that people and organizations are capable of conducting evaluation when provided with the necessary conditions in their organizational environment and with appropriate tools (e.g., process or outcome measures). Accordingly, empowerment evaluation incorporates user-friendly tools and concepts, whenever possible, to increase the probability that stakeholders can and will use these tools once they have built their capacities and once the empowerment evaluator and technical assistance teams have decreased their involvement.

PRINCIPLE 9: ORGANIZATIONAL LEARNING

Improvement is a basic principle of empowerment evaluation (see principle 1). Improvement is enhanced when there is a *process* that encourages learning (organizational learning) and an organizational *structure* that encourages learning (a learning organization). There is a vast literature on organizational learning and learning organizations in the organization and management literature (e.g., Ang & Joseph, 1996; Argyris & Schön, 1978, 1996; Argyris, 1999; Senge, 1990).

Organizational learning has been defined as the process of acquiring, applying, and mastering new tools and methods to improve processes (Schneiderman, 2003). Argyris (1999) concludes that in order for organizational learning to occur organizations must do the following:

1. Support learning and not just be satisfied with business-as-usual (i.e., organizations must be open to change).
2. Value continuous quality improvement and strive for ongoing improvement.
3. Engage in systems thinking. Organizational learning involves inquiring into the systemic consequences of actions rather than settling for short-term solutions that may provide a temporary quick fix but fail to address the underlying problem.
4. Promote new knowledge for problem solving.

Using data to inform decision making and developing a reflective culture within a program (and/or the host organization) encourages meaningful organizational learning (Preskill, 1994; Preskill & Torres, 1999). Therefore, organizations need to be ready to engage in an empowerment evaluation, and there are certain organizational structure and functioning characteristics that ensure a more successful implementation of empowerment evaluation (see Chapter 6 for a review of literature on organizational characteristics conducive to organizational learning and empowerment evaluation). When these characteristics exist, the structure for a learning organization exists and the sustainability of empowerment evaluation is enhanced. However, this does not mean that a program or organization needs to be operating smoothly or that every staff member needs to fully appreciate evaluation or change at the beginning of an empowerment evaluation process. In fact, empowerment evaluation uses tools and practices that are specifically designed to meet programs "where they are at" and to facilitate motivation and skills that support the development of an organizational learning culture—so long as some of the key ingredients of management and staff interest in an improvement process exist.

PRINCIPLE 10: ACCOUNTABILITY

Empowerment evaluation provides an innovative vehicle for helping programs to be accountable to administrators and the public by generating process- and outcome-oriented data within an evaluation framework that heightens an organization's sensitivity to its responsibility to the public and to itself (R. Miller, personal communication, March 12, 2004). Like most approaches to evaluation, empowerment evaluation is committed to accountability and focuses on the final outcomes achieved by a program. At the same time, empowerment evaluation is based on the proposition that the likelihood of achieving results is greatly enhanced when stakeholders collect process evaluation information and hold staff accountable for their activities and plans. Thus, because process evaluation is viewed as a vehicle toward results-based accountability, empowerment evaluation places a high priority on process accountability. In addition, the principle of accountability, in combination with other empowerment evaluation principles—especially improvement, community ownership, inclusion, and democratic participation—creates a self-driven, rather than other-driven, concept of accountability.

Empowerment evaluation views accountability as a mutual and interactive responsibility of funder, researcher/evaluator, and practitioner. This interdependence of roles is key to how empowerment evaluation conceptualizes process- and results-based accountability. In empowerment evaluation, accountability is not something someone else does *to* the program. All stakeholders work together to build upon one another's strengths to achieve results. The stakeholders are intertwined in a triple helix of accountability to one another to obtain results (Wandersman, 2003).

A description and assessment of program processes enables program staff and participants to create a chain of reasoning. This helps establish mechanisms for accountability on both process and outcome levels. The reason accountability is needed on both levels is illustrated with a sports example; players, coaches, and spectators at a football game want to win, and they want to know the score at the end of a game. However, in order to promote learning and ongoing improvement, coaches and players need to understand *why* they won or lost. The same is true of program evaluation. Outcomes are critical, but they are more meaningful if stakeholders understand how and why the program outcomes were or were not produced. If the outcomes were positive, stakeholders can pinpoint some of the processes that led to program success. Conversely, if the outcomes were less than expected, they can identify the factors that interfered with success.

Empowerment evaluation and results-based accountability (RBA) are concerned with the same issue—results. While empowerment evaluation is committed to learning from processes and implementation, its practitioners also need to know if the intervention worked. Based in part on Osborne and Graebler (1992), and on the Government Performance and Results Act of 1993, RBA moves practitioners away from collecting *only* process or output information (e.g., counting the numbers served) toward answering bottom-line questions about program effectiveness. In addition, RBA focuses on what can be learned from the program results. According to Cousins and Whitmore (1998), practical participatory evaluation is better suited to formative evaluation than to summative evaluation. Empowerment evaluation, however, is focused on both formative and summative forms of evaluation accountability. The more work put into formative evaluation, the more likely the program is to achieve at the summative phase.

The Getting to Outcomes (GTO) system (Wandersman et al., 2000) is an example of a tool that helps promote process- and results-based accountability by aiding program personnel in clarifying the goals of an intervention and in identifying the steps (process) necessary for achieving the goals. To be accountable, the interveners must proceed through the steps that help ensure an effective intervention (e.g., need and resource assessment, identification of clear goals, use of science and "best practices," fit, capacity building, planning, implementation, outcome evaluation, continuous quality improvement, and sustainability). A significant measure of accountability is assured after following these steps in ways that meet standards of quality for each step (see Chapter 6 for more information about GTO).

CONCLUSION

In this chapter, we have described the principles of empowerment evaluation that guide our decision making as empowerment evaluators and provide the basis for evaluation to be useful in everyday treatment, prevention, and education interventions. As stated at the beginning of the chapter, it is the set of empowerment evaluation principles taken as a whole that distinguishes it from other evaluation and participatory research approaches. The combination of principles creates a mindset for an empowerment evaluator and guides practice in terms of evaluator behaviors, responses, and attitudes. Chapter 3 and the case example chapters provide real-world illustrations of the application of empowerment evaluation theory and principles. Empowerment evaluation provides an innovative vehicle for supporting staff in being accountable to themselves and to the public by generating outcome-oriented data within an evaluation framework that heightens an organization's sensitivity to its responsibility to the public and to itself (R. Miller, personal communication, March 12, 2004).

Hopefully this chapter and the empowerment evaluation principles communicate how much can be gained when the traditional boundaries between funder, researcher/evaluator, and practitioner are strategically blurred and when evaluation concepts and tools are used routinely by program personnel for planning, implementation, and evaluation aims. The interdependence of funder, evaluator, and practitioner beliefs and practices is key to an empowerment evaluation approach. The evaluator, practitioner, and funder practices that correspond to the 10 empowerment evaluation principles are treated in the next chapter.

ACKNOWLEDGMENTS

We would like to thank Robin Miller for her very cogent comments on an earlier draft of this chapter. Some of her suggestions were so helpful that we actually incorporated a few of her suggested phrases into the text. We would also like to thank Meredith Minkler for her wise and encouraging comments and her suggestions and leads in the area of participatory evaluation and participatory research.

REFERENCES

Ang, S., & Joseph, D. (1996, August 9–12). *Organizational learning and learning organizations: Triggering events, processes and structures.* Proceedings of the Academy of Management Meeting, Cincinnati, OH.

Argyris, C. (1999). *On organizational learning.* Malden, MA: Blackwell Business.

Argyris, C., & Schön, D. (1978). *Organizational learning.* Reading, MA: Addison-Wesley.

Argyris, C., & Schön, D. (1996). *Organizational learning II: Theory, method and practice.* Reading, MA: Addison-Wesley.

Barnette, J. J., & Sanders, J. R. (2003). The mainstreaming of evaluation. *New Directions for Evaluation,* No. 99.

Bruins, J. (1999). Social power and influence tactics: A theoretical introduction. *Journal of Social Issues* (Special issue on Social Influence and Social Power: Using Theory for Understanding Social Issues), Spring.

Chelimsky, E. (1997). The coming transformation in evaluation. In E. Chelimsky & W. Shadish (Eds.), *Evaluation for the 21st century: A handbook.* Thousand Oaks, CA: Sage.

Chinman, M., Imm, P., & Wandersman, A.(2004). *Getting to Outcomes 2004: Promoting accountability through methods and tools for planning, implementation, and evaluation* (TR-TR101). Santa Monica, CA: RAND. Available free online at *http://www.rand.org/publications/TR/TR101/.*

Cousins, J. B., & Whitmore, E. (1998). Framing participatory evaluation. *New Directions for Evaluation,* No. 80, 5–23.

Dalton, J., Elias, M., & Wandersman, A. (2001). *Community psychology: Linking individuals and communities.* Belmont, CA: Wadsworth.

Dewey, J. (1940). Creative democracy—the task before us. In. S. Ratner (Ed.), *The philosopher of the common man: Essays in honor of John Dewey to celebrate his eightieth birthday* (pp. 220–228). New York: Greenwood Press.

Fetterman, D. M. (1998). *Ethnography: Step by step* (2nd ed.). Thousand Oaks, CA: Sage.

Fetterman, D. M. (2001). *Foundations of empowerment evaluation.* Thousand Oaks, CA: Sage.

Green, L. (2001). From research to "best practices" in other settings and populations. *American Journal of Health Behavior,* 25(3),165–178.

Jason, L. A., Keys, C. B., Suarez-Balcazar, Y., Taylor, R. R., Davis, M., Durlak, J. & Isenberg, D. (Eds.), *Participatory community research: Theories and methods in action.* Washington, DC: American Psychological Association.

Joint Committee on Standards for Educational Evaluation. (1994). *The program evaluation standards.* Thousand Oaks, CA: Sage. Available online at *http://www.eval.org/Evaluation/Documents/progeval.html.*

W. K. Kellogg Foundation. (1999). *Empowerment evaluation and foundations: A matter of perspectives.* Battle Creek, MI: Author.

Linney, J. A., & Wandersman, A. (1991). *Prevention Plus III: Assessing alcohol and other drug prevention programs at the school and community level: A four-step guide to useful program assessment.* Rockville, MD: U.S. Department of Health and Human Services.

Nonaka, I., & Takeuchi, K. (1995). *The knowledge creating company.* New York: Oxford University Press.

Osborne, D., & Graebler, T. (1992). Reinventing government: How the entrepreneurial spirit is transforming the public sector. Reading, MA: Addison-Wesley.

Patton, M. Q. (1997). *Utilization-focused evaluation* (3rd ed.). Thousand Oaks, CA: Sage.

Preskill, H. (1994). Evaluation's role in facilitating organizational learning: A model for practice. *Evaluation and Program Planning,* 17(3), 291–298.

Preskill, H., & Torres, R. T. (1999). *Evaluative inquiry for learning in organizations.* Thousand Oaks, CA: Sage.

Prilleltensky, I. (1999). Critical psychology and social justice. In M. Fondacaro (Chair), *Concepts of social justice in community psychology.* Symposium at the biennial meeting of the Society for Community Research and Action, New Haven, CT.

Rossi, P. H., Lipsey, M. W., & Freeman, H. E. (2004). *Evaluation: A systematic approach* (7th ed.). Thousand Oaks, CA: Sage.

Schneiderman, A. M. (2003). The art of PM/measuring learning/learning.htm. Available at *http://www.schneiderman.com/.*

Senge, P. (1990). *The fifth discipline: The art and practice of organizational learning.* New York: Doubleday.

Stufflebeam, D. (2001). Evaluation models. *New Directions for Evaluation,* No. 89.

Wandersman, A. (1979). User participation: A study of types of participation, effects, mediators and individual differences. *Environment and Behavior, 11,* 185–208.

Wandersman, A. (1999). Framing the evaluation of health and human service programs in community settings: Assessing progress. *New Directions for Evaluation,* No. 83, 95–102.

Wandersman, A. (2003). Community science: Bridging the gap between science and practice with community-centered models. *American Journal of Community Psychology, 31*(Nos. 3–4), 227–242.

Wandersman, A., & Florin, P. (2000). Citizen participation and community organizations. In J. Rappaport & E. Seidman (Eds.), *Handbook of community psychology.* New York: Plenum Press.

Wandersman, A., Imm, P., Chinman, M., & Kaftarian, S. (2000). Getting to outcomes: A results-based approach to accountability. *Evaluation and Program Planning, 23*(3), 389–395.

Wandersman, A., Keener, D. C., Snell-Johns, J., Miller, R., Flaspohler, P., Dye, M., et al. (2004). Empowerment evaluation: Principles and action. In L. A. Jason, C. B. Keys, Y. Suarez-Balcazar, R. R. Taylor, M. Davis, J. Durlak, & D. Isenberg (Eds.), *Participatory community research: Theories and methods in action.* Washington, DC: American Psychological Association.

Empowerment Evaluation Principles in Practice

ASSESSING LEVELS OF COMMITMENT

David M. Fetterman

Principles guide practice. This chapter discusses how empowerment evaluation principles guide empowerment evaluation practice. As noted in Chapters 1 and 2, the principles include (1) improvement, (2) community ownership, (3) inclusion, (4) democratic participation, (5) social justice, (6) community knowledge (knowledge closely related to practice), (7) evidence-based strategies (e.g., interventions, practices), (8) capacity building, (9) organizational learning, and (10) accountability. Practice represents the application of principles to real-world settings. However, practice is messy, often filled with nuance, compromise, and built-in tensions. Table 3.1, presented at the end of this chapter, highlights a few examples of each stakeholder's role in practice. In addition, the criteria for assessing high, medium, and low levels of each principle in practice are presented for each stakeholder in this table. This provides evaluators, communities,[1] and funders with guidance in the practice of empowerment evaluation.

IMPROVEMENT

Empowerment evaluations are designed to help people improve their programs and, in the process, their lives. The work is not neutral or antiseptic. Empowerment evaluators roll up their sleeves and help people to help themselves. They have a commitment to the people they work with. They help them to improve their programs through evaluation—specifically, evaluative thinking and feedback.

The commitment to improvement is an overriding orientation as much as a specific principle of practice. This commitment is manifested in many ways, including capacity-building domains such as helping people learn how to use evaluation concepts and tools to plan, implement, and evaluate.[2] It is also manifested in the effort to design and use evaluation to improve program practice. Empowerment evaluators and community-based organization staff members do not conduct research experiments without the purpose of, or prospect to, improving the program. Empowerment evaluation is never conducted for the sake of intellectual curiosity alone.

Funders are also typically focused on improvement (Millett, 1996; W. K. Kellogg Foundation, 1999, 2001; Yost & Wandersman, 1998). They have already made an initial assessment of the program or the implementing organization. Based on that assessment they have made an investment in the selected program. Evaluation is viewed as a tool to enhance the probability that the investment will pay off. This is similar to hiring a financial adviser to help them manage their money and achieve their financial goals (J. Bare, Knight Foundation, personal communication, 2004). The programs are more likely to accomplish their objectives with this kind of feedback, guidance, and assistance. Corrective feedback, validation of decisions and practices, as well as warnings about problems and "failures" are view as instrumental evaluative contributions aimed at helping programs to succeed, accomplish their objectives, and get to the desired outcomes.

COMMUNITY OWNERSHIP

Community ownership starts from day 1. The community (i.e., the specific group that is operating and shaping the program or set of activities) is responsible for the design and overall direction of the evaluation. In addition, its members specify their own goals and strategies to accomplish their objectives. The evaluator serves as a coach or critical friend to assist them, ensuring logic, rigor, and a systematic approach to inquiry (Fetterman, 2001). However, the community *owns* the evaluation

(Fetterman, 2001, p. 115). The more the group members control both the conceptual direction and the actual implementation of the evaluation, the more they are likely to use the findings and recommendations, since they are theirs. This is referred to as "process use" (Fetterman 2001, pp. 110–112; Patton, 1997).

The sense of ownership may vary in practice, based on the group's own stage of development, capacity, and history. Ownership starts from the beginning, but it is a cumulative experience. It gets deeper and stronger over time if it is reinforced. Ownership becomes stronger and more meaningful as a community uses its own evaluative findings to improve practice, finds evaluators supportive and helpful concerning the collection and interpretation of data, and experiences the trust of funders to take additional time (and the requisite detours, within reason) to accomplish its objectives. Community members come to learn that their judgment is valued and trusted. The process of doing evaluation in a climate of trust and good faith only enhances a sense of ownership and pride. Conversely, it is weakened if a funder takes charge of the effort in the middle, the evaluator shares findings without community approval, and if the community fails to follow through on its own self-assessment. The Community Toolbox provides online resources for evaluating community programs and initiatives at *http://ctb.ku.edu/tools/en/part_J.htm*. A few examples of each stakeholders role are provided in Table 3.1.

INCLUSION

Inclusion[3] means inviting as many stakeholders to the table as is reasonable or feasible and making a concerted effort to encourage their participation. It also is a basic prerequisite to building a family or community. Funders, program administrators, staff members, participants, and community members should be invited to participate in empowerment evaluation activities. Program participants have a tremendous amount to offer. They know their own condition. They can help ground program staff members and administrators in their reality, forcing them to reshape program implementation and practice.

Funders offer more than money. They have a tremendous amount of knowledge. They know how other similar programs work. Funders are often excluded (or exclude themselves). However, if they are included from the beginning, they are more likely to contribute to the knowledge pool and, as key participants in the process, are less likely to "pull the rug out" from under the group in mid-course.

Inclusion does not on the surface appear to be an efficient mechanism. The more groups represented, the more time required for scheduling and consensus building. However, it is more efficient to be "inefficient" when it comes to participation. Leaders or representatives of each constituency are busy, but they should be included in discussions about group goals and strategies. While it might appear to be more efficient to delegate such tasks as selecting group goals or developing strategies, deliberate exclusion makes later group consensus on such goals all but impossible. Thus, premature delegation is in practice inefficient. Groups, particularly diverse groups, need to spend time together deciding where they want to go and how they want to get there. Evaluation can be one of their guides. Efficiently delegating these kinds of tasks to select groups and failing to include other groups simply means revisiting the same issues over and over again until everyone has had a chance to "weigh in" with their views. Worse, the alienated or excluded group may undermine the collective good will of the community.

The principle of inclusion serves to remind empowerment evaluators of their obligation to advise the people they work with to include rather than exclude. Economics, schedules, deadlines, biases, as well as vested interests all militate against inclusion. It is easy to say that there was insufficient time or a group's schedule could not be accommodated. However, failure to include all the critical players results in a missed opportunity. All of the key players bring valuable insights and interests to the table. Multicultural contributions are a plus, not a minus (see Banks, 1981; Hakuta & Garcia, 1989; Davidman & Davidman 1997, pp. 9–10). They also ensure an authentic or meaningful consensus. This is required for any plan of action to move forward. A few examples of each stakeholder's role in practice are provided in Table 3.1.

DEMOCRATIC PARTICIPATION

The principle of inclusion is often confused with democratic participation. While inclusion means bringing all the pertinent groups together, democratic participation speaks to how the groups will interact and make decisions once they are together (see Dewey, 1940; Fetterman, 2001, p. 89; Wandsworth Community Empowerment Fund Network, 2003). The first ensures some measure of diversity (particularly of those groups that have been historically excluded from discussions and decision making). The second, democratic participation, ensures that everyone has a vote in the process. This may be a literal vote or a meaningful role in decision making. In practice, that may mean that everyone gets one vote (or sticky dot) to prioritize his or her evaluative concerns about program activities or implementation. It may mean that each tribe in an 18-tribe consortium gets 1 vote per tribe as decisions are made in the empowerment evaluation. Each patient may have a voice equal to the physician in a breast cancer screening program empowerment evaluation; in addition to equal representation, the patient's voice might provide the insight needed to ensure that women in rural areas participate in the program. Democratic participation also refers to another level, often cited as informed inquiry, deliberation, and action. In other words, democratic participation is both a means of ensuring equality and fairness and a tool to bring forth as many insights and suggestions about how to improve programs as possible. It also develops analytical skills that can be applied in society in general, such as reasoned debate (with evidence), deliberation, and action (see Table 3.1 for examples).

SOCIAL JUSTICE

Social justice is a fundamental principle guiding empowerment evaluation (Christie, 2003, p. 11; Fetterman, 2001, p. 142; Fetterman, 2003, p. 47). In practice, empowerment evaluators typically assist people in social programs aimed at ameliorating a specific social concern or injustice. The program may be designed to improve the health care or education of disenfranchised or minority populations. The populations might include the homeless, battered women, people with disabilities, children, or minorities. Programs might include shelters, literacy programs, teenage pregnancy prevention programs, drug and alcohol prevention programs, or HIV prevention programs (See Fetterman, Kaftarian, & Wandersman, 1996). Although there is a bias toward traditionally disenfranchised populations, an empowerment evaluator might work with middle- and upper-middle class communities in an effort to ensure equality of opportunity, due process, racial or ethnic diversity, or related issues.

One of the purposes of this principle is to remind us that we pursue social justice every day by working with certain people and specific kinds of programs. This principle of social justice keeps the evaluator, community, and funder's eye on the prize of social justice, equity, and fairness (Davidman & Davidman, 1997). In practice, this reminder may influence the funder to connect the organization he or she is funding with similarly oriented organizations (i.e., nonprofits being funded or other funders). When the common commitment to social justice is placed in front of the funders on a routine basis, they are more likely to make these kinds of connections and decisions. The community may seek out like community-based organizations in remote areas because the geographic differences disappear and the social justice agenda they have in common makes them more visible. They can see connections that are not apparent on the "ground" level of daily practice. Communities that make their social justice agenda explicit are also more likely to make programmatic decisions that are in alignment with their values on a daily basis. For example, evaluative data might suggest eliminating a social service program because it is not cost-effective. However, the social justice agenda might override that decision or force the organization to find other ways to subsidize that activity.

The social justice principle is instructive on many levels. On a personal level, it influences how we treat people. Respect becomes paramount. The pride of an individual is fiercely protected, and the struggle he or she is engaged in is honored. The social justice principle also informs our decisions about how we select and use specific methodological tools. Data collection is geared toward gathering information that sheds light on whether the program is making a contribution to the larger social good, as per program mandates and agreements. In some cases this simply means: Is the program accomplishing what it says it is doing? In other cases, the social justice principle focuses attention on issues of consequential validity, forcing us to question the impact or consequences of specific findings. Does the evaluation plan lead to invidious distinctions? Are the evaluation results likely to be misused and misinterpreted in ways that do not promote the social welfare or equity of the group? The principle of social justice places the image of a just society in the hands of a community of learners engaged in a participatory form of democracy. A few examples of each stakeholder's role in practice are provided in Table 3.1.

COMMUNITY KNOWLEDGE

Local community members have invaluable knowledge and information about their community and its programs. Respecting their knowledge and valuing it only makes sense from a pragmatic perspective. They know their children's day care and school schedules, the grocery store's hiring practices, and the hospital's policies concerning indigent care. Many conventional evaluations ignore this knowledge at their own peril. In addition to disrespecting and devaluing a community, ignoring this rich database is inefficient, resulting in needless redundant data collection efforts and misguided interpretations. In addition, local communities develop their own community knowledge within the organization. This is a bottom-up approach to knowledge sharing and development (see Palo Alto Research Center, 2004). This knowledge, if mobilized, can be an extraordinary catalyst for change in an organization (see McDermott, 2001; Wenger, 1998; Wenger, McDermott, & Snyder, 2002; Schön, 1983; see Table 3.1 for examples).

EVIDENCE-BASED STRATEGIES

Evidence-based strategies have much to offer developing programs. They offer programs strategies or interventions that have worked in other similar communities and populations. In essence, they offer a useful option that has a track record and external credibility. They allow local and scholarly communities to build on knowledge. Evidence-based interventions, however, should not be blindly adopted and expected to work in new communities. Instead, they should be adapted to the local environment, culture, and conditions.

Communities have been "burnt" by out-of-touch or off-target interventions introduced or mandated in the past. However, ignoring evidence-based strategies simply because they were inappropriately applied in the past is not a healthy prescription for the future. Some evidence-based strategies provide potential solutions to difficult problems. Communities that have been hurt by these interventions and consequently ignore these contributions should "move on" and with a more cautious and skeptical eye, selectively reconsider evidence-based strategies. They should not be considered "silver bullets" ready to solve a plethora of community problems— the silver bullet approach only sets communities up for failure. Instead, evidence-based strategies should be considered as useful ideas and models potentially adaptable to the local context and environment. A few examples of each stakeholder's role are presented in Table 3.1.

CAPACITY BUILDING

Capacity building is one of the most identifiable features of empowerment evaluation (see Fetterman, 2001, pp. 14, 111, 139, 144).[4] Program staff members and participants learn how to conduct their own evaluations. Communities should be building their skills in the following areas: evaluation logic, chain of reasoning, logic models, evaluation design, data collection methods (including qualitative and quantitative methods), analysis, reporting, and ethics. They should also be building evaluative capacity in the areas of making judgments and interpretations, using the data to inform decision making, and making formative and summative assessments about their programs. In some cases this might involve making a determination of merit or worth of the program. In most cases, their judgment focuses on program improvement. The bottom line is that people should be learning how to conduct their own evaluations. In practice, program staff members, participants, and funders should be engaged in some substantive part of the evaluation enterprise, ranging from data collection to reporting the findings and recommendations. In the process of internalizing and institutionalizing evaluation, they should be making evaluation a part of planning and management as well. In other words, as they improve their evaluative capacity they should be improving their own capacity to manage and operate their programs; see Table 3.1 for examples.

ORGANIZATIONAL LEARNING

Empowerment evaluation helps to create a community of learners (Fetterman, 2001, pp. 6–7; Lave & Wenger, 1991; Schön, 1983; Wenger, 1998; Wenger, McDermott, & Snyder, 2002). This community feeds back information about how the program or organization is working (or not working). This feedback loop is designed to make corrective or adaptive changes in organizational behavior. Empowerment evaluation makes organizations or groups more responsive to environmental changes and challenges. It also enhances an organization's receptivity to new adaptive strategies. Empowerment evaluation is able to accomplish these goals because it is focused on encouraging organizations to make data-driven decisions (data derived from their own self-reflection and analysis). In practice, the empowerment evaluator lobbies for the use of data to inform decision making at every opportunity. Empowerment evaluators encourage staff members and participants to continually evaluate their performance. This may be in the form of a simple question about how effective a staff meeting was or providing training concerning data collection, analysis, interpretation, and reporting functions.

The empowerment evaluator, as coach, has a role to ensure that communities receive help interpreting the data and putting it to good use. This is necessary if the organization is to learn and either maintain or modify its behavior. Timing is also critical. For example, empowerment evaluators encourage the use of evaluative data during critical phases of the budget cycle when the data is needed most. They act as historians to remind people what they found and what commitments they made in the past to help them follow through on what they have learned (and have subsequently committed to change).

Empowerment evaluators also have a responsibility to help make the environment conducive to organizational learning (see Argyris, 1992; Argyris & Schön, 1978; Fetterman & Eiler, 2001; Preskill & Torres, 1999; Schön, 1983) by making the processes simple, transparent, and trustworthy. Organization administrators have a significant role to play in practice as well. They take the lead in creating an environment conducive to taking calculated risks, experimenting, evaluating, and using data to inform decision making. They are effective when their decision making is transparent. In other words, they have a responsibility to communicate with clarity the criteria used for decisions. They also must ensure that the data is credible and used to inform decision making. Empowerment evaluation helps organizations develop both the climate and structures for generating reflective practitioners. It also helps communities focus on systemic issues and systems thinking rather than short-term solutions and quick fixes. A few examples of each stakeholder's role are provided in Table 3.1.

ACCOUNTABILITY

Empowerment evaluation is about accountability (Fetterman, 2001, p. 118). It is useful for external accountability, but its strength is in fostering internal accountability. External forms of accountability last as long as the external agency is present to exert its force. Internal accountability is built within the structure of the organization or program and is fueled by internal peer pressures and institutionalized mechanisms developed by members of the group or organization. Empowerment evaluation does not alter the existing authority structure. Supervisors remain supervisors. However, instead of imposing their independent and often autocratic will on their employees and staff members, they hold them accountable for what they agreed to do as part of the agency's efforts. The motivation changes because the work is in alignment with individual and group interests. In practice, this principle reminds people that they are both individually accountable and accountable as a group or community of learners. Individuals hold one another accountable for promises and commitments (including memoranda of agreement). The organization is also held accountable and expected to "walk its talk." The feedback mechanisms built into empowerment evaluation lend themselves to the development of this kind of internal accountability.

Accountability does not only refer to the community and the evaluator. The funder is also accountable to "walk its talk." If it commits to being a partner, then it has to be present in the program implementation and evaluation. If it promises to put funds in the hands of the community to help build the latter's capacity to make decisions, then it cannot suddenly and without cause take over operations. Funders have to be held accountable concerning their expectations. If they expect communitywide initiatives to take hold, they have to be willing to fund operations at a level that is meaningful and realistic.

External accountability is also a fundamental reality in empowerment evaluation. Empowerment evaluations are conducted within the context of external requirements and demands. This makes the process "real." Empowerment evaluation uses internal accountability to achieve both internal goals and external requirements or outcomes. A few examples of each stakeholder's role in practice are provided in Table 3.1.

CONCLUSION

These principles in practices are overlapping and interactively reinforcing.[5] For example, the focus on improvement instead of failure, compliance, or inadequacy is a positive and constructive force in people's lives.
People are receptive to approaches designed to help them accomplish their
objectives and improve programs and less receptive to destructive and off-
target forms of criticism. An improvement orientation also influences the
evaluation design. It ensures a constructive approach, including corrective
feedback, allowing for mid-course corrections and program enhancement.
It also typically builds on strengths.

Inclusion and democratic participation are also inviting features of
empowerment evaluation. These principles help to create an atmosphere
of respect, acceptance, and community. They help communities capitalize
on their own human capital (valuing their members' contributions).
Instead of reinventing the wheel, their knowledge is respected and used,
saving precious time and resources.

A social justice orientation attracts people committed to the same ideals. It conveys a unifying sense of purpose. It reminds people of their commitment by placing the larger picture in front of them. It is easy to forget
about the bigger picture when mired in the daily duty of program implementation. A social justice orientation provides a focal point for designing
and implementing a program and an evaluation. It provides a unifying
purpose that permeates both the program and the evaluation, shaping
daily decisions and actions.

Community knowledge is generated from a community of learners.
When the force of a community of learners is coupled with transparency in
decision making, organizational learning becomes possible. Community
ownership and capacity building make a learning organization sustainable.

Evidence-based strategies contribute to organizational learning. It is
more efficient to consider past evidence-based strategies when building a
learning organization. In addition, considering evidence-based strategies is
a form of respect. Valuing both local and scholarly communities' evidence-
based strategies recognizes the work of others who preceded the current
community. The use of evidence-based strategies also lends additional
credibility to the evaluation and to the program's implementation.

All of these principles in practice encourage and make possible internal accountability, one of the only sustainable forms of accountability.
Internal forms of accountability are in place day after day, long after the
external evaluators and funders have come and gone.

In conclusion, this chapter has discussed empowerment evaluation
principles in practice. The purpose was to provide scholars and practitioners with additional guidance in their pursuit of quality in their empowerment evaluation endeavors. Individual principles have been used to orga-

nize the discussion. In addition, a table of quality ratings has been used to assess the various (high, medium, and low) levels of commitment to empowerment evaluation principles in practice. These principles were assessed according to the specific roles in this collaborative enterprise, namely, that of the evaluator, the community, and the funder. This tripartite partnership is required to accomplish any meaningful empowerment evaluation. This discussion is not exhaustive but rather is illustrative of the collaborative and multilayered nature of empowerment evaluation principles in practice. In succeeding chapters we reflect on these principles in practice in greater depth by examining a series of empowerment evaluation case studies.

NOTES

1. The term "community" refers to the specific group using evaluation in the organization or local community—rather than the entire town or city.
2. Tools vary, ranging from the "three-step model" (Fetterman, 2001) to the 10-step "Getting to Outcomes" approach (Chinman et al., 2004). The emphasis is on both processes and outcomes (as well as impacts). Evaluators may help train staff members and participants to design a pretest and posttest survey in order to determine if the program or intervention had a desirable outcome. They might help them conduct interviews and write up case studies. The data would be used to reinforce successful efforts and question less effective strategies.
3. Empowerment evaluation has been influenced by the full-inclusion movement that relates to individuals with disabilities (see Fetterman, 1996; Hanson et al., 1998).
4. Capacity building is also a significant part of the United Nations agenda (see United Nations, 2003; One World Network, 2003; World Business Council for Sustainable Development, 2004, among many other organizations, including nongovernmental organizations and nonprofits.
5. The principles can also compete with one another. This can create conflicts in priorities. However, simple rules apply. Honesty and systematic inquiry are constant. Community ownership and control are a priority.

REFERENCES

Argyris, C. (1992). *On organizational learning.* Cambridge, MA: Blackwell Business.

Argyris, C., & Schön, D.A. (1978). *Organizational learning: A theory of action perspective.* Reading, MA: Addison-Wesley.

Banks, J. A. (1981). *Multiethnic education: Theory and practice.* Boston: Allyn & Bacon.

Chinman, M., Imm, P., & Wandersman, A. (2004). *Getting to Outcomes 2004: Pro-*

moting accountability through methods and tools for planning, implementation, and evaluation. U.S. Department of Health and Human Services, Centers for Disease Control and Prevention. Santa Monica, CA: RAND.

Christie, C. (2003). What guides evaluation? A study of how evaluation practice maps onto evaluation theory. *New Directions for Evaluation, 97*, 7–35.

Davidman, L., & Davidman, P. T. (1997). *Teaching with a multicultural perspective: A practical guide.* New York: Longman.

Dewey, J. (1940). Creative democracy—the task before us. In S. Ratner (Ed.), *The philosopher of the common man: Essays in honor of John Dewey to celebrate his eightieth birthday.* New York: Greenwood Press.

Fetterman, D. M. (1996). Empowerment evaluation: An introduction to theory and practice. In D. M. Fetterman, S. Kaftarian, & A. Wandersman (Eds.), *Empowerment evaluation: Knowledge and tools for self-assessment and accountability.* Thousand Oaks, CA: Sage.

Fetterman, D. M. (2001). *Foundations of empowerment evaluation.* Thousand Oaks, CA: Sage.

Fetterman, D. M. (2003). Fetterman-House: A process use distinction and a theory. In C. Christie (Ed.), *The practice-theory relationship in evaluation.* San Francisco: Jossey-Bass.

Fetterman, D. M., & Eiler, M. (2001). *Empowerment evaluation and organizational learning: A path toward mainstreaming evaluation.* St. Louis, MO: American Evaluation Association.

Fetterman, D. M., Kaftarian, S., & Wandersman, A. (1996). *Empowerment evaluation: Knowledge and tools for self-assessment and accountability.* Thousand Oaks, CA: Sage.

Hakuta, K. & Garcia, E. E. (1989). Bilingualism and education. *American Psychologist, 44*, 374–379.

Hanson, M. J., Wolfberg, P., Zercher, C., Morgan, M., Gutierrez, S. Barnwell, D., & Beckman, P. J. (1998). The culture of inclusion: Recognizing diversity at multiple levels. *Early Childhood Research Quarterly, 13*(1), 185–209.

Lave, J., & Wenger, E. (1991). *Situated learning: Legitimate peripheral participation.* New York: Cambridge University Press.

McDermott, R. (2001). *Knowing in community: 10 critical success factors in building communities of practice.* Available online at Community Intelligence Labs, *http://www.co-i-l.com/coil/knowledge-garden/cop/knowing.shtml.*

Millett, R. (1996). Empowerment evaluation and the W. K. Kellogg Foundation. In D. M. Fetterman, S. Kaftarian, & A. Wandersman (Eds.), *Empowerment evaluation: Knowledge and tools for self-assessment and accountability.* Thousand Oaks, CA: Sage.

One World Network. (2004). *Capacity building.* Available online at *http://www.oneworld.net/article/frontpage/232/3908.*

Palo Alto Research Center. (2004). *Community knowledge sharing.* Palo Alto, CA: Author. Available online at *http://www.parc.com/research/spl/projects/commknowledge.*

Patton, M. (1997). Toward distinguishing empowerment evaluation and placing it in a larger context. *Evaluation Practice, 18*(2), 147–163. Available online at *http://www.stanford.edu/~davidf/patton.html.*

Preskill, H., & Torres, R. T. (1999). *Evaluative inquiry for learning in organizations.* Thousand Oaks, CA: Sage.

Schön, D. (1983). *The reflective practitioner.* New York. Basic Books.

United Nations. (2003). *Issues in the negotiating process: Capacity building.* Available online at *http://unfccc.int/issues/capbuild.html* and *http://www.un.org/esa/subindex/gh15.htm.*

Wandsworth Community Empowerment Fund Network. (2003). *Strengthening democratic participation.* Available online at *www.wandsworth.gov.uk/wlsp/pdf/papers27may03/CEFN_Paper_SCreighton.pdf.*

Wenger, E. (1998). *Communities of practice.* Cambridge, UK: Cambridge University Press.

Wenger, E., McDermott, R., & Snyder, W. M. (2002). *Cultivating communities of practice: A guide to managing knowledge.* Boston, MA: Harvard Business School Press.

W. K. Kellogg Foundation. (1999). *Empowerment evaluation and foundations: A matter of perspectives.* Battle Creek, MI: Author.

W. K. Kellogg Foundation. (2001). *W. K. Kellogg Foundation logic model development guide.* Battle Creek, MI: Author.

World Business Council for Sustainable Development. (2004). *The WBCSD on capacity building.* Available online at *http://www.wbcsd.org/templates/TemplateWBCSD4/layout.asp?type=p&MenuId=NjU&doOpen=1&ClickMenu=LeftMenu.*

Yost, J., & Wandersman, A. (1998). *Results-oriented grantmaking/grant implementation: Mary Black Foundation's experience.* Paper presented at the 1998 annual meeting of the American Evaluation Association.

TABLE 3.1. Empowerment Evaluation Principles in Practice: Assessing Levels of Commitment

IMPROVEMENT	
Evaluator role in practice:	• Helps community build on strengths, instead of only focusing on problems • Helps focus evaluation on improvement-oriented goals • Suggests appropriate tools, tests, and instruments to measure change over time • Helps community internalize evaluation logic
High:	Encourages community to focus on improvement, helps design feedback mechanisms that are used for decision making, connects community with similar organizations guided by the same principles (of using evaluation to improve program practice)
Medium:	Minimal encouragement to focus on improvement, designs feedback mechanisms for community instead of with it, haphazard or random consideration given to making connections with other organizations
Low:	Does not spend time encouraging community to focus on improvement, does not provide (or help to provide) feedback mechanisms or tools to monitor change over time, does not connect the community with similar programs

Community role in practice:	• Uses evaluator to help keep the evaluation organized, rigorous, useful, and focused on improvement goals • Commits to the evaluation and assumes responsibility for both its direction and implementation in the spirit of program improvement • Uses the tools designed to monitor change over time and data for decision making to improve program practice
High:	Uses evaluation to improve program performance, uses tools to monitor change over time, uses data to inform decision making, follow up on recommendations to connect with similar organizations oriented toward evaluation-driven improvement
Medium:	Uses evaluation to monitor change over time with limited use of the findings to inform decision making, evaluation periodically used to guide program improvements, haphazard effort to make recommended connections with similar organizations
Low:	Does not monitor program performance or use evaluative data or insights to inform programmatic decision making, no effort to connect with similar organizations

EMPOWERMENT EVALUATION IN PRACTICE TABLE

Funder role in practice:	• Encourages community and the evaluator to create an evaluation design that generates data aimed at continual and long-term program improvement • Provides the financial support required of a community engaged in improvement-oriented evaluation efforts • Rolls up sleeves and helps problem-solve to improve the program • Respects community's right to govern itself and make its own evaluative and programmatic decisions
High:	Participates in community and evaluation efforts to problem solve, provides adequate funding to support improvement-oriented evaluations and initiatives, encourages the community and evaluators to design evaluations in a manner that will contribute to program decision making and improvement, respects the community's right to govern itself and make its own evaluative and programmatic decisions
Medium:	Participates periodically in problem-solving activities with the community and evaluator, provides minimal funds for improvement-oriented evaluation activities and program improvement, respects the community's right to self-govern but within limits
Low:	Not involved in problem solving with the community and evaluator, provides inadequate support for improvement-oriented assessments and initiatives, does not value an improvement-oriented paradigm nor respect the community's right to self-govern

COMMUNITY OWNERSHIP	
Evaluator role in practice	• Ensures that program staff and participants understand they own the evaluation from day 1 • Encourages staff members and participants to take responsibility for various components of the evaluation • Provide the community with the training and tools (including online self-help guides) needed to conduct its own evaluations • Support the community as it conducts its evaluations and use the findings for decision making
High:	Ensures the community understands it owns the evaluation from the beginning of the effort, enables the community to conduct its own evaluation (with training, guides, and guidance), encourages direct participation and control of the evaluation, creates opportunities for the community to take ownership of the evaluation, defends ownership of the evaluation on behalf of and/or in concert with the community when challenged (by the funder and others)

Medium:	Expects the community to take control of the evaluation without much encouragement by the middle of the evaluation, provides training designed to enable the community to assume ownership of the evaluation by the middle of the evaluation (instead of the beginning), provides a minimal role in supporting its efforts to assert control over the evaluation when challenged or differences of opinion arise concerning ownership
Low:	Accepts the community's allowing the evaluator to maintain control of the evaluation, provides training designed to help the community conduct its evaluations but without a sense of ownership

Community role in practice:	• Takes responsibility for the evaluation (and increasing levels of responsibility for specific evaluation activities and functions) • Uses evaluators to support and guide the evaluation, but under the direction of the community and/or organization • Respects the funder (as a partner offering more than funds alone) but establishes boundaries concerning decision making, governing responsibilities, and independence
High:	Takes responsibility for the evaluation from the beginning, uses evaluators and funders as partners to enhance the quality of the evaluation and program practice, defends the right to make decisions about priorities, conduct of the evaluation, and organizational behavior (based on evaluative feedback), takes the lead in informing the funder about evaluation findings and organizational behavior changes (based on evaluation feedback)
Medium:	Assumes ownership by the middle of the evaluation (instead of the beginning), relies heavily on the evaluator to shape the conceptual direction of the evaluation as well as implementation, accepts the evaluators and/or funder's mandates about the evaluation design without much discussion
Low:	Avoids assuming ownership of the evaluation, relies on the evaluator to design and implement the evaluation (including determining the community's goals and strategies to accomplish its evaluative objectives), depends on the funder to receive and digest evaluation findings

Funder role in practice:	• Respects the autonomy of the organization or agency to pursue the evaluation, as deemed appropriate (in conjunction with the evaluator) • Encourages institutional ownership of the evaluation • Supports evaluator's efforts to create opportunities to facilitate ownership by the community • Supports institutionalization of evaluation in the organization

EMPOWERMENT EVALUATION
IN PRACTICE TABLE

High:	Allows the community to own the evaluation (including conceptual direction and implementation) with the guidance and assistance of a trained evaluator, respects the autonomy of the community to make its own decisions based on the evaluative feedback, provides adequate support to enable the community to take ownership (including financial support to enable it to allocate staff time and resources to the effort), supports the evaluator's efforts to create opportunities to facilitate ownership, links up the community with similarly oriented evaluators to facilitate this process
Medium:	Allows the community to own significant portions of the evaluation, respects the autonomy of the community to make some critical decisions, provides minimal support to facilitate this process, makes minimal efforts to match up the community with the appropriate evaluator
Low:	Avoids allowing the community to take charge or ownership of evaluation, does not encourage the community to make its own decisions, does not provide sufficient support for the community to take ownership of the evaluation without straining its own budget

INCLUSION	
Evaluator role in practice:	• Reviews the demographics of the community • Asks community-based organizations to invite as many stakeholders or representatives of critical constituencies to empowerment evaluation activities • Requests the use of interpreters and/or translators for empowerment evaluation activities and documents • Respects, acknowledges, and invites cultural, political, and religious leaders in the community (as agreed to with the community) • Encourages multicultural participation in any empowerment evaluation activity
High:	Develops knowledge of the community demographics, encourages the community to include stakeholders from diverse backgrounds, encourages use of translators, facilitates multicultural participation in the evaluation
Medium:	Develops limited knowledge of or familiarity with the community, gives only minimal encouragement to invite diverse populations (typically due to time and scheduling constraints), encourages inconsistent use of translators, and minimal facilitation of multicultural participation (focused on whites and mainstream linguistic forms of expression)
Low:	Develops no knowledge of the community, does not encourage diversity among participants or use of translators, and facilitation is limited to the dominant culture or group

Community role in practice:	• Invites as many stakeholders or representatives from critical groups as possible • Ensures that voices are heard from a multicultural environment, both in evaluation activities and organizational decision making • Follows up with any group that fails to attend empowerment evaluations (to solicit its members' views and input) • Embraces diversity
High:	Invites stakeholders representing the diversity of the community or constituency, provides a framework for diverse opinions to be heard, engages a wide range of organizations and people, actively searches out voices that are not typically heard, and embraces diversity
Medium:	Invites selected stakeholders representing some measure of diversity in the community, provides a framework for evaluation but limits the diversity of opinions, engages select groups of people, rarely searches out voices that are not typically heard, and tolerates rather than embraces diversity
Low:	Does not aggressively invite stakeholders representing the diversity of the community (typically relying on a convenient sample or "old boys' network"), provides a framework for evaluation that precludes meaningful participation from diverse populations, limits the discussion by limiting participation, does not seek out diverse voices, prefers homogeneity instead of heterogeneity

Funder role in practice:	• Encourages the community and the evaluators to be as inclusive as possible • Supports inclusive efforts with advice (recommending the inclusion of relevant constituencies, as well as effective strategies promoting inclusion) • Provides appropriate funding for increased numbers and translators • Expresses an explicit expectation of inclusion
High:	Makes explicit statements supporting inclusion in the evaluation, advises the community and the evaluator concerning effective strategies promoting inclusion, provides adequate funding for increased numbers and translators and explicit expectations concerning inclusion
Medium:	Makes statements concerning inclusion but provides minimal advice concerning effective strategies, provides minimal funding to support the increased participation and little if any support for translators, and has implicit (rather than explicit) expectations concerning inclusion

Low:	Makes no statements concerning inclusion, provides no advice concerning successful strategies promoting inclusion, no funding to support participation outside the targeted or primary group, no support for translators, and no expectations concerning inclusion

DEMOCRATIC PARTICIPATION	
Evaluator role in practice:	• Sets up a framework for democratic forms of participation in the planning, implementation, and reporting of evaluation activities • Designs democratic forms of decision making at various junctures in the evaluation • Monitors the degree of democratic participation and decision making • Feeds back information concerning democratic participation to the community
High:	Designs evaluation activities that ensure fairness and equal representation, monitors the degree of democratic participation (such as voting, equal representation in forums, open dialogue), provides the community with feedback about its democratic participation and decision making
Medium:	Encourages democratic forms of participation but provides only a minimal role in actively designing evaluation activities that promote democratic participation, notes examples of democratic participation but collects no systematic data concerning this activity and provides minimal feedback in this area
Low:	Minimizes any encouragement concerning democratic participation, makes little if any effort to design activities that promote this principle, provides no data collection concerning the implementation of this principle

Community role in practice:	• Announces that a democratic form of participation and decision making will be used • Ensures that democratic participation and decision making are used • Allocates additional time that is required for democratic forms of participation • Responds promptly to complaints concerning democratic participation
High:	Explicitly commits to democratic participation as a principle in the program and evaluation, demonstrates examples of democratic participation in decision making, uses evaluation tools and activities designed to promote democratic participation, tracks and records adherence to this principle, uses evaluation feedback concerning this principle to improve practice

EMPOWERMENT EVALUATION IN PRACTICE TABLE

Medium:	Influenced by democratic forms of participation, periodically demonstrates examples of democratic participation, minimizes use of evaluation tools to promote this activity, does not provide tracking concerning this form of participation (except an occasional notation)
Low:	Demonstrates periodic examples of democratic participation but typically relies on traditional authority structure for decision making, uses no evaluation tools to facilitate this form of participation or tracking of this form of participation

Funder role in practice:	• Encourages the community and evaluator to adopt democratic forms of participation and decision making • Supports democratic participation with appropriate funding and an appreciation for the additional time required
High:	Explicitly states commitment to democratic forms of participation, encourages the community to adopt this principle in the program and evaluation practice, provides the financial support required to implement this principle
Medium:	Values this form of participation but makes no concerted effort to encourage the community in this direction, offers some support for this form of participation
Low:	Makes no effort to encourage the community to adopt and implement the principle, offers little or no funding to support activities associated with this endeavor

SOCIAL JUSTICE	
Evaluator role in practice:	• Works with people striving for social justice and self-determination • Focuses on projects aligned with a social justice and self-determination agenda • Helps design evaluations that contribute to a social justice agenda • Contextualizes evaluative findings and programmatic decision making within a social justice framework • Helps the community select evaluation tools that accurately measure whether the program is achieving its objectives within a social justice framework • Helps the community think through the potential consequences of the findings
High:	Works with people and programs aligned with a social justice agenda, helps design evaluations that contribute to a social justice agenda, helps the community conduct evaluations and interpret evaluation findings within a social justice framework

Medium:	Works with people with an interest in a social justice agenda but not completely aligned with these interests, helps design evaluations that contribute to a social justice agenda but does not help the community conduct the evaluation or interpret the findings with this frame of reference
Low:	Does not work with people interested in a social justice agenda, does not help design or conduct an evaluation within this framework

Community role in practice:	• Works with disenfranchised people and/or those committed to self-determination • Focuses on program activities and services aligned with a social justice agenda • Uses evaluation findings to improve programs contributing to the larger social good, including ameliorating social inequities • Factors in the welfare of those in greatest need when designing an evaluation, interpreting evaluation findings, and using evaluation findings to inform decision making
High:	Works with disenfranchised populations or others in the service of disenfranchised populations, focuses on program activities closely aligned with social justice issues, uses evaluation to improve programs and services to those in need, uses social justice issues as a lens in program and evaluation decision making
Medium:	Works with people interested in self-determination but not typically considered disenfranchised, focuses on some program activities aligned with a social justice agenda but is equally concerned with program activities only indirectly related or completely unrelated to these issues, only rarely uses social justice as a lens in making evaluative and programmatic decisions
Low:	Avoids working with disenfranchised populations or individuals pursuing self-determination initiatives, or focusing on program activities associated with social justice concerns, or using social justice as a lens in making evaluative and programmatic decisions

Funder role in practice:	• Works with people committed to a social justice agenda • Funds programs aligned with an agenda associated with social justice and self-determination • Helps bring communities and evaluators together that share a common social justice agenda • Fosters self-determination over dependency (by allowing groups to self-govern and develop capacity) • Helps make linkages with similarly oriented programs

EMPOWERMENT EVALUATION IN PRACTICE TABLE

High:	Works with people committed to social justice agendas, funds programs designed to help people help themselves, matches communities of evaluation use with similarly oriented evaluators, respects the right of communities to self-govern and make decisions (including evaluative and programmatic decisions) for themselves
Medium:	Works with people with an indirect relationship to a social justice agenda, funds programs designed to help people help themselves but without a central or overriding civil rights or similar agenda, manifests a minimal or haphazard role in matching communities with appropriate evaluators, respects the community's right to self-govern on selected evaluative and programmatic matters
Low:	Avoids working with people committed to a social justice agenda or funding many programs designed to help people help themselves, avoids involvement in matching communities with appropriate evaluators, adopts a position respecting the right of communities to self-govern but not allowing them to self-govern in practice (micromanagement is common)

COMMUNITY KNOWLEDGE	
Evaluator role in practice:	• Respects and values local community knowledge • Encourages multicultural participation • Uses and validates community knowledge in evaluation activities • Provides mechanisms for the use of community knowledge in the evaluation • Cultivates and validates the community knowledge generated by the community • Helps communities combine local community knowledge with external evidence-based strategies
High:	Values local knowledge, uses local knowledge to help design and implement evaluation, encourages community participation and contribution to the evaluation, provides mechanisms to use community knowledge in the evaluation, helps the community combine local community knowledge with external evidence-based strategies
Medium:	Values limited use of community knowledge in the evaluation, encourages local participation but limits local knowledge contributions to the evaluation, occasionally provides a mechanism to use local knowledge in the evaluation, allows external evidence-based strategies to dominate local community knowledge (but still combines approaches)

Low:	Does not value local knowledge concerning the design and implementation of the evaluation, does not encourage local contributions to the evaluation or create mechanisms to facilitate the use of local knowledge in evaluations, makes no attempt to combine local community knowledge with evidence-based strategies

Community role in practice:	• Recognizes the value of own contributions in evaluation • Uses community knowledge of demographics and conditions as part of the evaluation baseline data as well as part of the data collected to document change over time • Provides evaluators with cultural context in order to help them more meaningfully interpret evaluative data • Uses community knowledge to drive the evaluation
High:	Claims the right to assert the value of local knowledge, uses local community knowledge to design and conduct evaluation, works with the evaluator to ensure that local knowledge is combined with external evidence-based strategies
Medium:	Values local community knowledge but does not assert the right to use it to shape or contribute to the evaluation, minimizes the use of local knowledge to design and conduct evaluation, minimizes effort to inform or educate evaluator about community knowledge, allows external evidence-based strategies to dominate evaluation design and implementation
Low:	Does not value own community knowledge nor advocate for the role of local community knowledge in evaluation, does not make an effort to combine community knowledge with evidence-based strategies

Funder role in practice	• Encourages communities to use their community knowledge to help provide the context for the evaluation, the design of the evaluation, and the manner in which the evaluation findings are reported and used to improve community conditions • Encourages evaluators to find ways of validating and using community knowledge • Shares examples of how community knowledge has been useful in other funded projects
High:	Recognizes and explicitly validates the use of community knowledge in an evaluation, encourages the community to use community knowledge when designing and implementing an evaluation, encourages evaluators to listen to community members concerning the role of community knowledge to design and implement the evaluation as well as interpret meaningfully the findings, links the community with other organizations that have successfully used local knowledge to better inform their evaluations and programs

Medium:	Recognizes the value of community knowledge to provide context and a baseline for the evaluation but does not encourage the community to assert its right to guide the evaluation with its knowledge, encourages evaluators to make limited use of community knowledge, minimizes sharing of examples of how community knowledge has been useful in related projects
Low:	Is respectful of cultural differences and needs, but does not value community knowledge nor encourage the use of community knowledge to significantly shape the evaluation, avoids sharing knowledge of related project activity in this regard

EVIDENCE-BASED STRATEGIES	
Evaluator role in practice:	• Searches out and shares evidence-based strategies with the community in the organization and local community members • Help communities adapt evidence-based strategies to their own environment and populations • Help communities merge local community knowledge with evidence-based strategies • Help communities identify inappropriate or unworkable strategies for their communities • Help communities of evaluation to use, implement, and monitor the effectiveness of adapted evidence-based strategies
High:	Bring relevant and useful evidence-based strategies to communities for their own consideration and assessment, encourages the use of relevant evidence-based strategies, privileges local community knowledge over external evidence-based strategies when determining the appropriateness of a specific evaluation design or activity in practice, helps communities combine community knowledge with evidence-based strategies
Medium:	Brings only contractually mandated evidence-based strategies to the attention of a community, expresses minimal interest in and provides minimal encouragement for the use of evidence-based strategies, allows external evidence-based strategies to dominate local community knowledge in the design and execution of the evaluation
Low:	Ignores evidence-based strategies, misapplies evidence-based strategies, dominates the evaluation with external evidence-based strategies, fails to consider the local context and culture when applying or using external evidence-based strategies

Community role in practice:	• Requests evaluator assistance in identifying evidence-based strategies • Adapts evidence-based strategies to the community context and conditions • Combines local knowledge with evidence-based strategies • Uses evidence-based strategies used by comparable organizations • Rejects inappropriate or unworkable strategies
High:	Solicits evaluator's assistance in identifying appropriate evidence-based strategies, uses external evidence-based strategies (as tempered by community knowledge), adapts external evidence-based strategies to the local conditions, rejects unsound or inappropriate strategies
Medium:	Ignores or fails to consider external evidence-based strategies, engages in wholesale adoption of an evidence-based strategy without considering the local cultural context and conditions, displays indifference or ambivalence concerning the fusion of community knowledge and evidence-based strategies, gives only minimal or periodic consideration to the relative success or failure of external evidence-based strategies
Low:	Rejects external evidence-based strategies without due consideration for their usefulness in the evaluation, gives no consideration to combining local knowledge and external evidence-based strategies, readily adopts irrelevant or inappropriate strategies simply because they are mandated

Funder role in practice:	• Encourages the community to use evidence-based strategies with the caveat that they should adapt them, not adopt them without considering the local context • Shares evidence-based strategies that have been successful in similar funded programs • Encourages evaluators to help the community fuse evidence-based strategies with local knowledge • Respects the community's decision to use or abandon evidence-based strategies depending on the results of their experimentation with these strategies
High:	Encourages the community to adapt evidence-based strategies to the local context (instead of blind adoption), shares successfully adapted evidence-based strategies (based on the funder's knowledge of or experience working with similar programs and strategies), allows the community to determine if the external evidence-based strategies are useful (after due consideration and experimentation)

EMPOWERMENT EVALUATION IN PRACTICE TABLE

Medium:	Recommends evidence-based strategies with minimal consideration for local context and knowledge, rejects evidence-based strategies with minimal consideration or adaptation, only shares knowledge minimally about evidence-based strategies based on work with similarly funded projects/programs
Low:	Mandates the use of external evidence-based strategies regardless of the local condition, rejects evidence-based strategies without due consideration, fails to share what was learned from the use of evidence-based strategies in similar programs, fails to respect the local community's right to use or not use external evidence-based strategies

CAPACITY BUILDING	
Evaluator role in practice:	• Trains the community in how to use evaluation, ranging from the logic of evaluation to instrument development • Helps the community conduct its own evaluations • Encourages participation in and ownership of the community • Identifies ways to internalize and institutionalize evaluation (helps to make evaluation part of the planning and management of an agency or group)
High:	Places the evaluation in the hands of the community, provides training in conducting evaluation, creates a format that enables the community to immediately begin conducting parts of the evaluation itself, creates or structures opportunities for the community to engage in the evaluation, helps the community find ways to internalize and institutionalize evaluation
Medium:	Places the evaluation in the hands of community members halfway through the evaluation, provides minimal training, creates a format or system that enables the community to conduct parts of the evaluation itself over time, provides opportunities for the community to engage in the evaluation halfway through the evaluation, allow community members to find their own ways to internalize and institutionalize evaluation (without initial assistance)
Low:	Maintains control of the evaluation without a plan to transfer ownership of the evaluation, provides no training in evaluation, creates no opportunities for the community to engage in the evaluation gives no consideration to internalizing and institutionalizing evaluation

Community role in practice:	• Assumes responsibility for oversight and direction of the evaluation, as well as specific data collection, analysis, and/or reporting activities • Requests training as needed throughout the evaluation • Participates in evaluation training workshops and exercises • Works with an evaluator mentor (whenever possible) • Anticipates that mistakes will be made and plans to learn from them • Respects the process and the people engaged in the evaluation • Protects the rights of those engaged in the evaluation
High:	Assume control of the evaluation from the beginning, conducts various aspects of the evaluation (from the beginning), participates in training throughout the evaluation, learns and applies new skills, takes calculated risks, adheres to evaluation logic and guidelines, uses methods properly, acts in an ethical and appropriate manner that respects the rights of those engaged in the process
Medium:	Assumes minimal control of the evaluation, conducts a task or series of evaluation tasks midway through the evaluation, participates in initial evaluation training but haphazardly in additional training, learns evaluation skills and adheres to evaluation guidelines on most occasions, acts ethically
Low:	Does not assume control over the evaluation, not conduct part of the evaluation, not participate in training, not learn new skills, and has little conception of the evaluation logic or specific methods and little knowledge about ethical guidelines in evaluation

Funder role in practice:	• Specifies capacity building as an explicit expectation of the evaluation • Supports capacity building efforts by providing programs with additional experts and consultants as well as direct financial support for additional training, as needed • Shares program management and fund raising expertise as well as related knowledge with communities, as needed
High:	Explicitly values capacity building as part of program evaluation and implementation, provides experts, coaches, and related resources to facilitate capacity building, provides adequate funding to support capacity building activities, models by sharing funder management skills with communities
Medium:	Values capacity building minimally, provides little support in the area of external consultants or internal management expertise, models behavior only haphazardly
Low:	Places no value on capacity building, provides no support to facilitate capacity building, supplies little or no modeling in this area

ORGANIZATIONAL LEARNING	
Evaluator role in practice:	• Lobbies for the organizational learning approach with the community and funders • Creates workshops and training experiences that set the stage for organizational learning experiences • Helps the community meaningfully interpret and use data to inform decision making • Helps create learning organizational feedback loops (to inform decision making)
High:	Impresses on the community and the funder the importance of organizational learning and evaluation's role in creating a learning organization, provides training opportunities that prepare the community to engage in organizational learning, helps create structures and decision-making processes that facilitate organizational learning, helps the community interpret data in a manner that will enhance organizational learning, helps develop feedback loops
Medium:	Acknowledges the value of organizational learning, provides training to build capacity without helping to make the link to organizational learning, provides few opportunities to engage in organizational learning, helps the community of learning to interpret data for limited short-term decisions but rarely for larger organizational learning levels, makes a minimal effort to develop organizational feedback loops
Low:	Makes no mention of organizational learning as a goal, provides capacity building experiences focused on data collection but no training concerning what to do with the data after it is collected such as interpretation, decision making, and organizational learning, makes no effort to develop organizational learning feedback loops

Community role in practice:	• Commits to an organizational learning paradigm • Creates an atmosphere conducive to taking calculated risks, sharing successes and failures, and feeding back information into organizational decision making and behavior • Makes decision making transparent • Values staff member and participant engagement • Allocates time for staff members and participants to devote to the organizational learning enterprise
High:	Adopts an organizational learning paradigm, creates a climate conducive to organizational learning, values staff member and participant engagement, uses data for decision making and organizational learning, allocates time to organizational learning activities, makes significant changes in organizational behavior based on the evaluation

Medium:	Values but does not adopt an organizational learning paradigm, creates a climate conducive to conducting self-evaluation but not aware of the value of organizational learning (feeding the evaluative findings into decision making), values participation and evaluation activities but in a limited fashion, allocates minimal time to organizational learning activities rarely makes any change in organizational behavior based on evaluation findings
Low:	Does not value or adopt organizational learning paradigm, nor create an environment conducive to organizational learning, nor value participation, rarely uses evaluation for decision making or organizational learning, does not allocate time to organizational learning activities, makes no significant organizational changes based on the evaluation

Funder role in practice:	• Encourages the institutionalization of sustainable forms of organizational learning • Supports organizational learning with funding for staff support and tracking mechanisms • Shares knowledge about organizational learning, links up the funded agency with similar institutions and consultants possessing relevant expertise and a successful track record in this area • Asks what agencies are learning on this level and what they plan to do to institutionalize this form of organizational learning
High:	Explicitly states the value of organizational, learning, institutionalizing evaluation as a tool to foster organizational learning, provide adequate financial support to enable the community to engage in organizational learning activities, connects the community with organizational learning expertise and consultants, inquires about what the community and evaluators are doing and learning concerning organizational learning
Medium:	Values organizational learning but provides minimal support to engage in these activities, links up the community with appropriate organizational learning expertise but rarely inquires about what community members are learning
Low:	Does not value organizational learning, nor provide support to enable a community to become an organizational learning entity, nor connect the community with organizational learning consultants, nor inquire about what community members and evaluators are learning

EMPOWERMENT EVALUATION IN PRACTICE TABLE

ACCOUNTABILITY	
Evaluator role in practice:	• Trains community members to hold themselves accountable • Places the evaluation in the hands of community members to enable them to learn how to hold themselves accountable • Holds the funder accountable for agreements with the community in terms of community control of the evaluation (and program implementation) • Serves as a coach rather than dominating or controlling the evaluation
High:	Trains community members how to use evaluation tools to hold themselves accountable, encourages the use of internal accountability mechanisms (including positive peer pressure, evaluation measures, or benchmarks), encourages community participation in and implementation of the evaluation (to help the members learn how to take control of the evaluation by doing it), holds the community and the funder accountable for commitments (by serving as an historian or reminder), serves as a coach rather than an external expert in control of the evaluation
Medium:	Trains members in how to conduct an evaluation without a focus on how they need to hold themselves accountable and follow through on commitments, devotes minimal time to developing or encouraging the use of internal accountability mechanisms, minimizes participation in the conduct of the evaluation, takes a minimal role as an historian or reminder of commitments made by the community or funder, values internal control and ownership of the evaluation but dominates the design and implementation of the evaluation
Low:	Focuses minimally on the development or use of self-accountability measures, plays no role as an historian reminder, or archivist concerning commitments of the community or the funder, dominates the evaluation, makes community members' decisions for them, fosters dependency instead of internal accountability

Community role in practice:	• Holds each member accountable for implementing the program and conducting the evaluation • Holds the evaluator accountable for serving as a coach and critical friend and not dominating or controlling the direction or implementation of the evaluation • Holds the funder accountable for governance and ownership agreements

EMPOWERMENT EVALUATION
IN PRACTICE TABLE

High:	"Walks the talk," makes community members accountable for their own actions, including conducting the evaluation, being a member of the partnership, and following through on commitments, makes the evaluator accountable to serve as a coach and facilitator (and technical assistance agent), uses data to inform decision making (even when decisions are not popular), holds the community to the highest standards (methodologically, ethically, and in terms of social justice)
Medium:	Builds mechanisms designed to foster accountability but uses them inconsistently, occasionally uses data to inform decision making, overly relies on the evaluator and other experts to solve local problems, relinquishes control over the evaluation
Low:	Is not responsible for own actions, fails to build in mechanisms for self-reflection and accountability, fails to use data to inform decision making, blames others for own problems and mistakes, fails to hold community members to the highest standards possible under the circumstances, does not hold the evaluator or funder accountable for their commitments

Funder role in practice:	• Holds the community accountable for promised results • Holds the evaluator accountable for assisting the community in accomplishing its objectives • Holds the funder accountable for supporting these efforts in a manner that is realistic and sustainable
High:	Holds the community accountable for promises and commitments (with the understanding that modifications are often required but in consultation with each of the partners), the evaluator accountable for helping the program achieve its objectives in a constructive manner using evaluation, and the funder accountable for financial commitments and philosophical self-help commitments
Medium:	Pays attention haphazardly to community commitments, pays minimal attention to the evaluator's role or allows the evaluator to dominate, and minimal attention to the role of the evaluator in helping the community implement its programs and improve members' practice, pays only erratic attention to the funder's commitments
Low:	Does not hold the community responsible for or take charge of the evaluation, ignores own commitments to the community and the evaluator

CHAPTER 4

Lessons That Influenced the Current Conceptualization of Empowerment Evaluation

REFLECTIONS FROM TWO EVALUATION PROJECTS

Dana C. Keener, Jessica Snell-Johns, Melanie Livet,
and Abraham Wandersman

In this chapter, we reflect on our work as empowerment evaluators with two evaluation projects that began early in the history of empowerment evaluation. These projects and their contrasting features shaped our current conceptualization of empowerment evaluation by teaching us numerous lessons about how to facilitate program improvement and results-based accountability. After briefly describing the background and context for both evaluation projects, this chapter explores two important questions we regularly confront as empowerment evaluators: (1) when do we implement a particular evaluation task for program staff versus when do we show the staff how to implement the task themselves, while continuing to adhere to the empowerment evaluation value of building capacity? and (2) how do we address both program improvement and accountability in our work without compromising one or the other? In an effort to bring these questions to life, we share stories from our work that illustrate the benefits and disadvantages of key decisions made in each evaluation project. For each scenario, we consider the contextual factors that affected our decisions and examine the extent to which our work was consistent with the principles of empowerment evaluation. In sharing our real-life experiences, we hope the reader will gain a greater understanding of how to put the theory of empowerment evaluation into practice.

BACKGROUND AND CONTEXT OF THE PROJECTS

Both of the community programs presented in this chapter were funded by the Mary Black Foundation (MBF) of Spartanburg, South Carolina. Consistent with the philosophy of empowerment evaluation and informed by the Results-Oriented Grantmaking and Grant-Implementation framework (Crusto & Wandersman, 2004; Yost & Wandersman, 1998), MBF incorporated questions into its grant application that were intended to promote effective program planning, implementation, and evaluation. The foundation also selected the evaluation team, led by Abraham Wandersman from the University of South Carolina, to conduct the evaluation for both projects. A portion of the funds granted to each project was earmarked specifically for the evaluation efforts. In both cases, the evaluation team was introduced to project staff at the onset of funding, allowing the evaluation to begin during the planning stages of each project. This timing was made possible because of MBF's appreciation of the empowerment evaluation philosophy, which asserts that program outcomes are most likely to be achieved when evaluation begins in the early stages of program planning (Wandersman et al., 2004).

Although empowerment evaluation was the evaluation approach selected for both projects, the evaluation plans for each project developed differently. Table 4.1 provides a comparison of both evaluation projects in terms of their purpose, structural context, division of roles and responsibilities, and evaluation processes. Differences in the evaluation projects materialized for two reasons. First, there were differences between the projects (e.g., organizational structure, new versus existing program components) that called for distinct evaluation needs. Second, since the projects started 1 year apart from each other, the later project benefited from lessons learned during the first project.

The first project we evaluated was the Middle Tyger Community Center (MTCC)—a comprehensive family support center located in a rural community near Spartanburg, South Carolina. Approximately 1 year later, we began the second evaluation project with the Foundation for the

TABLE 4.1. Comparison of Middle Tyger Community Center (MTCC) and Foundation for the Future (FFF) Evaluation Projects

MTCC	FFF
Purpose of evaluation	
• Purpose: program improvement and accountability • Objectives: (1) develop and implement a process and outcome evaluation plan in collaboration with staff and (2) provide consultation regarding best practices	• Purpose: program improvement, accountability, and building evaluation capacity • Objectives: (1) develop and implement process and outcome evaluation by promoting self-evaluation among program staff and (2) evaluate the collaborative partnership
Structural context	
• Project started 1 year before the FFF project • Larger budget for evaluation team • Evaluation team composed of four individuals • No designated program staff person to coordinate evaluation efforts	• Project benefited from lessons learned from the first year of the MTCC project • Smaller budget for evaluation team • Evaluation team composed of two to three individuals • Designated program staff person with evaluation duties as part of job description
Division of roles and responsibilities	
Roles of evaluator	
• Developed and implemented evaluation plan with ongoing input from program staff • Provided consultation and recommendations on best practices • Conducted evaluation workshops, but to a lesser extent than FFF • Issued semiannual reports to the program and the funder regarding program implementation and outcomes	• Met individually with FFF partners to create individual evaluation plans • Worked with the FFF Collaboration Manager to create an infrastructure for sharing and reporting evaluation findings • Conducted extensive evaluation workshops • Evolved over time to include consultation on best practices and to assist in addressing barriers to effective program implementation • Issued semiannual reports providing feedback to the Boys and Girls Club regarding its role as the lead agency spearheading the collaboration
Roles of program staff	
• Provided input to evaluation team to help plan and implement the evaluation plan • Engaged in daily evaluation activity as specified by the evaluation plan developed by the evaluation team	• Involved in daily evaluation activity • Involved in developing, planning, and implementing their own evaluation plan with guidance from the evaluation team • FFF partners wrote their own program evaluation reports

(continued)

TABLE 4.1. *(continued)*

MTCC	FFF

- Over time, assumed a larger role in writing sections of the evaluation reports

Evaluation processes
Data collection procedure

• Specified and documented by the evaluation team	• Decided by FFF team in collaboration with evaluators
• Some data were collected entirely by MTCC staff, and some data were collected by the evaluation team	• All data were collected by FFF staff

Report process

• One report every 6 months	• Two reports every 6 months
• Evaluation team writes the first draft of the report	• Evaluation team helped develop a template for the partners to use for writing program reports
• In early years, lengthy meetings were held between evaluation team and MTCC administrative staff to collaboratively discuss and revise the reports	• FFF management team wrote reports about program process and outcome evaluation for the funder and received feedback from USC team
• In later years, MTCC administrative staff assumed a larger role in writing some sections of the report	• USC team wrote in-house reports on collaboration and received feedback from FFF management team
• The content and structure of the reports evolved over time to reflect changes in the collaborative structure and a shift in focus toward integrated services delivery	

Report usage

• The primary use of the report was to fulfill reporting requirements and accountability to the funder	• Evaluation findings prompted major structural changes to the partnership
• Key findings from evaluation reports were highlighted in presentations and publications to enhance public relations	• Reports were used to fulfill reporting requirements and accountability to the funder
• Findings and recommendations from each report were used to guide and improve programming for the next semiannual period. This purpose was achieved to a greater extent in later years of the evaluation, a sign of increased evaluation capacity	• Key findings from evaluation reports were often highlighted in presentations and publications to enhance public relations

Future (FFF) initiative—a collaborative effort designed to enhance exist-ing services for families and children in the metropolitan Spartanburg area by bringing existing agencies together in a partnership spearheaded by the Boys and Girls Club. Each project is described in greater detail below.

Middle Tyger Community Center

The overarching mission of MTCC is to promote healthy families. The idea for the center originated when a school nurse working in a small, rural community near Spartanburg, South Carolina noticed that a number of high school girls were becoming pregnant, having children, dropping out of school, and demonstrating difficulties coping with their life circum-stances. The nurse shared her observations with leaders in the school dis-trict, which led to a vision of a full-scale family resource center established to address the needs of adolescent mothers and other disadvantaged fami-lies living in the metro Spartanburg area. Funding was obtained from the Mary Black Foundation to (1) renovate an old elementary school building to house the center, (2) implement an educational support program for adolescent mothers and their children, including high-quality child care services, (3) implement an after-school program for middle school stu-dents designed to prevent teenage pregnancy, and (4) initiate, develop, and coordinate a collaborative partnership with existing agencies in the com-munity to serve the comprehensive needs of families in the region. The community center evolved into a model of service integration and a co-location for other partner agencies, including local branches of the Depart-ment of Social Services and the Department of Health and Environmental Control. Among the services offered were parent education classes, prena-tal clinic services, early childhood education programs, adult education programs, emergency financial assistance, and family therapy services.

The evaluation of MTCC began in 1998 during MTCC's pilot grant period. The MTCC evaluation team was hired to (1) assist with program development and (2) facilitate results and accountability by developing and implementing process and outcome evaluation in collaboration with the MTCC staff. In developing the evaluation plan, the evaluators empha-sized the critical elements necessary for effective programs—including needs and resource assessment, goal setting, use of science and best prac-tices, program planning, implementation, evaluation and sustainability.[1] See Table 4.1 for a more detailed description of the MTCC evaluation pro-ject.

Since the programs to be implemented at MTCC were new, the evalua-tion team played a key consultation role in terms of identifying and select-ing evidence-based programs. Given MTCC's needs and capacities at the time, the evaluators and the MTCC staff generally agreed that this was an appropriate role for the evaluation team; however, there was some confusion as to when the evaluators were acting as program consultants versus acting in a more traditional role of examining program outcomes. Although the evaluation team worked closely with the staff to develop the evaluation plans and guided staff in collecting data for the evaluation, the evaluation team assumed a lead role in writing the semiannual evaluation reports to be submitted to MBF. The first 2 years of the evaluation were heavily focused on the use of evaluation tools and information to support the design and implementation of the two anchor programs described above (i.e., the program for teenage mothers and the after-school program), but the evaluation focus later evolved into assessing MTCC as an integrated service delivery system.

Foundation for the Future

Realizing that the youths they served were exposed to multiple risk factors (e.g., poverty, lack of family support), the Boys and Girls Club of Metro Spartanburg created a grant to sponsor a community partnership (FFF) that would provide additional services to families of Boys and Girls Club members while simultaneously increasing the capacity of other existing agencies to reach populations their programs typically did not serve. The FFF partnership was founded on the belief that existing organizations and programs in the community (five arts programs, a Junior Achievement program, a Parents as Teachers program for parents of young children, and a Parent University program for parents of Boys and Girls Club members) could achieve more working together than each could do operating independently. Although each agency had its own unique set of desired outcomes, the partnership was unified around the overall goal of increasing families' sense of belonging, usefulness, influence, and competence.

The FFF evaluation developed differently than the MTCC evaluation, for a number of reasons (see Table 4.1 for a point-by-point comparison of both evaluation projects). First, the FFF initiative sought to capitalize on evidence-based programs that already existed in the Spartanburg area. This meant that FFF had less of a need for consultation regarding program selection, as compared to MTCC, which chose to create two brand-new programs. Second, each FFF partner agency had other funders to report to in addition to MBF (unlike the MTCC programs, which were initially housed under the same funding umbrella) and therefore needed to have their own process and outcome evaluation plans. Third, FFF had more programs to evaluate than MTCC; consequently, the evaluators had fewer resources they could devote to each individual program component. Based on these factors and because MBF was particularly interested in supporting capacity building in the community, FFF and MBF decided they would place a strong emphasis on self-evaluation. Accordingly, the evaluation contract stated that the first objective of the evaluation team was to help establish and maintain an effective self-evaluation system. To fulfill this task, the evaluation team worked closely with each partner to develop individual evaluation plans and products; however, the major responsibility for the evaluation belonged to the FFF initiative (and not to the evaluators).

The second objective of the FFF evaluation team was to provide feedback to the Boys and Girls Club and the collaborating partners regarding their self-evaluation and collaboration efforts. The evaluation team was asked to evaluate the effectiveness of the collaboration and to write a collaboration report twice a year. The collaboration report was a formal way for the evaluation team to provide feedback to the Boys and Girls Club and the other FFF partners regarding their efforts to collaborate and self-evaluate. However, based on the values captured in the empowerment evaluation principles of inclusion, community ownership, and improvement, the evaluation team agreed that the report was an internal, or "in-house," report. Nonetheless, FFF staff members voluntarily chose to include the collaboration report as an attachment with their semiannual evaluation reports submitted to MBF.

THE TIMING AND SELECTION OF STRATEGIES FOR BUILDING EVALUATION CAPACITY

Building evaluation capacity within community agencies is a primary task of the empowerment evaluator. In order to effectively build evaluation capacity, evaluators must be observant of the existing skills and attitudes among individuals and within a given organizational culture. Evaluators must also be attuned to opportunities to demonstrate and teach evaluation skills, especially in circumstances when the program staff does not yet appreciate the value of these skills. At times, it can be difficult to decide when it is appropriate to implement a particular task for community stakeholders, as an early step in the capacity-building process, and when to teach stakeholders how to do the task themselves, as illustrated in the following example.

In the later years of the MTCC evaluation project, the MTCC administrative staff gradually increased its consultation with the evaluation team when writing new grant proposals. For instance, MTCC requested assistance in developing a logic model for a grant proposal. The turnaround time was very short, making it unrealistic to collaboratively design the logic model. Believing that the logic model was a critical component to the grant proposal and wanting to support MTCC's efforts to secure new funds, a member of the evaluation team agreed to develop a logic model based on information provided by MTCC. The community center staff reported that they found the model very helpful in conceptualizing and organizing the purpose, goals, strategies, and desired outcomes of the new program. Later, the staff requested assistance in developing a logic model for a second grant proposal. This time, the evaluation team suggested that staff members work with the evaluation team to develop the model. The staff agreed to this and found the process and the resulting model helpful in conceptualizing their proposed program. As a result, the executive director requested a workshop on logic modeling for the entire administrative staff. Eventually, MTCC's primary grant writer was able to draft logic models on her own and simply requested that the evaluator review and refine her work.

The foregoing illustration reflects the developmental process of building the capacity of practitioners to value and utilize particular evaluation skills (in this case, logic modeling). First, the program developed an increased appreciation for how logic modeling can help link program goals and strategies in meaningful ways. As a result, MTCC staff members increased their motivation to gain the additional skills necessary for developing logic models on their own.

There are times when it is appropriate for an empowerment evaluator to implement an evaluation task for community stakeholders because this undertaking is seen as an early step in the capacity-building process. In the scenario presented above, there was not time to coordinate a collaborative effort. Therefore, the evaluator capitalized on the opportunity to model an activity that she believed would be valued by MTCC staff. In the end, the staff did value the product and wanted to learn the skill for future grant-writing efforts. Had the evaluator insisted on a collaborative effort upon the first request for assistance, or if she had refused to respond to the request due to the requirement for a quick turnaround, she would have missed an important opportunity to inculcate new and valuable evaluation skills.

In addition to being guided by the empowerment evaluation principle of capacity building, empowerment evaluators are also cognizant of other such empowerment evaluation principles as improvement and democratic participation. In certain situations, empowerment evaluators may implement evaluation tasks as one of many team players invested in working toward program improvement. This occurs when all the stakeholders agree that the evaluator's role is critical for ensuring improvement and/or accountability. This practice is distinct from other evaluation approaches because the empowerment evaluator's role is determined by all the stakeholders through a democratic process, and not assumed through the authority of the evaluator.

In a retrospective survey of evaluation capacity, MTCC staff members reported perceived increases in their ability to plan programs using evaluation concepts, to implement evaluation processes, and to measure and analyze evaluation data (Snell-Johns & Keener, 2000). While recognizing their gains in evaluation capacity, MTCC administrators continued to rely on the evaluation team (as consistent with the original evaluation contract) to design and write the evaluation reports. Staff members did not—and were not expected to—achieve a full-scale self-evaluation system.[2] In spite of the fact that it was sometimes uncomfortable for MTCC to have less control over report writing, MTCC staff members did not seek responsibility for this task, because their time and resources were fully exhausted by program implementation.

Unlike the MTCC evaluation, the FFF evaluation project was developed to emphasize self-evaluation from the onset. The FFF grant provided funds for a Collaboration Manager who would be responsible for coordinating the collaboration and evaluation of the initiative. Although FFF had fewer funds designated for evaluation than MTCC, FFF ultimately invested a comparable amount in evaluation by having their own staff member assume greater responsibility and time for the evaluation effort. As a result, the FFF evaluation team deliberately did not take responsibility for data entry or for writing the evaluation reports. At the same time, the evaluators spent significant amounts of time outlining the reports, writing sections of the reports, and editing reports based on the staff's capacities in these areas. The FFF evaluation team conducted numerous evaluation trainings intended to teach evaluation basics (e.g., valid methods of measurement, data collection, data analysis) to the Boys and Girls Club staff and other FFF partners. The evaluation team worked collaboratively with all partners to develop a measurement plan that fit their needs, helped select and design process and outcome surveys, created an evaluation workbook that included the individual measures and tools used by each program component, met with each partner to teach SPSS (Statistical Package for the Social Sciences) and data entry, and helped the partners organize and edit each of their individual reports. These strategies are highly consistent with the practices described under the evaluator's role in capacity building in Chapter 2.

Similar to MTCC, FFF staff members reported perceived increases in their evaluation capacity over time (Snell-Johns & Keener, 2000). Even more importantly, there was substantial evidence that evaluation processes had been institutionalized at FFF by the time the evaluation team left. For example, a web-based evaluation reporting system was fully implemented by FFF staff and was being utilized by all of the partners, demonstrating that evaluation had become part of their routine and daily activity, otherwise known as mainstreaming evaluation (Sanders, 2003). In the third year of the project, the Boys and Girls Club changed the position title of Collaboration Manager to Director of Collaboration and Evaluation, reflecting an increased emphasis on evaluation. In the last year of the program, the person who had held this position since the onset of funding left FFF to pursue other career interests. Before leaving, she had assumed a number of evaluation-related responsibilities with minimum involvement from the evaluation team. The new Director of Collaboration and Evaluation (DCE) had an appropriate educational background for the position (a BA in psychology) but had minimal previous evaluation experience. The new DCE was trained by the departing staff member and assumed the same duties with relative ease. The duties were written into her job description, reflecting an organizational culture that reinforced evaluation and learning from evaluation. The first evaluation report prepared by the new DCE was of a similar high quality as the previous reports, an indication that evaluation practices had become institutionalized within the organizational culture.

Lessons Learned about Building Evaluation Capacity

1. Self-evaluation is the highest form of evaluation capacity and is most consistent with the empowerment evaluation principles of community ownership and capacity building. At the same time, if a particular organization is not ready for full-scale self-evaluation or does not want to fully self-evaluate due to other factors (e.g., funding requirements), it can still utilize principles of empowerment evaluation in various forms and degrees. Empowerment evaluation is guided by its principles. Empowerment evaluation is not an "all-or-nothing" endeavor, nor is it guided exclusively by particular procedures or methods.

2. When an organization wants to develop a full-scale self-evaluation system (as did FFF), it is important that roles and responsibilities for evaluation tasks be defined clearly in a way that facilitates self-evaluation from the onset of the project. The program should be primarily responsible for the evaluation tasks, even if intensive coaching and assistance (or even implementing the task the first several times) is required in the early stages. Once the division of responsibilities for a given evaluation is established a certain way (e.g., the evaluators write the reports), it can be difficult to shift roles at a later time.

3. As empowerment evaluators, we strive to teach skills so that program staff can ultimately implement these skills on their own. However, at times it is appropriate to implement an evaluation task for a program. Specific decisions about when to implement a task for program staff are based on multiple factors, including stakeholders' current skill levels and attitudes. To make good choices regarding the timing and selection of strategies intended to build evaluation capacity, the evaluator must be attuned to

the organization's readiness to plan, implement, and sustain empowerment evaluation processes (see Chapter 6). If implementing a task for a program stakeholder eventually leads to an opportunity for teaching the same task later, then it still fits within the principles of empowerment evaluation. Consonant with the principles of democratic participation and program improvement, it is also appropriate for empowerment evaluators to implement tasks as a member of a team, working side by side with the program staff to carry out the evaluation plans.

4. The interplay between evaluation capacity and the principle of community ownership appears to impact the degree to which evaluation is mainstreamed within an organization. In other words, the greater the degree of community ownership over the evaluation process (i.e., the more control community stakeholders have over the evaluation), the more deeply evaluation seems to become engrained in the organizational culture. Furthermore, the principles of community ownership, inclusion, and democratic participation all contribute to the principle of organizational learning—the idea that the organization values knowledge and insight for the purpose of achieving outcomes. Reflecting these concepts through our own experiences, we observed both MTCC and FFF demonstrate important gains in evaluation capacity. However, the FFF project was more successful at mainstreaming evaluation practices throughout its organization. We attribute this difference in capacity to the fact that FFF had a larger degree of community ownership over the evaluation process than MTCC (e.g., FFF wrote its own reports and was primarily responsible for implementing the evaluation plan). Having more responsibility for these tasks from the beginning facilitated a degree of skill at FFF that was not required from the MTCC staff. Although the MTCC evaluation was intended to be an empowerment evaluation, looking back in hindsight, some of the features of the evaluation more resemble participatory evaluation than they do empowerment evaluation, with the primary distinction in this case being a lesser degree of community ownership over the evaluation process itself and ultimately a lesser degree of organizational learning and capacity to self-evaluate.

SELECTING PRACTICES THAT FACILITATE IMPROVEMENT AND ACCOUNTABILITY

An important benefit of empowerment evaluation is that it does not force evaluators to choose between program improvement and accountability; instead, it conceives these goals as intimately connected. Empowerment evaluation serves the dual roles of providing valuable information to programs that can be utilized to improve programs while also remaining accountable to funders and community stakeholders about implementa-

tion and outcomes. This requires that both positive and negative evaluation findings be valued (Wandersman et al., 2004) and that negative
results not be used against the program unless the program fails to implement changes designed to address them.

Our work has taught us that in order to achieve both improvement
and accountability we must establish clear expectations among all stakeholders regarding the manner in which evaluation results will be reported
and used. Specifically, the purpose, scope, and target audience of evaluation reports must be defined and agreed upon by all stakeholders. We also
found that when community agencies have greater ownership over the
reporting process, it is easier to maintain the desired balance between
improvement and accountability.

About 2 years into the MTCC evaluation, a lack of clear expectations
regarding how a particular outcome measure would be reported led to a
difficult period of tension between the empowerment evaluation principles
of improvement and accountability. Despite what led up to the problem,
the values and practices of empowerment evaluation helped resolve the
problem and restore trust between program staff and the evaluation team.
In this particular situation, a member of the evaluation team presented a
formative evaluation tool to an MTCC staff member. The tool was
intended to assess the program's adherence to established best practices in
an after-school program. The staff member and evaluator agreed the tool
would be helpful in identifying and documenting areas of the program that
needed improvement and would help the staff member advocate for more
resources to develop the program. They also agreed to have the evaluator
conduct the assessment to ensure the objectivity of the results. The evaluator conducted the assessment, scored the measure, and included the
results in the body of an early draft of a semiannual evaluation report. The
assessment was scored using a Guttman scale (McIver & Carmines, 1981).
Accordingly, in order to receive a high score on the scale, a program must
demonstrate all of the elements necessary for that score as well as every
element under all of the lower scores. Therefore, even if a program has all
of the elements under the highest score of the scale but is missing an element of a lower score, the program will receive a low score and not receive
credit for the elements under the higher score. Aside from the scoring
structure of the scale, some of the program features measured by the tool
were not seen as desired components of the MTCC after-school program
and were deliberately not implemented by the program. As a result, the
program received low to average scores on the measure.

In keeping with a previously agreed-upon timeline for completing the
semiannual evaluation report to the funder, a member of the evaluation
team faxed an early draft of the report to the program, which included
results from the assessment just described. However, no discussion of the
results had taken place prior to sending the report, and little communica-

tion had occurred between the evaluators and the program staff about whether the results of the assessment would be included in the evaluation report and, if so, in what form they would be presented. Even though the staff initially sought out the measure to identify areas of the program that needed improvement, they were surprised and confused by the scores from the assessment and anxious about the results being shared with MBF. In subsequent discussions with members of the evaluation team, the program staff members expressed their understanding that the results were not part of the original evaluation plan and should not be included in the evaluation report. Staff also felt that the score did not accurately or fairly reflect the positive things being implemented by the program. At the same time, the member of the evaluation team that conducted the assessment felt uncomfortable removing the results from the report on the basis that the results were negative, especially considering that there was no request to omit the positive results found from a similar tool for a different MTCC program. In addition, the evaluation team felt that there was important information to be shared with all stakeholders about areas of the program that needed improvement.

In keeping with the empowerment evaluation principle of inclusion, the executive director of MTCC requested a meeting with the funder (MBF) and the evaluators to discuss the problem (a testament to the strong relationships and trust facilitated by MBF). The meeting was initially uncomfortable for all stakeholders—the program staff, the funder, and the evaluation team. When everyone was at the table, every voice was valued and heard (i.e., demonstrating democratic participation), allowing an open and honest dialogue to take place among all stakeholders. The discussion revealed that the intent of the assessment in question was program improvement, which was consistent with the interests and desires of all three stakeholders. The foundation was most interested in hearing about the process of program improvement that resulted from the evaluation rather than the specific score of the assessment. Furthermore, respect of community knowledge helped the evaluators understand that many of the items were not appropriate and thus everyone agreed that the numerical score was not a valid measure of the overall quality of the program. As a result, the findings from the assessment were included in a descriptive format, and the numerical score was omitted from the report. It was also concluded that detailed evaluation results would be shared and discussed with appropriate staff members and remain "in-house" for the purpose of program improvements, while a summary of the results and their resulting implications would be included in the evaluation reports submitted to the funder.

The FFF partnership also contended with negative evaluation results. However, the dynamics of reporting negative findings were different for FFF, as compared to MTCC. For one, the evaluation team did not know about negative findings before the FFF staff because the staff was directly involved in the data collection and analysis, which seemed to prevent tension from arising between the program staff and the evaluation team. Second, the FFF staff was responsible for writing its own reports and including negative findings in its reports. While both the MTCC and FFF staff were committed to using negative results in the spirit of program improvement, we found that the FFF staff was more comfortable revealing negative results in evaluation reports to MBF. We believe that the FFF's comfort was in part due to the ownership it had over the process (i.e., it can be easier at times to be self-critical than to be criticized by someone else) and in part due to the evaluation team's continuous emphasis on plans and actions to address negative findings as more important than the initial findings themselves. As a result, FFF staff members understood that the purpose of the evaluation was program improvement and had little fear that MBF would punish them (e.g., take away funds) due to negative results unless they never chose to address them.

While the FFF program staff remained in the decision-making role, the evaluation team actively observed the strengths and weaknesses of the programs, discussed problem areas, and made recommendations to address negative findings. For instance, evaluation data revealed that the arts programs were not attracting and retaining the desired number of teenage participants for the after-school program, and the Boys and Girls Club was not meeting its average daily attendance goals. Initially, the partnership was discouraged by these findings and thought that continued efforts to attract youths might not be an effective use of resources. The evaluation team strongly believed that the Boys and Girls Club and the arts partners needed to further examine program implementation (through process evaluation) and organizational factors that could be limiting the partners' abilities to implement their programs as intended. Although the evaluation team did not require that the partnership conduct further process evaluation, they actively challenged the partners' thinking on the matter through lengthy and vigorous discussions. Following these discussions, the partnership decided on its own to expand the arts programs to target elementary-age children, and the Boys and Girls Club agreed to design and implement a new process for evaluating aspects of its after-school programming that previously was not a part of the evaluation plan.

Evaluation results regarding FFF's Parent University (PU) program provided additional opportunities to explore empowerment evaluation strategies that support program improvement and accountability. A major goal of the FFF initiative was to engage parents of low-income, multi-problem families in order to teach parenting skills and to help parents build a sense of competence, influence, usefulness, and belonging in their families. However, data from the pilot year, collected and analyzed by the program staff, revealed that the PU program was not reaching the desired number of parents. After initial attempts to increase parent attendance did not work, the FFF staff considered eliminating the program out of fear that future efforts would also fail. Concerned, the evaluation team encouraged the FFF administrators to consider the needs they themselves had identified in their community that spurred the parenting program in the first place. The evaluation team also provided literature and conducted training regarding science and best practices germane to engaging hard-to-reach parents. Program staff and the evaluation team collaboratively reviewed best practices and made several changes to the original program design, such as the selection of an evidence-based parenting program designed for use with low-income parents and increased use of incentives for parent participation.

In addition to the problem with parent attendance, data from the quantitative, knowledge-based parenting survey suggested that knowledge gains were not occurring among PU participants. Upon further examination, the knowledge-based survey (originally suggested by the evaluation team) was found to be inappropriate for the community context. In addition, the survey produced a ceiling effect in scores, which failed to capture the positive changes that seemed to be occurring among families based on staff members' observations. The evaluation team, program staff, and program participants worked together to design a more sensitive method to assess desired changes in parenting practices through individualized goal logs for each family. Following the programmatic and measurement changes described above, the PU program was sustained in the Spartanburg community and has been so successful that it is now being adopted in additional South Carolina counties.

Lessons Learned about Improvement and Accountability

1. When evaluation is consistent with all of the principles of empowerment evaluation, a natural balance can occur between program improvement and accountability demands. It is when one or more of the principles are emphasized at the expense of the others that tension occurs. In the MTCC example described above, the evaluation team had more control over the reporting process than was appropriate to maintain the principle of community ownership. In an attempt to fulfill traditional evaluation commitments, such as reporting results to funders, the evaluation team slipped into the role of taking charge instead of ensuring that program staff controlled the lines of communication about results to the funder. This produced tension and fear among program staff. At the same time, the empowerment evaluation principles of inclusion and democratic participation, as well as the strong emphasis on relationships, allowed this tension to be resolved through open dialogue among all stakeholders.

2. Making distinctions between in-house and external reporting is a useful way to address both improvement and accountability demands.

Specification of what data and information are maintained internally versus reported to funders and other stakeholders must be made clear in advance to all stakeholders.

3. Established tools of measurement (representing the principle of evidence-based strategies) need to be adjusted to serve the individual needs of programs. This requires respect and validation of community knowledge (e.g., knowledge of the unique context, needs, and resources within a given community). In the MTCC and FFF examples described above, the evaluators suggested the use of established measurement tool and surveys, which was consistent with empowerment evaluation practices designed to promote program improvement and evidence-based strategies. However, the initial use of these tools did not fully take into account community knowledge (e.g., the tool used at MTCC for after-school programs did not support some of the unique features of the program that were chosen based on the identified needs in the community). Therefore, the tools were either adapted or replaced by more appropriate measures, as guided by the empowerment evaluation principle of community knowledge.

4. Sensitivity to the manner in which unexpected or negative findings are communicated to the program is important to maintaining positive relationships among stakeholders and to reducing fears associated with evaluation. It is more effective to share negative results in a personalized manner (e.g., during a face-to-face meeting with key staff members) as opposed to sending the results in a written report for the first time. In addition, it is important that the strengths of a program be recognized and emphasized by the evaluator, especially when there are shortcomings that must also be addressed. When full-scale self-evaluation is taking place, the issue of communicating negative findings by evaluators is moot because program administrators discover and report their own results.

5. The principles of community ownership, inclusion, and democratic participation are essential aspects of achieving both improvement and accountability because they provide the mechanisms for reducing fears associated with negative evaluation findings. Although the events surrounding the negative findings at MTCC were painful and difficult for members of the program staff and for the evaluation team, in the end the experience was an excellent test of the principles of democratic participation, inclusion, and community ownership that define the empowerment evaluation approach. In this instance, the open dialogue with the funder was critical to resolving the problem in a way that felt appropriate to all parties. Although the damage to relationships among members of the evaluation team and program staff required some time to heal, the process eventually resulted in greater trust among the program administrators, funder, and evaluation team.

6. Program improvement and accountability demands can both be fulfilled when program administrators are responsible for writing their own reports. The reports for the FFF partnership, which were written by the program partners (and not the evaluators), were equally revealing—and at times perhaps even *more* revealing—of negative findings as the MTCC reports, which were written by the evaluation team. The fact that FFF was in control of reporting their own findings seemed to reduce the anxiety associated with negative findings and to encourage ownership over decisions related to addressing negative findings.

7. Although program staff members are the decision makers in empowerment evaluation, the evaluators can have a strong influence on the decisions that are made. In the FFF initiative, the evaluators acted as critical friends and spoke up when they saw that the program was considering choices that conflicted with its stated goals. This was consistent with the principles and practices of program improvement, accountability, and democratic participation (the evaluators have a voice in the process). At the same time, the evaluator's influence did not diminish the program's ownership of decision making.

CONCLUSION

This chapter presented experiences from two evaluation projects that heavily influenced the conceptualization and practical applications of empowerment evaluation. Although the defined principles and practices of empowerment evaluation provide us with a rich framework that can guide our decisions as evaluators, the empowerment evaluation principles cannot determine our actions in every context and challenging situation. Doing effective empowerment evaluation is a learning process for evaluators as well as for the organizations that participate in the approach. We learned the following lessons from our work:

1. Empowerment evaluation is not defined by the methods employed but rather by its principles.
2. When stakeholders want to pursue full-scale self-evaluation, roles that facilitate self-evaluation should be established from the very beginning of the evaluation project.
3. Implementing a task for a program can be consistent with the practice of capacity building when it has the potential to lead to new opportunities for growth or when it supports program improvement and/or accountability.
4. Community ownership over the evaluation-process (i.e., control over evaluation related decision making and implementation)

appears to correspond to greater institutionalization of evaluation practices.

5. When one or more of the principles is emphasized at the expense of others, undesirable tensions can arise that signal empowerment evaluators to make adjustments in their work.

6. Distinctions between in-house and external reporting help address both improvement and accountability demands.

7. Established tools of measurement and best practices should be custom tailored to serve the individual context of programs.

8. The principles of community ownership, inclusion, and democratic participation provide the mechanisms for reducing fears associated with negative evaluation findings.

9. Program improvement and accountability demands can both be fulfilled when program administrators are responsible for writing their own reports.

10. Although program staff members are the decision makers in empowerment evaluation, the evaluators can and should influence the decisions that are made.

In addition to the specific lessons we gained from our experiences, our work confirmed much of what we already believed to be true. For instance, relationships are important to the success of empowerment evaluation. Mistakes can be repaired. Being a good empowerment evaluator does not require perfection, but it does require that we know what is important, we have consistent strategies that promote our values, we reflect on our work, we build relationships among all stakeholders, and we are willing to acknowledge and correct our mistakes. In doing these things, we hope to model the very process that we believe creates effective programs.

ACKNOWLEDGMENTS

We are grateful to the many exceptional program leaders and staff who dedicated their time and energy to evaluation and taught us important lessons about our work. We are especially grateful to Wanda Fowler at the Middle Tyger Community Center of Lyman, South Carolina, and to Joan Moore, Greg Tolbert, and Molly Jones with the Foundation for the Future Initiative and the Boys and Girls Club of Metro Spartanburg. From the Mary Black Foundation, we would like to thank Jan Yost (former President) and Allen Mast (Vice President for Programs) for facilitating and supporting the use of results-oriented evaluation among grantees. Past and current members of the evaluation team for the Middle Tyger Community Center project include Abraham Wandersman, Kevin Everhart, Dana Keener, Lisa Johnson, Melanie Livet, and Patricia Keith. Past and current members of the evaluation team for the Foundation for the Future Initiative include Abraham Wandersman, Jessica Snell-Johns, Julia Mendez, and Melanie Livet. We thank Jennifer Duffy, David Fetterman, Alice Fields, Wanda Fowler, Laura Gambone, Molly Jones, Allen Mast, Robin Lin Miller, Joan Moore, Greg Tolbert, Elizabeth Whitmore, Annie Wright, and Jan Yost for reviewing and providing valuable comments on earlier drafts of this chapter.

NOTES

1. These elements of effective prevention programs are based on the Getting to Outcomes framework, a user-friendly tool that can be used in the context of empowerment evaluation (Wandersman, Imm, Chinman, & Kaftarian, 2000).
2. It is important to note that continued use of an outside evaluator does not necessarily mean that a program lacks evaluation capacity. Accountability demands of funders often require that programs use outside evaluators to fulfill evaluation requirements, regardless of their capacity to self-evaluate.

REFERENCES

Crusto, C. A., & Wandersman, A. (2004). Setting the stage for accountability and program evaluation in community-based grant-making. In A. Roberts & K. Yeager (Eds.), *Evidence-based practice manual: Research and outcome measures in health and human services*. New York: Oxford University Press.

McIver, J. P., & Carmines, E. G. (1981). *Unidimensional scaling* (pp. 40–59). London: Sage.

Sanders, J. R. (2003). Mainstreaming evaluation. In J. J. Barnette & J. R. Sanders (Eds.), *The mainstreaming of evaluation: New directions for evaluation* (No. 99, pp. 3–6). San Francisco: Jossey-Bass.

Snell-Johns, J., & Keener, D. C. (2000, November). *The past and current evaluation capacity of two community initiatives*. Paper presented in a Presidential Strand symposium at the 2000 meeting of the American Evaluation Association, Honolulu, HI.

Wandersman, A., Imm, P., Chinman, M., & Kaftarian, S. (2000). Getting to outcomes: A results-based approach to accountability. *Evaluation and Program Planning, 23*(3), 389–395.

Wandersman, A., Keener, D. C., Snell-Johns, J., Miller, R., Flaspohler, P., Dye, M., Mendez, J., Behrens, T., & Bolson, B. (2004). Empowerment evaluation: Principles and action. In L. A. Jason, C. B. Keys, Y. Suarez-Balcazar, R. R. Taylor, M. Davis, J. Durlak, & D. Isenberg (Eds.), *Participatory community research: Theories and methods in action*. Washington DC: American Psychological Association.

Yost, J., & Wandersman, A. (1998). *Results-oriented grantmaking/grant implementation: Mary Black Foundation's experience*. Paper presented at the 1998 annual meeting of the American Evaluation Association, Chicago.

CHAPTER 5

Empowerment Evaluation

FROM THE DIGITAL DIVIDE TO ACADEMIC DISTRESS

David M. Fetterman

The purpose of this chapter is to highlight empowerment evaluation principles in practice using two case studies. The principles highlighted include improvement, community ownership, inclusion, democratic participation, social justice, community knowledge, evidence-based strategies, capacity building, organizational learning, and accountability.

The first case study is the $15-million Hewlett-Packard Digital Village project. The second is an empowerment evaluation of academically distressed Arkansas Delta school districts for the Arkansas State Department of Education. The common theme running through both of these highly publicized communitywide initiatives is that they used empowerment evaluation to help develop, implement, assess, and improve their programs. A brief discussion about the specific empowerment evaluation process used in both is presented below.

THE PROCESS

Empowerment evaluation can take many forms. The format used in these studies followed a three-step approach: mission, taking stock, and planning for the future (see Fetterman, 2001, for details). A critical friend (in the form of an evaluation coach) facilitated each step in the process. However, the group remained in charge of the content throughout the evaluation.

Mission

First the critical friend/evaluation coach facilitated a discussion about the group's mission. The group's members determined who they were as a collective and what they wanted to accomplish as a collective. This represented the group's values. It should be noted that the groups were not initially cohesive. However, this process enabled them to find common interests. It also provided individual and divergent interests to find a "home" where multiple interests could operate under the same umbrella.

Taking Stock

Second, the critical friend helped the group to prioritize. Group members determined what they thought was important to assess as a group. This involved brainstorming about the most important activities the group engaged in to accomplish its mission. Sticky dots were used to vote for the most important activities. Only members of the community were allowed to vote. The facilitator counted the votes. The top 10 activities were selected (by counting the activities with the most dots). This prioritized list of activities was placed in an Excel spreadsheet. Each member of the group rated how well the group was doing in each activity on a 1- (low) to 10-point (high) scale. Members of the community valued the opportunity to have their voices heard with their ratings. This provided everyone, including even the most marginalized individuals, with an opportunity to express their opinions about the state of affairs. An effort was made to invite some of the most outspoken and cynical individuals in the group as well, because when they complained it makes any other comment seem tame by comparison. This opened up a space in the dialogue for people to speak up and make comments that they otherwise might not have made in the group. The ratings were averaged vertically and horizontally. The group could immediately see who was the most optimistic and pessimistic by reviewing the vertical averages (by person). This provided them with an insight into each other from an evaluative perspective. They were able to interpret each other's ratings more precisely in the future because they were contextualized within the group's rating pattern. For example, the next time a pessimistic participant praised an activity, other members of the group took notice. They realized that if, say, Suzanne thought we were doing well, then "it really meant something." The more important scores, however, were horizontal. The average ratings concerning each activity provided the entire group with an insight into how well they were doing in terms of the activities required to accomplish their objectives. More to the point, the ratings provided a launching point for discussion and dialogue. The critical friend probed and asked why members of the group rated an activity a 3 or an 8. This helped to build a culture of evidence, as participants had to justify or explain the basis for their ratings. This process also helped people to understand the basis for each other's ratings. Both processes were a form of norming. Everyone knew where they stood within the larger context of the group. Taking stock represented the baseline assessment. Solutions to problems were generated in the dialogue and saved for the next step in the process: planning for the future.

Planning for the Future

Planning for the future is rooted in the group's taking-stock activity, which is rooted in the group's mission (or values). This provides the group with a thread of coherence and an audit trail throughout the engagement. The evaluation coach asks members of the group to use the same prioritized list of activities from the taking-stock activity and use them in the planning for the future exercise. The critical friend asks the group to generate goals and strategies for each of these activities. For example, the goal might be to improve communications. Strategies might include developing and disseminating a newsletter, creating a web page, or constructing an Internet-based calendar. The group is also asked to generate a list of credible forms of evidence to determine whether the strategies are being implemented and working to accomplish specified objectives. This third step in the process represents the group's intervention.

Traditional evaluation tools can be used at this point, because the group has specified the intervention and theory of change. Online surveys, interviews, focus groups, and even traditional achievement tests might be selected to determine whether the strategies are working. If the data suggest the strategies are not effective, the group substitutes new strategies for the less effective strategies. The point of the process is to use data to inform decision making in real time and make mid-course corrections as needed (before it is too late). These minitests are conducted on an ongoing basis to improve the probability that the strategies are working and in alignment with the overall objectives. A formal taking-stock exercise is conducted about 6 months later to compare the baseline assessment (the results of the initial taking-stock exercise) with the current status of the organization's efforts, documenting change over time. The results are important. They either confirm that the work is on track and should continue or that changes in goals or strategies are needed. The cycle is a continuous loop of action and assessment with the aim of improvement and results.

PRINCIPLES

The principles are discussed at length in Chapter 2. However, a brief review of these principles is presented to orient the discussion in the case studies.

Improvement

Improvement involves making things better than they were. Improvement can be incremental or radical transformative change. It can focus on a specific program or entire communities. The concept of improvement is dependent on a monitoring system to measure change over time. All of the programs discussed in this chapter were aimed at improvement on many levels, ranging from programmatic to comprehensive communitywide initiatives.

Community Ownership

Community ownership means that the group is in charge of the conceptual orientation and execution of the evaluation. They also own the data and the knowledge generated from the evaluation. Group ownership of the evaluation enhances commitment to the project or program. It is an empowering experience for a community's members, as they take charge of their lives and the future direction of their program.

Inclusion

Inclusion is an important principle in empowerment evaluation. It involves inviting critical stakeholders to contribute to the evaluation, particularly people who have been systematically excluded. The principle of inclusion in empowerment evaluation represents a form of multicultural respect. In addition, it is more efficient to include various constituencies as early as possible. Otherwise, the conceptual foundation will be faulty and the structure continuously in need of repair. The assumption about inclusion in empowerment evaluation is that it is additive, rather than subtractive, enhancing the final assessments and plans for the future.

Democratic Participation

Democratic participation has two levels. The first is the simple act of voting or consensus building. Everyone has a vote or substantive role in decision making. No matter how high or low the individual is in the organization, he or she has a voice in determining the future. The second level of democratic participation is the process of intellectually engaging in informed inquiry, debate, and action. This second level cultivates analytical skills and behaviors that are generalizable to all aspects of society.

Social Justice

Social justice issues are typically related to clear and compelling concerns. They may be social or economic inequities. People who are disenfranchised or low-income, individuals with disabilities, and minorities are often the "target" populations. Disparities in access to educational opportunities, the web, adequate health care, and employment are common themes. Social justice agendas attempt to redress these inequities and burnish our democratic ideals.

Community Knowledge

Community knowledge is the cultural information the group brings to the project and evaluation as well as the knowledge developed as a group in the course of implementing the project and evaluation. This includes practitioners' knowledge about the program. The evaluator, funder, and community should value this knowledge and use it to design the evaluation so as to ensure sensitivity to the local group, program, and environment. Community knowledge is also invaluable when implementing or adapting an innovation in the local community.

Evidence-Based Strategies

These are strategies that have been tested and demonstrate effectiveness in a specific setting. Ideally program staff members conduct a literature search to identify evidence-based practices or strategies. This helps them plan and implement their program on a more solid foundation. However, many initiatives are exploratory in nature. Often there is no evidence-based strategy to select from with these kinds of initiatives. However, there are often best practices or evidence-based practices concerning procedures or approaches that can be adapted to specific programs.

Capacity Building

Capacity building is one of the most identifiable features of empowerment evaluation. People learn how to conduct evaluations by actually conducting the evaluation in practice. They learn the logic of evaluation, specific techniques and procedures, and how to use evaluation to improve program performance. Empowerment evaluation enhances both evaluation and program capacity, since community members use evaluation to inform their program decision making. The same skills needed to conduct evaluations are applied to program decision making and implementation efforts.

Organizational Learning

Organizational learning involves the use of data for decision making. The data-driven decisions enable organizations to achieve their specific goals and objectives. However, using data for decision making is a necessary but not sufficient factor. The focus is on systemic and underlying issues rather than short-term solutions to superficial problems. In addition, the community of learners' commitment to inquiry, knowledge development, and action is ongoing. One of the ideas associated with organizational learning is to make data-driven decisions to facilitate the organization's mission. The initial taking-stock activity established a baseline for each program. The group's plans for the future represented the intervention. Surveys, interviews, and observations were designed to test the effectiveness of these strategies. Corrective action was taken when the strategies were not effective. This enhanced the likelihood that appropriate or effective strategies were being selected and used to accomplish the group's goals. This feedback loop of effectiveness and organizational decision making is at the heart of organizational learning (see Argyris & Schön, 1974; Argyris, 1999; Senge, 1990; Preskill, 1994).

Accountability

Accountability is both internal and external. Internal accountability is required for long-term sustainability. It is a driving force in an organization and is present on a day-to-day basis. Accountability also involves reporting to an authority. It involves being held responsible for delivering specific outcomes or results at specified times. Accountability is also conceptualized in terms of process accountability and results accountability. The first, process accountability, focuses on program implementation and fidelity to the "model," or plan. The second, results, focuses on outcomes and specified objectives (or results, as discussed in Chapter 2). Did the program accomplish its goals and objectives? This can be viewed as a four-way matrix. Internal accountability and external accountability can both be viewed in terms of processes and outcomes (see Figure 5.1).

Everyone is accountable to someone. Accreditation agencies hold schools and hospitals accountable. Regulatory agencies hold businesses and government accountable. Funders hold nonprofits accountable for serving their clients. Empowerment evaluation is not conducted in a vacuum; it is conducted within the context of internal and external accountability. An evaluation approach that helps people accomplish their goals and deliver services or products in a timely manner is valued. Empowerment evaluation enables people to contribute to group or organizational goals and produce results.

This brief review of the principles sets the stage for the next part of this discussion. Two case examples have been selected to illustrate how the principles work in practice.

CASE STUDIES

The empowerment evaluation principles are used to organize the presentation of each case study. The principles highlighted in each case study include improvement, community ownership, inclusion, democratic participation, social justice, community knowledge, evidence-based strategies, capacity building, organizational learning, and accountability. The projects highlight a variety of topics, including the digital divide and academic distress.

Hewlett-Packard

The first case study is the $15-million Hewlett-Packard Digital Village project. The aim of this ambitious project is to help three communities leap-

	Internal	External
Process		
Outcome		

FIGURE 5.1. Four-way matrix: Internal and external by process and outcome accountability.

frog across the digital divide[1]: one African American urban community in the northeast, a Latino and African American low-income community in northern California, and 18 American Indian tribes in California. The individual projects included distributing laptops in schools, providing community centers with computers and access to the Internet, helping people grow small businesses, and developing web-based tools to enhance community access to local resources. This discussion will draw primarily on examples from the Tribal Digital Village because it was successful (as were the other Digital Villages) and most of the relevant information is readily available on the Internet, in Federal Communications Commission (FCC) documents and communications, and in related public documents.[2]

Improvement

The Digital Villages all sought improvement in such areas as education, health, business, housing, security, and employment. The most common vehicle or tool used to pursue the improvement was the Internet. Community members were provided with computers and/or computer training to enhance their capacity to use the Internet. Pretests and posttests were conducted to determine whether they were being taught effectively and/or were learning the requisite skills. If they consistently answered a posttest question incorrectly, the training associated with that question was revised and/or the related question was revised as well. The aim was to improve the training in order to ensure greater capacity building.

The Tribal Digital Village established a baseline in January/February related to the most important activities associated with implementing its plans, including equipment delivery (to the tribes), communication (within the Digital Village), training, management, cultural documentation, organizational structures, seeking funds, increasing community awareness, and governance. The community's members discussed the ratings for their baseline assessment and then created a plan to improve in each area. The baseline ratings were compared with the second data measurement in September, highlighting the extent of improvements in each activity (see Figure 5.2). While success was documented in all areas, there was room for additional improvement in each area.

The communities also assessed larger issues such as communications, community involvement, and knowledge transfer. The process was the same. A baseline assessment was created, an intervention strategy was developed and implemented, and tests were conducted throughout the implementation to determine whether the intervention was being successfully implemented and whether the strategies were working. The process documented change over time and facilitated improvement.

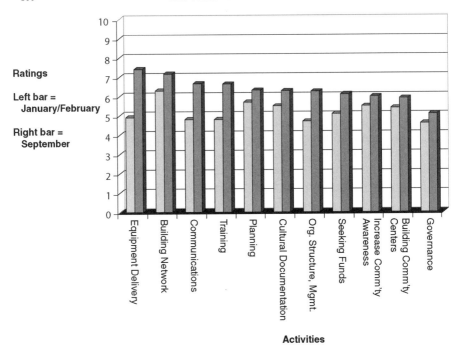

FIGURE 5.2. Tribal Digital Village rated the status of many of its activities in January/February, including equipment delivery, communications, and cultural documentation. The tribes rated the same activities in September. An increase was documented in each area over time.

Community Ownership

Hewlett-Packard understood the philosophy behind empowerment evaluation and demonstrated respect for community ownership from the inception of the project, allowing the Digital Villages to design and conduct their evaluations with the assistance of the team of evaluators. The Digital Villages were in charge of the content of every stage of the evaluation. They produced, with the assistance of their evaluators, their own online surveys, training programs to collect stories from elders, digital photographs of the construction of their towers for wireless transmission, and Quicktime videos of critical stages of the evaluation (see Figure 5.3 and *http://homepage.mac.com/profdavidf*).

An additional measure of Hewlett-Packard's respect for local control and ownership occurred when one Digital Village suggested that the company not participate, explaining that the evaluation team had not yet finished working with its members to prepare for the visit. The sponsor

FIGURE 5.3. Tribal Digital Village video of empowerment evaluation workshops.

understood and complied with the request. The sponsor respected the community for assessing its lack of preparedness accurately and the community's plan to remedy the problem with evaluation assistance.

Inclusion

The Digital Villages were inclusive by design. The aim was to use the Internet to connect people with one another, as well as needed services. The Digital Villages provided community members with the opportunity and the means to participate. Community members were invited to share their knowledge on the community web page. They were also encouraged to use the web page to complain to city officials about lingering problems. Laptops were distributed to teachers and students in an effort to include critical members of the learning community. Community centers were equipped with computers and a connection to the Internet. This type of programmatic inclusiveness invites if not demands evaluative participation and inclusiveness as well. Community executives, program directors, faculty, students, and parents participated in the collection of baseline data. They also created surveys and administered them. They used the data to inform decision making. There were two levels of inclusiveness that were noted in the Digital Village: ethnic diversity and technological capacity. In one community, African Americans invited Latinos to participate and take charge of the evaluation with them, in spite of significant difference in interests and backgrounds. Pacific Islanders, often excluded from significant discussions were also actively recruited. In addition to ethnic diversity, people were invited to participate regardless of their level of technological sophistication. Basic computer training was provided for novices to ensure their participation in the Digital Village efforts. An extraordinary effort was made to invite as many groups and organizations in the community as possible. An error was made on one occasion when an important housing advocacy group was overlooked at a weekend evaluation workshop. After mending fences for this oversight, representatives of the housing advocacy group were contacted to solicit their input in the community plan and assessment. The revised plan was considered by the entire community. Leaving an important group out of the discussion, even by accident, was costly in terms of trust and time.

Democratic Participation

Democratic participation and local cultural knowledge merged in the Tribal Digital Village. During the taking-stock step of the process, the tribes recognized that there wasn't equal representation at the sessions. For example, there were three members of a tribe represented at the first meeting and only one member of another tribe at the same meeting. In addition, staff members from the supporting agencies were present at the same taking-stock exercise. If everyone got one vote the supporting agencies would have been overrepresented and would have outweighed the tribal vote. One of the tribal empowerment evaluators[3] suggested a novel twist on the voting process to respond to this problem. Each tribe was asked to assign a representative to vote for the group. They agreed to the representative approach. Each tribe or group discussed the issues and came to a consensus about their ratings. The tribal representative was entitled to cast one vote as a member of the larger empowerment group. The same applied to the supporting agencies. The result was a much more democratic approach than equally dividing the vote based on attendance. Local cultural knowledge was used to meaningfully interpret the situation and conceive of a more democratic form of participation. Cultural knowledge informed practice and ensured that the group met the spirit of the law concerning democratic participation.

Democratic participation contributed to intelligent reasoning and judgment. Evidence was required as each assessment was analyzed and discussed. A culture of evidence evolved from the discussions and self-assessments. The community of learners engaged in a dialogue about the status of their efforts. This engagement helped them build and refine skills in discourse and reasoning. These skills were generalizable to many other facets of their life. It also contributed to building a trusting relationship in the process.

Social Justice

The Hewlett-Packard Digital Village project was aimed at addressing a variety of social justice issues. Equity in education, housing, employment, and health were paramount. The communities were selected in part because of their specific pressing needs. They were communities largely left behind in the digital age. They were also selected for their potential to develop successful programs to address specific socially relevant concerns. The communities assumed responsibility for addressing specific social justice issues most relevant to their environment. In two Digital Villages, teachers and students received laptops and computer training. The projects were designed to enhance teacher skills and student access to Internet resources. Ideally this effort will reduce the gap between upper-middle and lower socioeconomic class access to the Internet. Access to the Internet as well as technology-related skills can enhance the quality of education, improve access to employment opportunities, and provide health-related information. All of these are social justice issues in this context.

All three villages provided community centers with the equipment and expertise required to help community members search for jobs on the Internet. The centers also provided assistance in the preparation of resumes and online applications, as well as related employment documents. Enhancing access to the Internet was a useful step toward reducing the gap in employment opportunities. All three villages provided Internet-based health information on web pages or "community portals." They also facilitated access to health centers and treatment centers.

One of the goals of the Tribal Digital Village was the preservation and development of the tribes' rich cultural heritage. Tribal members received ethnographic and video recording training to help them collect life histories of elders and record their languages, rituals, and artifacts. The simple act of recording tribal knowledge represented a powerful counterbalance to concerted government efforts in the past to decimate Native American cultures. The Bureau of Indian Affairs took children away from their homes and enrolled them in boarding schools, where they were separated from their communities and culture. In addition, they were typically prohibited from speaking their native language. The physical layout of the reservation itself was designed to isolate individuals, inhibit communication, and fragment cultural knowledge. Simply installing a wireless system to enable communication among the tribes constituted a step toward addressing fundamental inequities and injustices. The Tribal Digital Village went beyond preservation and maintenance of Native cultures. The Tribal Digital Village addressed equity issues by providing computer training (including Cisco router training) to enable young people to maintain the wireless system they constructed. This represented an investment in their future as well as their past. This was an effort to make social justice sustainable and long-term.

Community Knowledge

The Digital Villages relied on community knowledge to inform the initial design of the projects. The funder requested projects that were meaningful and relevant to community concerns. They also encouraged the development of culturally sensitive innovations and practices throughout the evaluation. For example, the Latino community arranged for translations of our dialogues and brochures. American Indian communities arranged for all evaluation reports to be reviewed and approved by the tribal elders, respecting community protocols. African American communities enlisted the support of local churches and related religious organizations to communicate about Digital Village programs. This sincere respect for community knowledge shaped the evaluation at every stage.

The community knowledge about technology also pervaded the entire project, specifically technology linked to the Internet. Senior and junior members of the Digital Village compared notes on emergent web designs and computer equipment. The projects were almost exclusively technology-related, ranging from the Tribal Digital Village's wireless system to the distribution of laptops in Californian and East Coast school districts. Solutions to problems were typically conceptualized or framed in terms of the Internet. For example, publishing a web calendar on the Internet was proposed at each of the sites to facilitate communication with the community. During breaks the discussion revolved around the latest tech gadgets, from the size of flash drives to digital cameras.

The technology-oriented community knowledge provided a common ground and language across sites, socioeconomic levels, ethnic groups, genders, and geographic regions. This shared set of understandings enabled the communities to experiment with new strategies and interventions without complex explanations or presentations at every turn.

Evidence-Based Strategies

There weren't any prepackaged models or strategies to select from with this initiative. The fiscal scale of the project ($15 million), the national breadth, and the scope of the endeavors are all unique. However, each group sought out the best practices associated with its own programs. These included computer training programs, virtual classroom and conference software, standardized protocols, html, cross-platform programs, reading programs, business models, and exemplary parenting skills programs. Each had to be adapted, but an effort was made to identify evidence-based practice at each site.

Capacity Building

Hewlett-Packard and the Digital Villages selected empowerment evaluation in large part because it builds capacity. Empowerment evaluation helps people help themselves and in the process acquire new skills and knowledge. Community members learned how to use evaluation to enhance the probability of accomplishing their objectives. A senior staff member associated with the project at Hewlett-Packard observed, "We accomplished both of the objectives in this evaluation, to demonstrate that the programs had an impact and that there was [evaluation] skill transfer." Participants acquired new tools to plan, implement, evaluate, redirect their energies as needed, and produce results. Community members determined their own needs, proposed solutions, took risks in addressing those community challenges, and assessed the effectiveness of their own efforts. In one program, laptops were distributed to students and teachers in school districts. In another program, community members were provided with access to computers and digital cameras in community centers or hubs. Training was provided in both cases to teach the members how to maximize the potential of their technological tools.

Evaluation capacity was developed by assessing these programs. The members developed their own pre- and posttests for many of their training workshops, with the assistance of trained evaluators. Some of the pre- and posttests were online surveys. They also conducted interviews and observations of training sessions. Sharing stories (based on systematic inquiry and documentation) was a prominent part of the evaluative process. The stories were compelling and had an impact on decision making. The evaluative information was fed back into the organizations to improve training. Evaluation was also used to make sure strategies adopted by the group were being implemented and effective.

The Tribal Digital Village used empowerment evaluation to help community members produce results, including building the largest unlicensed wireless network in the country (an accomplishment noted by the head of the FCC), a high-resolution digital printing press business, and a parenting skills program. Members assessed the status of their activities and developed plans for the future to accomplish their goals. The capacity-building theme ran through the entire project, including training youths to maintain the towers and the network long after the funding cycle expired. Each of the Digital Villages applied evaluation logic to funding issues, programmatic implementation, and sustainability concerns as well.

Organizational Learning

Hewlett-Packard's chief executive officer, Carly Fiorina, made the pledge of $15 million to the Digital Villages. The company wanted to help these communities, and its executives wanted to learn from their philanthropic endeavors. Bess Stephens, Vice President and Worldwide Director of their Corporate Philanthropy and Education Program, made a personal commitment to organizational learning throughout the project. In addition to providing support for an evaluation approach that helps each Digital Village learn from its experiences, her team requested evaluative feedback on their own performance as philanthropists. The aim was to learn from their experience in order to improve their work with these Digital Villages. This knowledge would also be used to improve philanthropic efforts with others in the future. For example, they readily accepted criticism over Hewlett-Packard's merger with Compaq, which temporarily had an adverse impact on equipment delivery to the Digital Villages. They also appreciated positive feedback from the Digital Villages. On balance, the Digital Villages viewed the team executives as respectful, committed, and courteous problem solvers. Staff member observations were used as part of the data to document the behavior and demeanor of Hewlett-Packard consultants; providing grist for the organizational learning cycle. Members shared stories about how respectful the Hewlett-Packard consultants were, explaining how "they emptied the garbage like anyone else" and how "they rolled up their sleeves and got to work." The institutional feedback was important, reinforcing "good behavior" on the part of the consultants and remedying internal problems (such as product delivery) that had an impact on their performance.

The Digital Villages used evaluative feedback to change their priorities organizationally, to initiate new projects, and to eliminate or minimize less successful efforts. The evaluation served as a rudder for many of the Digital Villages at critical points in their development, including prioritizing projects.

Overall, executives from the Digital Villages found empowerment evaluation to be a "good fit." It provided senior management in Hewlett-Packard's philanthropy division, local staff members, and other Digital Village community members with a compatible approach to data collection and analysis. It also provided them with an approach that enabled them to use evaluation to inform organizational decision making and action. Empowerment evaluation became a useful tool to further engage in institutional learning and growth.

Accountability

The Digital Villages were all held accountable for specified goals and objectives. Empowerment evaluation was used to achieve their goals. The Digital Villages set their goals and monitored their progress as a group or collective. They altered their strategies when they were not working out as planned. Each Digital Village used evaluation as a feedback mechanism to help it monitor its progress and accomplish its objectives.

The feedback system was used for a variety of purposes. Programmatically it was a useful tool to keep track of the number of laptops distributed in schools. Community members had external requirements, specific numbers they promised the funder. On another level, the feedback was used to monitor internal and external forms of communication. Each Digital Village developed a chain of reasoning, or theory of change. The theory of change always ended with an outcome or result. Accountability was a routine part of the empowerment evaluation process—stretching from the beginning to the end of the project.

What was delivered was neither small nor trivial. The Tribal Digital Village created the largest unlicensed wireless system in the country. It also started a high-resolution printing press business. In addition, it developed computer training and parenting skills programs. The Tribal Digital Village also reflexively demonstrated its accomplishments by teaching one of my empowerment evaluation classes by videoconferencing from the community's towers to my classroom at Stanford University (see Figure 5.4). The community's members had internalized evaluation well enough to teach about it. Moreover, they were teaching about it using the very tools they had made a commitment to build. The Digital Village held itself accountable and produced concrete outcomes. One of the tribal leaders declared that the project's greatest accomplishment was that "it was an empowering experience" for the entire community. Bess Stephens, Hewlett-Packard's Vice President and Global Director for Corporate Philanthropy and Education, praised the empowerment evaluation effort because it produced concrete results and because "it placed the work squarely in the hands of the community" (B. Stephens, personal communication, 2004).

Arkansas Delta

The second case study is an empowerment evaluation of rural and impoverished Arkansas Delta school districts classified as being in "academic distress" (see the typical rural landscape, as shown in Figure 5.5, and the typical economic decay of a local downtown district, as depicted in Figure 5.6). Academic distress is defined as having more than 40% of the students in the district scoring at or below the 25th percentile on the statewide assessment. One district was in academic distress for over 6 years. The initial objective was to increase students' scores and improve their learning, so as to move the schools out of distress. Firing all the schools' principals and teachers was not deemed an appropriate or realistic option, as the schools often were the largest, and sometimes the only, employer in the district. Also, the remote and isolated nature of these impoverished communities made it difficult to recruit credentialed teachers to these districts. The effort, therefore, had to focus on building existing capacity.

FIGURE 5.4. A Tribal Digital Village videoconference with Dr. David Fetterman and his empowerment evaluation class at Stanford University.

FIGURE 5.5. Cotton fields in the Arkansas Delta.

FIGURE 5.6. Typical Downtown scene in one of the Arkansas Delta school districts.

Improvement

The aim to *improve* the Delta schools was paramount. Since the school districts were officially classified in the state as being in the "distressed" mode, the state had the right to "take over" the districts. Instead, we arranged to engage in a partnership (Fetterman, 2002, 2003). The initial needs assessment documented that there was potential for improvement (in fact, there seemed little way to go but up). The aim was to build individual, program, and school district capacity in order to construct a firm foundation for future improvements. Everyone was focused on improvement in critical areas (which participants identified as a group). Specifically, we focused on improving test scores, discipline, parental involvement, and administrative support and follow through. School district teachers, administrators, staff members, and community members documented their improvement or progress, using the taking-stock (baseline) data and comparing the baseline data with a later second assessment (a posttest following the intervention of improved teaching and discipline). Improvements were made in each of the areas identified by the districts (see Figure 5.7 for 10-measure comparison in the Altheimer Unified School District).

In addition, overall improvement in the student test scores was a proxy for learning and the key requirement for shedding the "academic distress" status, as determined by the Arkansas Department of Education. School district teachers, staff members, and administrators tested students in order to

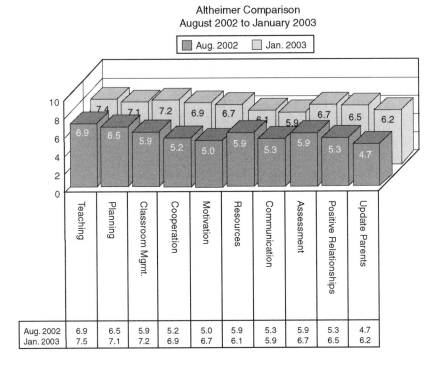

Altheimer Comparison
August 2002 to January 2003

	Teaching	Planning	Classroom Mgmt.	Cooperation	Motivation	Resources	Communication	Assessment	Positive Relationships	Update Parents
Aug. 2002	6.9	6.5	5.9	5.2	5.0	5.9	5.3	5.9	5.3	4.7
Jan. 2003	7.5	7.1	7.2	6.9	6.7	6.1	5.9	6.7	6.5	6.2

FIGURE 5.7. Comparison of August 2002 baseline data with January 2003 posttest data, documenting gains in the school district on measures relating to, respectively, teaching, planning, classroom management, cooperation, motivation, resources, communication, assessment, positive relationships, and updating parents.

document change over time. Improvements were recorded in a variety of areas, documenting the effectiveness of the self-reflective process. The school districts that adopted empowerment evaluation made gains in literacy and mathematics according to the Arkansas Benchmark Exams, as documented by the Arkansas Department of Education and the National Office for Research on Measurement and Evaluation Systems (NORMES) (McKenzie & Mulvenon, 2004; Smith, 2004; Wilson, 2004).

Community Ownership

There were two levels of community ownership in the academically distressed Arkansas Delta school districts: within the school and at the school–community level. The first level in the school included the teachers, administrators, and students. The teachers and administrators were fully invested in the evaluation and conducted their own assessment of critical aspects of the school, ranging from test results to discipline. Students provided digital video camera interviews about the school, truancy, and discipline issues. Many of these digitally recorded interviews were emailed to the evaluation team as part of the ongoing data collection regarding discipline, truancy, and administrative control.

The second level involved the community outside the school walls. Parent involvement was needed to make the intervention work, for example, following up on student homework, truancy behavior, and confronting oppositional behavior. Serendipity played a part in solidifying a bond with the community in this project. While interviewing one of the ministers in the community, it became apparent that we (the evaluator and the minister) had met previously. The minister interrupted the interview and said he remembered me. I apologized for not remembering his name, although I remembered his face. He reminded me that we had worked together in a dropout prevention program over 20 years earlier in the Northeast. The odds of our meeting again after so many years seemed astronomical. However, that coincidental meeting solidified the evaluation team's rapport with community members and helped enlist their support with the school initiative and the empowerment evaluation. The serendipitous meeting and reconnection helped strengthen community involvement in support of the schools and the evaluation effort. Parent groups recorded their meetings to document parental involvement and action on agreed-upon initiatives. The clergy took the lead in the community to secure additional funding for communitywide initiatives directly associated with the empowerment evaluation. Community ownership was necessary on both levels in order for the empowerment evaluation to be successful.

Inclusion

The evaluation included teachers, staff members, administrators, clergy, the mayor (a former teacher), and many others. A local foundation officer was invited to participate in the discussions. News media were involved (covering the story while the empowerment evaluation workshops were being conducted). Their presence was particularly important. Having an open-door policy toward the press meant that local reporters were able to cover "the story" when things went well, rather than being focused on potentially negative developments. Dramatic changes were needed, and inclusion became a necessity to accomplish district objectives. School personnel were needed to teach, counsel, and administer. Parents were needed to reinforce academic and disciplinary standards. Clergy were needed to organize and unify the community with a common purpose. Making a significant change in local students' learning and test scores required an inclusive and comprehensive community level of involvement.

Democratic Participation

Entire districts were engaged in the empowerment evaluations in the Arkansas Delta. Almost every teacher and administrator—even janitor—was involved. The mayor of the town, clergy, and parents were also present. They were engaged community members. The discussions ranged from test scores to discipline, as well as parental involvement. Teachers, staff members, administrators, clergy, and others in the community participated in the vote concerning how best to prioritize community concerns associated with the schools. They also rated how well they were doing concerning each prioritized activity. They also worked together to come up with a plan for the future. The butcher block and poster paper used to record everyone's ratings stretched from one end of the school cafeteria to the other. The level of engagement and enthusiasm was high and contagious. The widespread participation of district residents increased the credibility of the effort. It also encouraged community members to continue their participation. The effort was transparent and real. It represented their views. This created a trust in the process. It also created an opportunity to engage in thoughtful inquiry. In some instances the rationale for participation was less altruistic, with some members wanting to make sure they were heard and that others would not take over. In either case, the inclusive and democratic nature of the communitywide participation enhanced the resulting dialogue.

Social Justice

The Arkansas Delta is one of the most impoverished and isolated areas in the country. The communities are only a few hours away by car from Little Rock, the state capital. These communities are surrounded by miles upon miles of cotton and soybean fields. There is little industry apart from agribusiness in the Delta. People are leaving the area in search of employment and educational opportunities, and many of the area's towns are on the decline economically. As with the Hewlett-Packard Digital Villages, the location of the communities is no accident. The southern Delta communities were segregated by law in the past. Blacks or African Americans went to one school, while whites went to another. The discrepancy between the education provided blacks and whites in terms of facilities, textbooks, and teachers was stark and incontestable. The legacy of this separate-but-unequal educational opportunity in the past continues to the present, most visibly in terms of test scores. The effort to close the educational gap in terms of test scores is a belated response to educational inequities that have persisted for generations. This Arkansas empowerment evaluation represents a clear commitment to social justice, focusing on people long deprived of access to basic educational opportunities.

Community Knowledge

The common thread of Delta school district community knowledge was a commitment to improving the educational system. Everyone had an opinion about public education in the Delta. That common link provided much of the basis for exchange and dialogue. The mayor, a former teacher in the school, provided his historical perspective about the schools in his community. He pointed out how graduates of these same schools were admitted to some of the top universities in the country when he taught. This was an important perspective to share with the community. It eliminated any doubt about the potential of these children and pointed the finger of responsibility squarely at the school and the family. If low-income minority students from the same rural community could succeed in the past, there was no reason why they could not succeed at this time. This helped convince school, local community, and foundation officials that a turnaround was possible and squarely within the purview of their own responsibility.

The districts developed their own cultural knowledge about what worked and what did not work in their schools. They generated their own solutions to their problems. The solutions made sense to the communities, because they were informed by local knowledge. State officials and local administrators also paid attention to local community knowledge and context. They realized that teachers would lose face if they were temporarily removed and replaced by technically more qualified teachers. These teachers had to remain in the community long after this attempt to transform the district. Consequently, team teaching became the strategy of choice, instead of replacing teachers even on a temporary basis. A partnership instead of a takeover approach was adopted at all levels in the districts. Expertise was brought in on every level, including literacy instructors, math coaches, curriculum specialists, administrative coaches and leaders, and school board specialists. Although they brought in external materials and standards, they were introduced with sensitivity to the local context and conditions. The evaluation was also a partnership with the local school districts, the State Department of Education, and the evaluator. This community knowledge-based approach contrasts with the traditional authoritarian, top-down "school takeover" model.

Evidence-Based Strategies

The academically distressed school districts agreed to teach to the standards. Although much debate surrounds the adoption of standards, they represent a compelling evidence-based strategy. One of the areas identified as needing particular attention and improvement was math. Student math scores were well below the national average. The teachers and administrators tested the students and found rounding in math to be a common problem. Based on this diagnostic information, they provided specific training on rounding. After teaching students about rounding, they tested the specific students who had problems with rounding. If there was no progress or improvement, the instruction was modified, and if there was improvement, instruction shifted to the next topic. A formal pre- and posttest was conducted (by local teachers and math coaches) to document improvement in specific areas in math. They administered the tests, used the data to inform decision making, and took appropriate action based on the data.

The district also identified weaknesses in literacy instruction. The community, based on its own assessment, decided to search for literacy coaches. The entire community also identified chronic administrative problems. Instead of pointing the figure at one individual, administrative consultants were recruited. The same process applied to disciplinary problems. In that case, evidence-based strategies such as teaching to the standards were identified and implemented. The gains in test scores were so dramatic in most of these areas that the districts attracted TV and news media attention (see representative TV news coverage and print media coverage at *http://homepage.mac.com/profdavidf*). The cycle of inquiry and evaluation was applied to most of the areas of concern in the district, including discipline, curriculum, administration, and community involvement.

Capacity Building

The entire premise of the partnership was based on capacity building. Literacy coaches were brought in to team teach with local teachers to enhance their capacity (without their losing face by being temporarily replaced). Similarly, math coaches were recruited to enhance the capacity of local math teachers. The same process applied to superintendents and even the local board of education in one district.

Participants also conducted their own self-assessment concerning critical areas of concern, as well as student learning. The distressed school districts used evaluation to establish a baseline. This baseline was the launching point for their plans for the future, or the intervention, specifying what needed to be done to get the districts out of academic distress and to enhance learning.

The community learned how to internalize the logic of evaluation and conduct pre- and posttests in order to monitor the progress of its students, teachers, and administrators (see Figure 5.8, for a 10-measure comparison in the Elaine School District). They enhanced their evaluation capacity and their teaching, learning, and administrative capacity simultaneously.

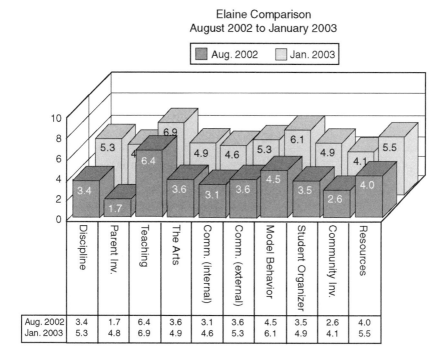

Elaine Comparison
August 2002 to January 2003

| | Aug. 2002 | | | Jan. 2003 | | | | | | |

	Discipline	Parent Inv.	Teaching	The Arts	Comm. (internal)	Comm. (external)	Model Behavior	Student Organizer	Community Inv.	Resources
Aug. 2002	3.4	1.7	6.4	3.6	3.1	3.6	4.5	3.5	2.6	4.0
Jan. 2003	5.3	4.8	6.9	4.9	4.6	5.3	6.1	4.9	4.1	5.5

FIGURE 5.8. Comparison of August 2002 baseline data with January 2003 posttest data, documenting school district gains in, respectively, measures of discipline, parental involvement, teaching, the arts, communication (internal), communication (external), model behavior, student organizations, community involvement, and resources. The change is also an indication of capacity building in specific areas.

Capacity building extended beyond the evaluation and the school districts. Teachers, administrators, and community members reported applying empowerment evaluation to their personal life as well, ranging from their church activities to their family disputes or concerns.

Organizational Learning

The Arkansas Department of Education used empowerment evaluation to critique its own performance in assisting academically distressed schools. The department changed technical assistance strategies based on evaluative feedback from the academically distressed school districts. Coaching and partnership models were adopted instead of the "heavy hand" of a state takeover. This strategic decision was based on a needs assessment of the academically distressed districts, national experts in the field, and the past performance of previous state takeover efforts.

Districts used evaluative data to target initiatives ranging from truancy reduction to violence prevention. They also used evaluative data to refocus participants' energies on testing, teaching, and learning. The old approaches were not working. Data concerning new approaches in each of these areas was compelling and convinced students, teachers, and administrators to adopt new strategies in their school districts, ranging from teaching math twice a day in one district to the adoption of new literacy programs.

Accountability

The primary outcome was to raise student test scores and increase student learning. According to Arkansas Department of Education educational accountability officials who partnered in this effort, "Empowerment evaluation was instrumental in producing Elaine and Altheimer school district improvements, including raising student test scores" (Smith, 2004; Wilson, 2004). At the beginning of the intervention in the fall of 2001, 59% of Elaine School District students scored below the 25th percentile on the Stanford 9 Achievement Test. By the end of the empowerment evaluation intervention in the spring of 2003, only 38.5% of students scored below the 25th percentile, representing an improvement of more than 20 percentage points (see Figure 5.9).

Similar gains were made in the Altheimer Unified School District. Approximately 44% of Altheimer students scored at or below the 25th percentile in the fall of 2001. At the end of the empowerment evaluation in the spring of 2003, 28.6% scored at or below the 25th percentile, representing a 35% decline in lowest-quartile scores. This is an improvement of more than 15 percentage points (see Figure 5.10). The improvement in Stanford 9 test scores was impressive. Improvements in related scores were also recorded. For example, according to the National Office for Research on Measurement and Evaluation Systems, overall Altheimer students made "gains in both the Literacy and Mathematics portions of the Arkansas Benchmark Exams"[4] (McKenzie & Mulvenon, 2004). The gains are presented in Figures 5.11 and 5.12.

Similarly, Elaine students made gains "in both the Literacy and Mathematics portions of the Arkansas Benchmark Exams" (McKenzie & Mulvenon, 2004). The graphs are presented in Figures 5.13 and 5.14.

The press, both television and print, held the schools accountable as well. Their routine coverage was at times demoralizing for teachers and administrators. However, their vigilance ensured support for the districts. In addition, they reported on the positive gains as well as the remaining problems in the districts. (See Figure 5.15.)

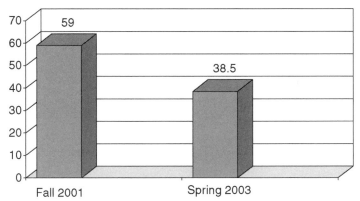

FIGURE 5.9. This graph depicts the decrease in students scoring at or below the 25th percentile. In the fall of 2001, 59% scored below the 25th percentile on the Stanford 9 test. In the spring of 2003, at the end of the empowerment evaluation intervention, only 38.5% of students scored below the 25th percentile.

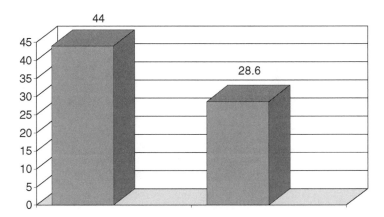

FIGURE 5.10. This graph depicts the decrease in students scoring at or below the 25th percentile in the Altheimer Unified School District on the Stanford 9 Achievement Test.

Literacy Mean Scaled Score

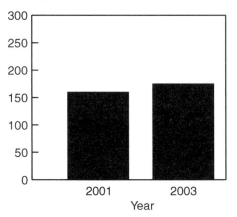

FIGURE 5.11. Altheimer: All students' literacy mean scaled scores (2001 = 158 and 2003 = 168). Courtesy of the National Office for Research on Measurement and Evaluation Systems. Reprinted by permission.

Mathematics Mean Scaled Score

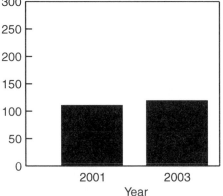

FIGURE 5.12. Altheimer: All students mathematics mean scaled scores (2001 = 114 and 2003 = 128). Courtesy of the National Office for Research Measurement and Evaluation Systems. Reprinted by permission.

Literacy Mean Scaled Score

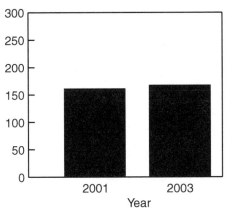

FIGURE 5.13. Elaine: All students' literacy mean scaled scores (2001 = 159 and 2003 = 169). Courtesy of the National Office for Research on Measurement and Evaluation Systems. Reprinted by permission.

Mathematics Mean Scaled Score

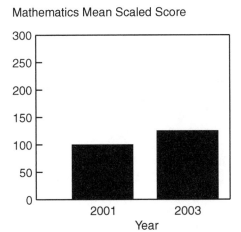

FIGURE 5.14. Elaine: All students' mathematics mean scaled scores (2001 = 98 and 2003 = 125). Courtesy of the National Office for Research on Measurement and Evaluation Systems. Reprinted by permission.

FIGURE 5.15. Channel 7 (KATV)—Arkansas News.

The parents, teachers, students, and administrators also held themselves accountable for improving discipline, parental involvement, community participation, and improved governance and management. Gains
were made in each of the activities selected by the districts (see Figures 5.7
and 5.8).

CONCLUSION

These two cases highlight empowerment evaluation principles, ranging
from improvement to accountability. The same principles guide related
empowerment evaluations for the Western Knight Center for Specialized
Journalism (Bare, 2004; Fetterman, 2004),[5] the MOSAICS art-oriented
teacher education project (Fetterman & Thibeault, 2004), and the NASA
Mars Rover educational program (Fetterman & Bowman, 2002; Choy,
2004). The case examples highlight both the strength of specific principles
in guiding practice and the overlapping and reinforcing nature of the principles, as discussed in Chapter 3. A social justice orientation lends credibility to the initiative and motivates community members to participate.
Community ownership, respect for community knowledge, and democratic participation provide a day-to-day basis for continued participation
and action. These principles build a foundation of community trust. This
relationship is enhanced when capacity building is a part of the process.

People know they are learning on an individual and group basis as they see their own growth. Couple this foundation of trust with growth in capacity and a logical next step is the development of a learning organization. Accountability becomes a by-product, in many instances, of a normal organizational learning culture. Although this brief presentation can only scratch the surface of these communities' accomplishments, the chapter does serve to highlight significant empowerment evaluation principles that operate across ethnic groups, organizations, regions, and socioeconomic classes.

NOTES

1. The digital divide refers to the "haves" and "have-nots" in a technological world. Typically low-income and minority groups have not had the same access to computers and the Internet that middle-class white groups enjoy. This represents the "digital divide."
2. In addition, I made a personal commitment to share some of the highlights of their success.
3. Linda Locklear was a co-empowerment evaluator on this project. She recognized the problem and proposed the representational solution.
4. The Benchmark Exam gains are only important when placed in the cumulative context of Stanford 9 test scores and districtwide gains made in such areas as discipline, teaching, motivation, classroom management, and parental involvement. The intervention began in 2001, highlighting collaborative forms of Web instruction. The needs assessment and empowerment evaluation are documented on the Web at *http://homepage.mac.com/profdavidf*.
5. "In empowerment evaluation they all work together as a team, transcending the traditional boundaries between implementation and evaluation" (J. Bare, Vice President for Strategic Planning and Evaluation, Blank Family Foundation; formerly Director of Planning and Evaluation at the John S. & James L. Knight Foundation, personal communication, 2004).

   "What I like about empowerment evaluation is the seamless way in which we work together planning, implementing, assessing, and revising. It is a true learning experience" (V. Porter, Director of the Western Knight Center for Specialized Journalism, personal communication, 2004).

REFERENCES

Argyris, C. (1999). *On organizational learning*. Malden, MA: Blackwell Business.
Argyris, C., & Schön, D. (1974). *Organizational learning*. Reading, MA: Addison-Wesley.
Bare, J. (2004). On evaluation and philanthropy: Evaluation in a new Gilded Age. *The Evaluation Exchange* (Harvard Family Research Project, Harvard Graduate School of Education), 9(4), 20.

Choy, C. P. (2004). *Connecting novices with experts, students with science.* Harvard Graduate School of Education. Available online at *http://www.gse.harvard.edu/news/features/bowman03012004.html.*

Fetterman, D. M. (2001). *Foundations of empowerment evaluation.* Thousand Oaks, CA: Sage.

Fetterman, D. M. (2002). *Improving school performance: Partnering for success: A needs assessment report.* Stanford, CA: Stanford University. Available online at *http://homepage.mac.com/profdavidf*

Fetterman, D. M. (2003). *Interim report on districts in Phase III: Empowerment evaluation report to the State Board of Education.* Stanford, CA: Stanford University. Available online at *http://homepage.mac.com/profdavidf*

Fetterman, D. M. (2004). *Teleconferencing and web broadcasting for the Western Knight Center for Specialized Journalism.* Stanford, CA: Stanford University.

Fetterman, D. M., & Bowman, C. (2002). Experiential education and empowerment evaluation: Mars Rover educational program case example. *The Journal of Experiential Education, 25*(2), 286–295.

Fetterman, D. M., & Thibeault, M. (2004, April 12–20). *Stanford University's empowerment evaluation of the MOSAICS Project: Combining internal and external evaluation approaches.* Paper presented at the American Educational Research Association, San Diego, CA.

McKenzie, S., & Mulvenon, S. (2004). Personal communication. National Office for Research on Measurement and Evaluation Systems (NORMES). University of Arkansas, Fayetteville.

Preskill, H. (1994). Evaluation's role in facilitating organizational learning: A model for practice. *Evaluation and Program Planning, 17*(3), 291–298.

Senge, P. (1990). *The fifth discipline: The art and practice of organizational learning.* New York: Doubleday.

Smith, C. (2004). Personal communication. Assistant Director, Educational Accountability Section of the Arkansas Department of Education, Little Rock.

Wilson, R. (2004). Personal communication. Senior Coordinator, Educational Accountability Section of the Arkansas Department of Education, Little Rock.

CHAPTER **6**

Organizational Functioning

FACILITATING EFFECTIVE INTERVENTIONS
AND INCREASING THE ODDS OF PROGRAMMING SUCCESS

Melanie Livet and Abraham Wandersman

mportant lessons for effective interventions can be gleaned from the Columbia shuttle disaster of 2003. Launching the shuttle takes evidence-based
knowledge and systematic planning and implementation. An evaluation of
the disaster found that this was not enough. Strained relationships within the
agency led to a lack of communication and fear about raising issues during the
flight that may have led to ameliorative steps (Poor NASA Management,
2003).

What lessons can be learned from this? Previous chapters in this book discuss the importance of obtaining results in educational, health and social service programs. Many literatures suggest that what we need to do to obtain
results is to have greater use of evidence-based interventions ("science"). As
the shuttle disaster suggests—whether we are talking about rocket science,
prevention science, or clinical science—"For any intervention to succeed,
whether at the individual level (e.g., therapy) or at the organizational level
(e.g., violence prevention programs for a school), it is necessary to have both
appropriate content of the intervention and a good structure that delivers it"
(Wandersman, 2003, p. 234).

In the shuttle example, there is a connection between organizational characteristics (such as the chain of command and communication channels) and rocket science (e.g., the types of insulation needed to protect the rocket from heat generated by hitting the earth's atmosphere) that is also linked to outcomes (successful or unsuccessful landing). In education and in health and human services, we look for links between organizational characteristics, interventions, and outcomes. For example in the education of our children, we look for links between organizational characteristics (e.g., administrative leadership), interventions (e.g., phonics reading curriculum), and outcomes (reading achievement scores). This chapter is about organizational characteristics and the successful implementation of effective interventions. Whether we are talking about an intervention *as a specific program or curriculum* (e.g., DARE [Drug Abuse Resistance Education]) or *as a process or way of doing things* in an organization (e.g., using a management information system), it is critical that an organization be receptive to the intervention and implement it with quality. For example, empowerment evaluation is an example of a process. As previous chapters have noted, empowerment evaluation has values, principles, methods, and tools to help organizations increase the probability of obtaining favorable outcomes. Therefore, introducing empowerment evaluation into a program should be considered as being an intervention into the culture ("the way of doing things") of the program and of the organization that hosts the program. Our work and the work of others make it clear that not all organizations are immediately ready to implement empowerment evaluation and the tools associated with it. As described in Chapter 2, one of the core values of empowerment evaluation is organizational learning. The empowerment evaluation approach and the use of its tools will only be effective in an organization that is ready to learn and shares some key organizational prerequisites that will facilitate the adoption and implementation of empowerment evaluation. While we recognize that organizational learning is a dynamic process that occurs in cycles, this chapter focuses on organizational readiness to use empowerment evaluation and its tools rather than on empowerment evaluation as a way to facilitate learning and build organizational capacity. In this chapter, we will examine the organizational characteristics that have been found to be related to the effective implementation of an intervention. We will focus on interventions *as a process or way of doing things* (e.g., empowerment evaluation tools such as Getting to Outcomes); however, many of the ideas in the chapter are also applicable to interventions that are *specific programs or curricula* (e.g., DARE).

In order to make the organizational ideas in this chapter more tangible, we have written it using the perspective of a community agency that has been entrusted with planning, implementing, and sustaining intervention programming designed to provide services to families in need of assistance with a number of issues, including teenage pregnancy, illiteracy, poverty, and other health and mental health issues. As the director of this agency, you have decided that in order to increase the likelihood of your program's succeeding you need to adopt a process that would facilitate your programming activities. You chose to use the "Getting to Outcomes" system, which is an empowerment evaluation program development and evaluation tool that consists of 10 programming steps (e.g., conducting a needs assessment) that was developed to help practitioners achieve results with their interventions while demonstrating accountability (Wandersman, Imm, Chinman, & Kaftarian, 2000; Chinman, Imm, & Wandersman, 2004). Having a good tool or evidence-based intervention is one thing, but having your organization be interested and capable of delivering it is another. There may be political issues and organizational capacity issues that will ease or inhibit putting the intervention into place. The question then becomes: What organizational factors will help implement the intervention? This chapter aims to answer this key question based on an extensive review of the literature on organizational characteristics needed in program planning, implementation, success, improvement, and sustainability.

Whether you are a community practitioner, empowerment evaluator, or funder, you need to be aware of the cultural and structural aspects of the organization to make the best use of its capacities and to be able to strengthen its weaknesses. Some of the research findings and recommendations (e.g., better communication) might appear evident at first glance. However, if they are that obvious, then the question becomes: Why don't many organizations implement them? Common sense is obviously not common practice. More importantly, previous work by Wandersman and colleagues (e.g., Florin, Chavis, Wandersman, & Rich, 1992) has taken the approach that it is important to move from a level of findings about what works (whether obvious or not) to tools and processes that can help practitioners improve what they do. In this vein, we also present practical implications of the literature and checklists in this chapter. If you are a practitioner, you can use this chapter as a briefing and checklist to make sure that your organization is prepared to plan, implement, and sustain an intervention. The assessment can identify which organizational resources and capacities need to be built up. If you are an empowerment evaluator, you can use this chapter to assess the organizational readiness of the organization that you are working with as well as to help pinpoint the potential organizational issues that might hinder or facilitate program success and adoption of programming and evaluation processes by the organization.

Finally, if you are a funder, you can use this chapter to think about organizational enhancements that would help organizations carry out more effective programs or projects.

To summarize, understanding and assessing the organizational characteristics of the agency that is responsible for implementing the intervention is crucial to increasing the likelihood of programming success (by programming, we are referring to the process of putting an intervention in place). While we are aware that external macro-system variables, including political and social forces, are at play in the success of social programs, our specific focus is on understanding the influence of both *general organizational factors* and *intervention-specific factors* on programming within an empowerment evaluation framework. Our chapter is intended to provide you with an overview of the organizational elements that will help you most in achieving programming success. First, it provides a comprehensive synthesis and analysis of the quantitative and qualitative empirical literature linking organizational conditions to program planning, implementation, and maintenance. As already noted, these research findings are presented from the perspective of a community agency director who is responsible for planning, implementing, and maintaining an intervention. In addition, we use examples from the Middle Tyger Community Center (MTCC) case (see Keener, Snell-Johns, Livet, & Wandersman, Chapter 4 of this volume, for further description of this case) to guide you, the reader, through this literature review and bring our organizational ideas to life. Finally, we describe the practical implications and recommendations that derive from these findings.

THEORETICAL FRAMEWORK

In order to guide our work, we developed a theoretical model (see Figure 6.1) based on Goodman and Wandersman's action model that simultaneously tracks implementation of an intervention with coalition functioning (1994) and on Wandersman et al.'s "Getting to Outcomes" (GTO) paradigm (2000; see Table 6.1 for a brief description of the GTO approach). Following the logic of the Goodman and Wandersman model and the GTO model, our framework conceptualized two parallel processes in program development: the development of the agency/partnership itself and the progression of intervention-specific activities. When being involved in programming, you therefore need to be attuned to two types of organizational characteristics: (1) the overall functioning of your agency (e.g., communication within the agency) and (2) the organizational capacities that are intervention-specific, including human (e.g., staff knowledge of

ORGANIZATIONAL CHARACTERISTICS   PROGRAM STAGES

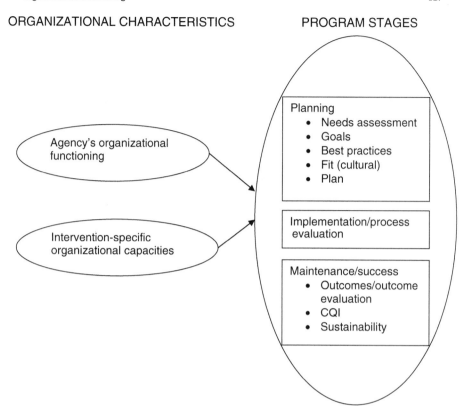

FIGURE 6.1. Theoretical model.

the specific intervention), technical (e.g., technical assistance for the intervention), and fiscal (e.g., funding for a given intervention) resources. As seen in Figure 6.1, programming was defined as including three stages based on the 10 GTO programming steps: planning, implementation, and maintenance. Planning involved completion of a needs assessment, development of program goals, use of evidence-based research and information, fit/cultural competency, and conceptualization of a program plan. Due to the lack of empirical research on program goals, this step was dropped from the literature review. The program implementation phase referred to the assessment of program activities that were put in place, including level and quality of service delivery. Finally, program maintenance included research on program outcomes, use and implementation of continuous quality improvement strategies (CQI), and factors affecting the sus-

TABLE 6.1. The 10 GTO Accountability Questions and How to Answer Them

The accountability questions	Literatures for answering the question
1. What are the needs and resources in your organization/school/community/state?	1. Needs assessment; resource assessment
2. What are the goals, target population, and desired outcomes (objectives) for your school/community/state?	2. Goal setting
3. How does the intervention incorporate knowledge of science and best practices in this area?	3. Science and best practices
4. How does the intervention fit with other programs already being offered?	4. Collaboration; cultural competence
5. What capacities do you need to put this intervention into place with quality?	5. Capacity building
6. How will this intervention be carried out?	6. Planning
7. How will the quality of implementation be assessed?	7. Process evaluation
8. How well did the intervention work?	8. Outcome and impact evaluation
9. How will continuous quality improvement strategies be incorporated?	9. Total quality management; continuous quality improvement
10. If the intervention is (or components are) successful, how will the intervention be sustained?	10. Sustainability and institutionalization

tainability of the program after the end of initial funding. Continuous quality improvement refers to strategies used to refine the process, including the working through of the GTO questions on a periodic and cyclical basis. Based on our framework, organizational characteristics identified in the literature, each represented by a set of proxy variables, were grouped and classified in an effort to synthesize findings (see Figure 6.2). Inclusion criteria for the review and the methodological considerations of the literature examined are described in Appendix 6.1.

CASE EXAMPLE

In order to illustrate the findings from the literature, we use examples from the MTCC case study (see Keener et al., Chapter 4 of this volume, for

AGENCY'S ORGANIZATIONAL FUNCTIONING/STRUCTURE	
Organizational conditions	Make sure you have:
Staff skills and expertise	
Staff skills	
Staff tenure	
Staff education level	
Interpersonal Processes	
Staff–organization relationships √ Leadership √ Interagency communication, collaboration, and cohesion √ Staff–organization fit	
Staff–client relationships	
Community–organization relationships √ Participation in networks √ Community involvement √ Reputation	
Organizational structure	
Complexity	
Formalization/flexibility	
Centralization	

ORGANIZATIONAL CAPACITIES FOR INTERVENTION-SPECIFIC ACTIVITIES (e.g., GTO)	
Organizational conditions	Make sure you have:
Human capacities	
Knowledge	
Attitudes √ Commitment √ Compatibility √ Perceptions of benefits and payoffs/fears	
Behavior √ Involvement (e.g., program/process champion) √ Timing	
Technical capacities	
Availability/compatibility of information	
In-service training	
Technical assistance	
Fiscal capacities	
Overall budget	
Other financial factors	

FIGURE 6.2. Checklist.

further description of this case). Both of us were involved in this project as evaluators. Briefly, the overarching mission of the initiative was to create healthy families in the community. While the original goals were to prevent teenage pregnancy and school dropouts, the project quickly expanded to include other programs designed to serve the unique needs of each family member (e.g., adult education, family therapy, family support services, prenatal services, assistance to seniors, etc.). Additional partners were also located at the center, including the Department of Social Services and the Department of Health and Environmental Control. Over time, the center grew from two original programs and a co-location model to become a model of integrated services. While this journey had its challenges, programs offered by this community center were successfully planned, implemented, and sustained. With hindsight, it is now clear that their successes and challenges were partly due to the organization's infrastructure and culture.

OVERALL ORGANIZATIONAL FUNCTIONING

In terms of overall organizational functioning, the research literature shows three salient clusters of organizational characteristics that were involved in programming success: (1) staff skills and expertise, (2) interpersonal processes, and (3) organizational structure. Skills and expertise refer to the competencies that the staff member brings to the agency, including previous experience with similar programs and/or programming activities, as well as more general competencies, such as interpersonal, communication, and community-related skills. Interpersonal processes focus on the relationships within the organization (e.g., between staff members and the target population) as well as between the organization and the rest of the community (e.g., volunteers). Organizational structure can be understood as the way the agency is organized in terms of intricacy and complexity, existence of policies and other formalized processes, and authority hierarchy/participation in decision making

Staff Skills and Expertise

Research Findings

Your first order of business is to ensure that your staff has skills and expertise that will increase the likelihood of program success. The makeup of your agency or partnership staff—that is, their expertise, professional experience, and education level—has a significant impact on programming. Providers need to have the skills and expertise necessary to undertake both the process activities (process skills, such as conducting a needs assessment, choosing best practices, etc.) involved in program planning, implementation, and maintenance, as well as program activities (expertise or experience related to the program chosen). Interestingly, experience with process-related skills seems to be slightly more important than program-related skills. Furthermore, knowledge about process-related activities is influential in the program planning and continuous quality improvement stages, while program-related expertise plays a role in program implementation and sustainability. If your staff is knowledgeable and has had experience in conducting any of the GTO activities, the programming process is likely to go much smoother (Barnette & Clendenen, 1996; Dearing, Larson, Randall, & Pope, 1998; Hanlon et al., 1998; Humphris, Littlejohns, Victor, O'Halloran, & Peacock, 2000; Maciak, Guzman, Santiago, Villalobos, & Israel, 1999; Robins, 1982). Some knowledge of the program itself acquired through training or past experiences with similar types of programs will also increase the likelihood of successful program implementation and sustainability (Bossert, 1990; Cooke, 2000). Based on these findings, it is clear that preference should be given to either choosing staff members with previous experience in conducting *process* activities or in providing training to staff on how to perform those activities, rather than focusing on the level of *program* knowledge staff members have.

Tenure in the agency and educational level also appear to make a difference when planning, implementing, and maintaining an intervention. Interestingly, staff members with longer tenure have been found to be more hesitant in using best-practices research to guide program development (DiFranceisco et al., 1999; Johnson, 1985). It is possible that members who have been in the organization longer have an increased awareness of the barriers associated with this process, including limitations in personnel and budget, and are therefore less willing to undertake it. If you want to use evidence-based research in your choice of programming, it therefore may be preferable to entrust a newer staff member with this task while ensuring that everyone in the organization, especially more experienced supervisors, understands the importance of this process. Findings in the literature also point to the possibility that the general level of education, as defined by the number of years in school, might not be as important as the specificity of professional education received and its fit with the organization's purpose and program choice (Boehm & Litwin, 1997; Friedmann, Alexander, & D'Aunno, 1999a; Smith, 1998). In other words, your staff should have had some professional education that is a good fit with your agency's mission. Findings also suggest that it is more important for executive decision-making administrators to have a higher level of education, while the average educational level of frontline staff members is not as important in the program planning and implementation process (Johnson, 1985).

Example

In the case of the community center, direct providers and management staff had excellent general skills. They were able to relate to others on a personal level, clearly communicated and expressed their needs to one another, and worked very closely with one another. For instance, in the meetings that we attended, time was devoted for individuals to interact with one another on a more personal basis prior to the meeting. In addition, many of them had been involved in community initiatives previously and therefore had had experience with needy families. The director of the teenage pregnancy prevention program, for instance, had worked as the director of a church child care center prior to joining the community center, and her hands-on experience allowed her to build wonderful relationships with the teens. Interestingly, staff members were generally not familiar with the process of planning, implementing, and maintaining an intervention. However, they were receptive to new information and actively pursued opportunities to further their knowledge base. Furthermore, while members of the management team held at least a bachelor's degree, frontline staff members were hired based on their professional capacities and interpersonal skills rather than their educational background.

Interpersonal Processes

Research Findings

Once you have adequately matched the staff members' skills and expertise to the positions, you need to examine the relationships within and outside your organization. Interpersonal processes are the organizational factors that are most consistently associated with all three stages of programming. As you plan, implement, and maintain your program, you need to take into consideration the relationships between staff and the organization, staff and the target population, and the organization and the rest of the community, as they will influence programming success. There is overwhelming evidence supporting the importance of key organizational factors pertaining to the *relationship between staff and the agency/partnership*, including the leadership management style, the staff's cohesion and communication style, the level of clarity each has about his/her and others' roles and expectations, and the level of staff–organization fit. First, it is crucial to have a *leadership* that is democratic and egalitarian, stable, strong, and committed. The leader must possess certain qualities, including a "can do" attitude, a high degree of respect from others, strong negotiation skills, an ability to obtain resources, a high degree of political knowledge, an ability to foster collaboration and to maintain staff and community enthusiasm when they are faced with what appear to be insurmountable challenges, an ability to establish priorities and define accountability, as well as access to the decision makers in the community (Korr & Joseph, 1996; Maciak et al., 1999; Stanton, Kennedy, Spingarn, & Rotheram-Borus, 2000). In short, leadership should be empowered and empowering to others (Dohlie et al., 1999; Handler, Geller, & Kennelly, 1999; Shortell et al., 1995). You will find that certain leader characteristics are more important for certain stages of programming. For instance, the use and quality of continuous quality improvement strategies are facilitated if leadership is comfortable with a data utilization approach and insists on obtaining results during the process (Barnette & Clendenen, 1996; Hermann, Regner, Erickson, & Yang, 2000). Extrapolating from these findings, we hypothesize that leadership is particularly important during the adoption phase of any new activity rather than when this activity has been implemented and routinized.

Second, the fostering of effective *intraagency communication, collaboration, and cohesion* will greatly facilitate programming success. Your staff members need to be encouraged to communicate openly and to collaborate with one another (Barnette & Clendenen, 1996; Dohlie et al., 1999; Glisson & Hemmelgarn, 1998; Hermann et al., 2000; Johnson, 1989; Korr & Joseph, 1996; Maciak et al., 1999; McGrew & Bond, 1997; Riley, Taylor, & Elliott, 2001; Shortell et al., 1995; Stanton et al., 2000). Group processes, such as conflict resolution, need to be handled with care, as they will affect progress on programming (Dearing et al., 1998; Glisson & Hemmelgarn, 1998; Kieler, Rundall, Saporta, Sussman, Keilch, Warren, Black, Brinkley, & Barney, 1996). Certain strategies that have been found to be particularly useful are the use of group consensus building as a participatory decision-making approach (Maciak et al., 1999; Loue, Lloyd, & Phoombour, 1996) and utilization of a multidirectional multimodal information flow (Hodges & Hernandez, 1999; Streefland, 1995). In other words, two-way communication should be promoted, with staff communicating with management and vice versa. Finally, everyone needs to understand what his or her and others' roles are in the initiative, and be clear on what he or she and others are expected to be doing. General confusion about roles and expectations in the agency or partnership as well as lack of understanding regarding one's responsibilities in conducting or using data for a specific GTO activity have been found to correlate negatively with all three stages of programming (Amodeo & Gal, 1997; Bracht et al., 1994;

Glisson & Hemmelgarn, 1998; Hermann et al., 2000; Hilderbrandt, 1994; Kieler et al., 1996).

Third, every effort should be made toward ensuring *staff–organization fit* and avoiding turnover and unstable staffing, which have negative impacts on programming. Low turnover not only allows for the building of networks and relationships between staff members and between staff and the rest of the community, but also facilitates the development of staff enthusiasm for the programming of the project (Amodeo & Gal, 1997; Becker, Dumas, Houser, & Seay, 2000; Elder et al., 1998; Hodges & Hernandez, 1999; Kieler et al., 1996; O'Loughlin, Renaud, Richard, Sanchez Gomez, & Paradis, 1998; Stanton et al., 2000). Other proxy variables of staff–organization fit that are associated with programming success and therefore need to be carefully monitored are loyalty to the organization and leader, high levels of job satisfaction, low frequency of burnout, perceptions of fairness, and the extent to which the staff personal vision is aligned with the organization vision (Barnette & Clendenen, 1996; Glisson & Hemmelgarn, 1998; Scheid & Greenley, 1997).

In addition to the relationships of staff with the organization, the *relationships between the staff and the target population* and *between the personnel of the organization and the community* have also been investigated in the literature, although to a lesser extent, and have been associated with a greater likelihood of programming success. Your frontline providers need to build a rapport of trust with clients, which is likely to more readily occur if clients perceive them as being involved and interested in their lives and as having a flexible and responsive approach to their needs (Clark, Teague, & Henry, 1999; Dohlie et al., 1999; Friedman, Glickman, & Kovach, 1986; O'Loughlin et al., 1998; Sormanti, Pereira, El-Bassel, Witte, & Gilbert, 2001; Streefland, 1995). Participation of the organization and employees in *community and other informal networks*, *community involvement* (e.g., volunteerism, collaboration with other agencies), and the agency's *reputation* are also positively associated with successful programming. Having access to a network of colleagues and consultants, for instance, allows individual staff members to problem-solve and overcome challenges related to best-practices information seeking, and therefore facilitate research utilization in program planning (Tyden, 1996). Involving other community members in programming, either through volunteer activities or by creating collaborations with other agencies, is likely to result in an intervention that is well planned and culturally sensitive (Dearing et al., 1998; Kieler et al., 1996; Loue et al., 1996; Maciak et al., 1999; Williams & Becker, 1994), is more fully implemented (Moss, 1983; Riley et al., 2001), and, because of high levels of interest in the community, will ultimately be more readily improved and sustained (Barnette & Clendenen, 1996; Bossert, 1990; Bracht et al., 1994; Dohlie et al., 1999;

Goodman & Steckler, 1987; Hodges & Hernandez, 1999; Korr & Joseph, 1996; Loue et al., 1996; Miller, 2001; Streefland, 1995). If your agency has been around for a while, its reputability and prestige will also play a role in the successful adoption and development of a new program (Moss, 1983; Stanton et al., 2000).

Example

One of the definitive strengths of the community center's staff was their ability to build relationships. The center was characterized by an atmosphere of warmth and close interpersonal relationships. Sharing of professional and personal stories among staff members was a common occurrence, and they seemed to pull together through difficult times. As a visitor, you were always welcome and greeted by a volunteer receptionist at the front door and frequently offered refreshments by staff members before and during meetings, as if you were also part of the center's family. In satisfaction surveys, clients reported being very satisfied with the center's staff and with the services that were provided to them. Observations by the evaluation team were consistent with client reports. Staff members seemed to be genuinely concerned with the families they were serving and were eager to share their enthusiasm with the evaluators when they had successfully helped a family, by relating stories and anecdotes.

The agency also had very strong leadership, with an executive director (ED) who was able to inspire and mobilize staff and other resources. Having lived and worked in the community for many years, she and her team also had access to an extensive social and personal network and were acutely aware of the politics surrounding the project. Her interpersonal style allowed her to foster collaboration between the center and other partners in the community and played a major role in the formation and growth of the partnership that came to characterize the center. She empowered staff members by encouraging them to voice their opinions and participate in decision making, and cultivated commitment from others to the project. Staff members at all levels felt comfortable enough to give her and one another feedback. The ED also had a vision for the center and worked tirelessly to achieve it. Because she invested so much of herself in the center, she was protective of the way it was portrayed to outsiders. While she was committed to improving the project, the presentation of unexpected and/or negative findings by the evaluation team that were intended to be used for improvement were at times met with fear and skepticism, especially at the beginning of the project. One such event is recalled in detail by Keener et al. in Chapter 4. As the ED and her team learned to know and trust the evaluation team and as the evaluation team learned how to best communicate unexpected findings, however, these concerns waned, and the center's management staff became more comfortable with understanding and using evaluation data as a tool for program improvement rather than as punishment.

Finally, it was clear that staff demonstrated strong loyalty to both the ED and the center. Over the course of 6 years, all but one individual who had been involved with the center from its very beginning were still employed by the agency in one capacity or another. Management was also committed to accommodating staff members by allowing them to modify their position, if needed. For instance, the director of one of the original programs decided to cut her workload by half in order to be able to raise her children. The center created a new position for her. It was clear to the authors that individuals believed in what they were doing and were strongly committed to making a difference in their community.

Organizational Structure

Research Findings

In addition to managing the human aspect of the agency, including staff and relationships within and outside the organization, you need to consider the structure and culture of the organization, including degrees of organizational complexity, flexibility/formalization, and centralization. *Organizational complexity* refers to the degree of structural intricacy, or the "amount of differentiation that exists within different elements constituting the organization" (Dooley, 2002, p. 5013). It is represented by the amount of variation in the workforce, organizational processes and activities, levels of command or overall number of levels in the organization, program activities, geographical location, and clients. While it is evident that you need to have enough staff to carry out the programming tasks and enough clients to utilize the services offered (DiFranceisco et al., 1999; Humphris et al., 2000; Johnson, 1990; Kieler et al., 1996; Kim & Cho, 2000; Miller, 2001), the size of your agency (i.e., the number of staff members and clients) is not as important in predicting successful programming as the organizational structure of jobs and services offered. Smaller staff–client ratios and lighter workloads are precursors of more successful implementation (Becker et al., 2000; Ethier, Fox-Tierney, Nicholas, Salisbury, & Ickovics, 2000; Friedmann et al., 1999a; Healton et al., 1996; Sosin, 2001), and the integration of new services into an already existing structure will increase the likelihood of positive outcomes and program sustainability (Altman, 1995; Bossert, 1990; Bracht et al., 1994; Clark et al., 1999; Dohlie et al., 1999; Shediac-Rizkallah & Bone, 1998). Furthermore, the type of agency that is most successful in the programming process also tends to encourage public ownership and to focus on a specific intervention that fits with the organization's overall vision (Friedmann et al., 1999a; Friedmann, Alexander, Jin, & D'Aunno, 1999b; Healton et al., 1996; Kim & Cho, 2000; Scheid & Greenley, 1997).

The amount of formalization and flexibility in organizational administrative procedures is just as important as having an organizational work structure and/or service structure that can carry out the planning, implementation, and maintenance of the intervention. *Formalization* refers to the extent to which organizational policies are explicitly stated and routinized, while *flexibility* is defined as the organization's ease and comfort with creativity and adaptability (level of adherence to policies). If the culture of your organization is able to encourage risk taking and demonstrates some willingness to adjust and change while at the same time providing flexible guidelines and routinization of processes, you will increase the odds of successful programming (Altman, 1995; Barnette & Clendenen, 1996; Becker et al., 2000; Cooke, 2000; Dohlie et al., 1999; Kieler et al., 1996; Kim & Cho, 2000; Moss, 1983; Robins, 1982; Shediac-Rizkallah & Bone, 1998; Shortell et al., 1995). Interestingly, levels of organizational formalization and flexibility might be differentially influential on programming activities, with flexibility being particularly important for organizational planning (e.g., negotiating with supporting systems, dealing with clients), while the presence of clear and obvious guidelines is necessary for successful rational planning activities (e.g., methodical gathering of data) (Boehm & Litwin, 1997). The task of balancing levels of organizational formalization and flexibility is therefore facilitated if careful attention is paid to the types of programming activities involved, with more mechanical tasks being eased if a formal process is in place and more dynamic activities being positively associated with a more flexible responsive style.

Consistent with the findings on organizational formalization and flexibility, the degree of centralization that is most likely to predict programming success depends on the activity at hand. *Centralization* is defined as the extent to which activities in the organization are centrally coordinated and the organizational structure clearly hierarchical. In other words, it refers to the distribution of formal control and power within the organization. The likelihood of achieving program planning, implementation, and maintenance is facilitated by decentralizing decision-making tasks and by centralizing information-seeking tasks (Barnette & Clendenen, 1996; Becker et al., 2000; Boehm & Litwin, 1997; Bossert, 1990; Cooke, 2000; Dearing et al., 1998; Dohlie et al., 1999; Hermann et al., 2000; Shortell et al., 1995; Streefland, 1995). Empowering staff to make decisions about policy, resources, recruitment, and other issues will maximize participation and ultimately affect programming. Likewise, having a clear chain of control and central coordination eases the completion of more mechanical and performance-oriented tasks (e.g., compiling information tools about a particular intervention) by ensuring accountability. Again, in order to achieve the ideal balance, the degree of centralization needs to be adjusted, depending on the type of activity engaged in by community practitioners.

Example

While the MTCC started out as a simple infrastructure (two core programs, two program directors, an executive director, and direct service providers), it eventually reached higher levels of organizational complexity in terms of the number of agencies involved, diversity of work roles, and the number of services provided. The center was located in an old school that had been renovated and the premises were shared by several other agencies, including the Department of Social Services and the Department of Health and Environmental Control. Some of the classrooms were also used by the center's partners. For instance, the Department of Education was utilizing classrooms to run their Basic Education and GED programs.

The structure and diversity of roles was also quite complex, as some staff members shared their time between several agencies and fulfilled different roles. While individuals appeared to be comfortable with their understanding of what they were supposed to do, they were not always clear on what their coworkers were responsible for accomplishing. This sometimes led to confusion over duties and responsibilities. Because of the closely knit culture of the center, however, these issues were easily resolved through good communication. Furthermore, the services provided were quite complex in their breadth and depth since they were designed to address the needs of each family member. Understandably, staff members and even the management team of the center were not always aware of the services provided by the other agencies sharing the same premises or participating in the partnership. In order to remediate the problem, it was decided that information about each agency and about the services offered at the center and by its partners be compiled in a resource manual to be distributed to each employee and partner, the ultimate goal being that familiarizing oneself with the manual would become part of new employee and partner training. While high levels of complexity can slow programming success, it is also necessary for the organization to reach a certain level of complexity if services are to be integrated. In this case, the center was able to problem-solve and successfully manage a complex infrastructure, and was ultimately able to successfully sustain the programs it had developed and implemented, under one "umbrella."

The center also successfully balanced organizational formalization and flexibility. It grew to understand the importance of having a certain level of formalized processes, such as written policies and documentation. Because of the nature of their work, it was not always a simple task for the center's employees to learn to document what they were doing. For instance, the evaluation team had to slowly build the center's evaluation capacity by teaching the employees the importance of using data internally for program improvement purposes. One of the center's strengths, however, was the staff's willingness and ability to learn and adjust to changes in the environment. Depending on the needs, the center constantly readjusted its structure and jobs. For instance, a program that had been started by the agency was later adopted by one of its partners to ensure sustainability, which changed the structure of the center. The administrative team had to choose whether to reassign the employees who were part of this program to other positions at the center or come up with some type of creative solution to have them continue working with that program.

Finally, given the democratic leadership style of the agency, the staff was encouraged to participate in decision making about programming as well as administrative issues. For example, when the evaluation team met at the center, the meetings were often attended by the management team as well as other personnel from each program. Each individual was encouraged to provide feedback and voice his or her opinion regarding planning, implementation, and evaluation activities. Decisions were clearly made not only by the executive director but also by the rest of the staff. When it came to specific activities, such as compiling data for the evaluation, however, decisions regarding who was responsible for what tended to be made by the individual's direct supervisor.

Implications

Having examined the research, we now describe some key points relating to the elements of overall organizational functioning that you need to have in place to increase the odds of programming success, especially when you use empowerment evaluation tools such as the Getting to Outcomes steps to plan, implement, and sustain your program:

- Match your *staff's skills, expertise, and education* to the appropriate professional positions in the agency.
- Examine the *interpersonal processes within and outside your organization*, including the relationships between your staff and the agency, between your staff and target population, and between your organization and the community, and ensure that you have (1) *leaders* who not only adopt a democratic participatory style, which appears to be more advantageous in social settings, but also possess the skills and flexibility to adapt to the needs of their staff; (2) management and personnel who are *cohesive and able to collaborate and communicate effectively* by means of team approaches (e.g., consensus building) when making decisions and a two-

way communication process that is particularly relevant to program development effectiveness; (3) a good *fit* between your team and the organization, which will allow for low turnover, high loyalty, high levels of job satisfaction, and closer alignment of the staff's personal vision and organizational values; (4) employees who are able to *build rapport* with clients; (5) an organization that is able to participate in *community and other informal networks* (e.g., volunteerism, collaboration with other agencies); and (6) individuals who are able to build your agency's *reputation*.

• Consider the *structure and culture of the organization*, including degrees of organizational *complexity, flexibility/formalization, and centralization*, and ensure that you (1) organize the work structure and service structure so as to keep small staff–client ratios and integrate new services into already existing structures; (2) have an organizational culture that encourages risk taking and willingness to adjust and change while providing flexible guidelines and routinization of processes; and (3) support the centralization of more mechanical and performance-oriented tasks while decentralizing decision-making tasks, which will empower your staff.

INTERVENTION-SPECIFIC ORGANIZATIONAL CAPACITIES

So far, we have proposed ways to maximize the overall functioning of your organization to increase the odds of successful programming. We now turn to the organizational capacities that are specifically related to the intervention and that should be put in place before or while you plan, implement, and attempt to maintain the intervention. These factors, which are both related to the program chosen and to programming processes (e.g., GTO steps), can be classified into human, technical, and fiscal organizational characteristics. Human capacities refer to the skills and capabilities of your staff that are directly related to the program and the GTO process. Technical capacities include the availability of information and expertise as well as access to databases and other office equipment, and fiscal capacities refer to funding resources.

Human Capacities

Research Findings

Extensive knowledge in, positive attitudes about, and high involvement in both program- and process-related activities from staff and management are key to programming success. Lack of *knowledge* and understanding of the target program and of the programming steps was consistently cited as hindering all stages of programming success (Bedell, Ward, Archer, & Stokes, 1985; Dearing et al., 1998; Hanlon et al., 1998; Kim & Cho, 2000; Tyden, 1996). Just as crucial as knowledge are your and your staff's *attitudes* toward the intervention and processes (e.g., commitment and support, fit, and benefits vs. drawbacks). First, senior management, staff, and board members should be highly *committed* to and supportive of both implementing the project and using the steps outlined in GTO (Becker et al., 2000; Dohlie et al., 1999; Hanlon et al., 1998; Healton et al., 1996; Hodges & Hernandez, 1999; Kim & Cho, 2000; Maciak et al., 1999; Robins, 1982; Stanton et al., 2000; Tyden, 1996). Interestingly, the staff's attention span changes longitudinally during the life of a program, with the intensity of services being impacted over time by declining enthusiasm (Sosin, 2001). Therefore, it is particularly important to maintain the staff's motivation and interest once the initial enthusiasm has waned. Community practitioners need to be continuously encouraged and reinforced by their supervisors and other leaders for engaging in program- and process-related activities, which will greatly facilitate programming (Barnette & Clendenen, 1996; Becker et al., 2000; Dohlie et al., 1999; Hermann et al., 2000; Hilderbrandt, 1994; Redman, Levine, & Howard, 1987; Scheid & Greenley, 1997). As mentioned above, developing strong community support is also an additional asset to programming success (Bracht et al., 1994; Stanton et al., 2000).

Second, make sure that the intervention chosen as well as the GTO activities are *compatible* with your organization's philosophy. Program values need to fit with organizational values (Altman, 1995; Becker et al., 2000; Bedell et al., 1985; Bossert, 1990; Bracht et al., 1994; Elder et al., 1998; Hodges & Hernandez, 1999; Johnson, 1989; Kaluzney & Veney, 1973; Miller, 2001; O'Loughlin et al., 1998; Riley et al., 2001; Stanton et al., 2000), and intervention-related steps (e.g., doing a needs assessment, choosing best practices) should be considered a priority in the successful planning, implementation, and maintenance of the program (Amodeo & Gal, 1997; Hanlon et al., 1998; Robins, 1982). Third, you need to address the *fears* associated with the project and maximize *perceptions of benefits and the degree of visible payoffs*, to ultimately increase buy-in (Bedell et al., 1985; Elder et al., 1998; Kaluzny & Veney, 1973; Redman et al., 1987). One of the most common drawbacks accompanying program development and use of intervention-related steps (GTO steps) are perceptions of increases in workload (Hanlon et al., 1998; Humphris et al., 2000). You need to ensure that the staff has enough time to devote to both the implementation of the program and processes associated with programming (Altman, 1995; Becker et al., 2000; Humphris et al., 2000; Moss, 1983; Robins, 1982; Tyden, 1996).

Once the individuals involved have sufficient knowledge and positive attitudes toward the program and GTO processes, you need to capitalize on this wealth of human resources and enthusiasm and make sure that it gets transformed into *action and behaviors*. *Involvement* of both the organization's staff and the community in the diverse activities associated with programming will increase program ownership, and facilitate the successful completion of programming stages (Altman, 1995; Amodeo & Gal, 1997; Becker et al., 2000; Bracht et al., 1994; Clark et al., 1999; Dearing et al., 1998; Goodman & Steckler, 1987; Scheid & Greenley, 1997; Robins, 1982; Shediac-Rizkallah & Bone, 1998; Stanton et al., 2000). For instance, in terms of community involvement, the use of community "gatekeepers" to access otherwise linguistically and culturally isolated communities is key to facilitating culturally competent programs (Loue et al., 1996). The presence of information brokers and higher linkage levels with outside research sources positively influence the use of best-practices research (Johnson, 1985). Having a process advocate will facilitate the use of intervention-related process steps and ultimately affect outcomes (Amodeo & Gal, 1997), while having a program champion will directly impact all programming stages and particularly sustainability (Altman, 1985; Elder et al., 1998; O'Loughlin et al., 1998; Shediac-Rizkallah & Bone, 1998). In terms of employees' involvement, a recommended strategy to increase staff ownership of the continuous quality improvement process, for example, is to empower staff members by encouraging them to choose their own performance measures and tools (Barnette & Clendenen, 1996; Dohlie et al., 1999; Hermann et al., 2000).

When engaging in any of these process-related activities, you need to pay close attention to your *timing*. Allow enough time between the completion of each activity but not enough for the initial enthusiasm and interest to decline significantly (Amodeo & Gal, 1997). Planning should occur before implementation, continuous quality improvement should be an ongoing process rather than occurring at one point in time for a given duration, and sustainability should be planned for from the very start of the project (Barnette & Clendenen, 1996; Cooke, 2000; Dohlie et al., 1999; Goodman & Steckler, 1987; Shediac-Rizkallah & Bone, 1998). Implementing these strategies will increase the likelihood of programming success.

Example

Key to the success of the MTCC were the attitudes and behavior of the staff, which reflected a strong belief in what they were trying to accomplish. Furthermore, while not explicitly using the GTO steps in programming, they had been exposed to GTO on repeated occasions and understood the importance of planning, implementation, process and outcome evaluation, program improvement, and sustainability. They were obviously committed to helping families in need and often went beyond their duties by organizing community events on weekends and nights. For instance, an annual weekend retreat was held at a neighboring conference center for staff and families who were served by the center. Staff and management were very involved with and proud of their center. They were program champions to a certain extent, talking about their work to others in the community and always on the lookout for clients to serve. The ED made it a point to ensure that outreach events, including presentations to community groups, fairs, and retreats, were conducted each month and that the center also served as a meeting place for other community groups, including Alcoholics Anonymous, the Chamber of Commerce, and Mary Kay consultants. The center was even used for family celebrations, including wedding receptions and birthday parties. Staff members' choice of programs also reflected their and the community's beliefs. For instance, one of the grants they applied for was a faith-based initiative designed to promote abstinence as a way to prevent teenage pregnancy, which appeared to fit with the values of many of the staff and of the community.

In terms of process activities, while staff members were committed to programming, they were also fearful of the additional amount of work and time it represented, especially at the beginning. For instance, the evaluation team had to demystify evaluation and teach staff members the importance of collecting data for program improvement purposes before they willingly engaged in the process. Once their attitudes had been modified, however, it became easier for them to justify the additional work that this process represented, therefore improving their capacity to improve their initiative. Another key to the success of the center was the ED's ability to time programming activities. For instance, she was able to start thinking about and planning for sustainability early in the process, therefore leaving her enough time to consider all of her options. All of the programs that had been implemented by the center ended up being successfully sustained either through additional funding or by other partners who adopted them.

Technical Capacities

Research Findings

Even if the staff has sufficient knowledge and positive attitudes, and is highly involved in the project, members may need to increase specific capacities related to the intervention. The availability and compatibility of information as well as access to in-service training and technical assistance are crucial to programming success. *Additional information* on both program-related and process-related topics has been found to facilitate programming. Program-related materials such as summary assessments of intervention effectiveness will familiarize staff with research and best practices for the program chosen and ease the planning process (Dearing et al., 1998), and teaching materials (in English and other languages) will aid staff with implementation of the intervention (Redman et al., 1987). In terms of process activities, the creation of a community resource manual listing available services in the community will be helpful when assessing the fit of the chosen intervention with the community (Dearing et al., 1998). In addition, implementation and program improvement will be easier if staff has access to a procedure manual, evaluation information, and data management materials, including measurement tools, checklists, tables, and chart forms, and presentation tools (Dohlie et al., 1999; Gilman & Lammers, 1995; Hermann et al., 2000; Kim & Cho, 2000; Redman et al., 1987). If possible, staff should have access to and be able to use computer databases, which are likely to facilitate access to and adequacy of services and effective use of improvement strategies (Hodges & Hernandez, 1999; Tiamiyu & Bailey, 2001).

Knowledge of the program and of the programming process can be further consolidated by organizing *in-service training sessions* or offering recurrent continuing education opportunities. Training in how to implement and use needs assessment findings, frequent education sessions on utilization of research findings, availability of diversity-related continuing education programs, training in CQI and TQM (total quality management) methods, and education in program maintenance strategies have all been found to play a major role in programming success (Altman, 1995; Amodeo & Gal, 1997; Barnette & Clendenen, 1996; Bossert, 1990; Bracht et al., 1994; Dohlie et al., 1999; Handler et al., 1999; Hanlon et al., 1998; Hermann et al., 2000; Humphris et al., 2000; Kim & Cho, 2000; Shediac-Rizkallah & Bone, 1998; Smith, 1998; Streefland, 1995). Teaching staff about the program that will be adopted is also important to increase the odds of successful planning and implementation (Becker et al., 2000; Dearing et al., 1998; Redman et al., 1987).

While in-service trainings are important sources of information, individuals in the organization cannot be expected to fully integrate all the material presented during the training and correctly use and implement it without additional help. For this reason, it is often recommended that *technical assistance and consultation* be available in place of or in addition to in-service trainings. While you and your staff possess unique knowledge about the community, experts and consultants can assist you with the implementation of mechanisms that will facilitate conducting and using needs-assessment findings, utilizing best practices, ensuring adequate cultural sensitivity, program planning, program implementation, implementation of successful CQI strategies, and program sustainability (Altman, 1985; Amodeo & Gal, 1997; Becker et al., 2000; Dearing et al., 1998; DiFranceisco et al., 1999; Hermann et al., 2000; Hilderbrandt, 1994; Kieler et al., 1996; Kim & Cho, 2000; Riley et al., 2001; Williams & Becker, 1994). A close and positive relationship with a group of experts and consultants has consistently been found to be an important factor in successful programming (Dearing et al., 1998; Handler et al., 1999; Johnson, 1999), suggesting that your organization should develop a network of experts and consultants that can provide you with the assistance needed.

Example

While the MTCC started out with very little technological availability, the management team decided to acquire a computerized client tracking system to ease both program- and process-related aspects of the project. They wanted a system that would facilitate efficient documentation of family information that could be easily accessed by multiple service providers and ease service integration, and that could also be used for evaluation and program improvement purposes. After careful consideration of several systems, they finally chose the one that they thought would best fit their needs.

The ED was also careful to provide several training opportunities for her staff, both to increase their knowledge of the programs they were responsible for implementing and to increase awareness of the importance of programming activities. For example, she asked the evaluation team to conduct a 1-day training on "Getting to Outcomes." The training was attended by the entire center staff as well as by some of the partners. This training was followed by the implementation of weekly GTO meetings designed to discuss issues pertaining to the day-to-day operation of the center and attended by the administration and program coordination personnel.

In addition to being offered frequent continuing education opportunities, staff members also had access to consultation and technical assistance from the evaluation team. In the spirit of empowerment evaluation, we acted as consultants when we assisted them in selecting the appropriate best-practice programs. We also played the role of evaluators by developing outcomes and implementing process and outcome evaluations in collaboration with the center's management team. The relationship between the center's staff and the evaluation team grew to become more comfortable over the years, making the sometimes blurred boundaries of consultant and evaluator easier to manage for both the staff and the evaluation team. Center personnel came to view the evaluation team more as members of their "family" than as outsiders, which facilitated a true collaboration and the use of evaluation findings (even negative ones) by center staff for program improvement (this is covered in more detail by Keener et al., Chapter 4).

Fiscal Capacities

Research Findings

While human and technical capacities are important, you will not be able to plan, implement, and sustain your intervention without financial resources. Programming activities will be impacted by the initial level of funding assigned for the project and for programming activities. Having a financially sound plan and an awareness of budget issues at all organizational levels has been found to impact all programming stages (Altman, 1995; Barnette & Clendenen, 1996; Becker et al., 2000; Campbell, Baker, & Mazurek, 1998; Dohlie et al., 1999; Goodman & Steckler, 1987; Hanlon et al., 1998; Kaluzney & Veney, 1973; Kim & Cho, 2000; Maciak et al., 1999; Miller, 2001; Robins, 1982; Shediac-Rizkallah & Bone, 1998; Tiamiyu & Bailey, 2001). Do not be afraid to be creative when your initial funding ends and you need to sustain the program with other financial resources. In addition to ensuring that you have multiple sources of funding (Stanton et al., 2000), some of the strategies that have led to successful program sustainability include cost control, cost recovery, and income generation (Bratt, Foreit, & de Vargas, 1998). While no single method has a large impact on the overall cost recovery of the head agency, using several of these strategies at once will increase the likelihood of program maintenance.

Example

The center had the chance to be initially funded by a 3-year implementation grant for $1.3 million obtained by the local school district. The original grant allowed for the restoration of an old school building and for funding the two original core programs, that is, an after-school program for middle school students and an educational support program for adolescent mothers and their children. In addition, a partnership between the school district and a number of other existing agencies in the community was to be created. The center's ED was always highly aware of funding issues and consistently planned for sustainability of programs, starting early in the project. She aggressively went after continuing grants and even hired an individual whose initial job duty was to find and apply for these grants. Grants were only one strategy used by the center to ensure funding. Some of the programs, such as family therapy, implemented a sliding scale fee schedule. Others were sustained through funding from business and individual donations or by being adopted by partner agencies. Finally, the ED was able to save enough money from different funding streams to invest it in an interest-bearing savings account. More recently, the organization launched a 3-year capital campaign to raise funds for sustainability.

Implications

Based on the literature on intervention-related organizational capacities and programming success, we can infer that, when planning, implementing, and maintaining your intervention, whether this intervention is a process such as empowerment evaluation and implementation of empowerment evaluation tools and activities, or a program, you need to:

• Assess and build *your staff knowledge, positive attitudes* (e.g., high commitment levels, compatibility of intervention, perceptions of benefits and visible payoffs), and *involvement* in both the program and the programming activities, with particular attention being paid to the *timing* of programming phases and to making sure that you have a *program champion*.

• Have access to *technical resources*, including: (1) additional *information* about the program and process activities, including resource and procedure manuals, evaluation and data management tools, and ability to use computer databases; (2) *in-service trainings* to build your staff's knowledge of the intervention and programming process activities; and (3) *technical assistance* and consultation from outside experts, which can assist you with the implementation of the GTO steps.

• Have a financially sound plan and enough *financial resources* to plan and implement the intervention as well as continue and sustain the program after the *initial funding* has ended. You should start thinking about fiscal resources for sustainability early in the process and ensure that you have multiple funding streams. Make use of *several creative strategies*, such as cost control, cost recovery, and income generation.

SUMMARY AND CONCLUSIONS

This chapter focused on the organizational characteristics needed to plan, implement, and maintain interventions, and especially interventions related to *processes or ways of doing things* such as the use of empowerment evaluation tools (e.g., GTO). As stated previously, while we are aware that the use of empowerment evaluation tools helps build organizational capacity and learning, we concentrated on the use of GTO-related activities as a process to engage in empowerment evaluation and on the subsequent organizational readiness necessary to use this process and therefore facilitate it. In reviewing the research on the role of organizational characteristics in program planning, implementation, and maintenance, we have identified important factors relating to both overall organizational functioning and intervention-related capacities that affect the odds of programming success. While certain factors appear to be more influential in certain program phases (e.g., the presence of information brokers for use of best-practices research in program planning), most factors impact program development across stages. Among the agency's organizational functioning variables were staff expertise/experience, interpersonal processes within the agency, and relationships between the agency and outside constituents, and organizational structure, including complexity, formalization, and centralization levels. Organizational capacities for intervention-specific activities included human capacities, that is, knowledge, attitudes, and behavior toward the program and the GTO approach; technical capacities, including the availability and compatibility of materials or hardware, training, and technical assistance and consultation; and financial capacities, including the size of budgets and fiscal strategies. The findings suggest that these organizational conditions should be in place or built before planning, implementing, and maintaining your intervention (see Figure 6.2 for a checklist).

Our framework highlights three core areas of an organization: its structure, functioning, and capacities (see Figure 6.3). The structure of the organization is reflected in its complexity, formalization, and centralization. Organizational functioning refers to the processes by which the organization operates, including relationships within and outside the agency (e.g., leadership, communication, collaboration, cohesion, and networking). Finally, organizational capacity is determined by its human, technical, and financial resources. While it is beyond the scope of this chapter to discuss the Columbia shuttle disaster in detail, the $400-million investigation (evaluation) notes that the immediate technical cause of the disaster was influenced by communication and other organizational problems within levels of the team (e.g., engineers and management), between the space centers in Houston and Huntsville, and between suppliers and NASA. This led to recommendations that included technical changes in the shuttle and in the organizational culture of NASA. The message that can be generalized to all organizations (whether we are talking about NASA and rocket science or community organizations and prevention science) is: Good organizational functioning facilitates the adoption of empowerment evaluation processes and tools, such as GTO, and subsequently increases the odds of programming success.

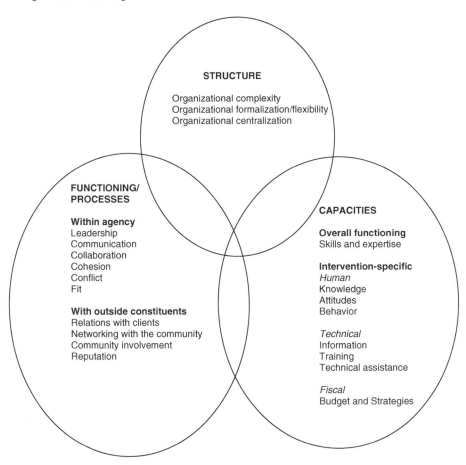

FIGURE 6.3. Three core areas of an organization.

APPENDIX 6.1

These results are based on a review of articles that were included, based on the following criteria: (1) programming was related to health or mental heath issues; (2) programming focused on outpatient interventions and consisted of community-based projects for the most part; (3) only quantitative and qualitative empirical articles that had been published in peer reviewed journals were included; and (4) the focus was on the impact and relationship of organizational characteristics with programming capacity rather than on capacity-building programming. We used several search engines including PsycLit, Social Work, Sociological Abstracts, and Medline to find relevant articles.

While the findings are suggestive and interesting, the current literature is not without its limitations. First, studies focusing on a given GTO activity/step usually use different definitions and assessment tools to measure organizational characteristics (e.g., organizational complexity might be defined as the number of staff members, clients, or program components, depending on the study). Second, assessment methods (e.g., lack of standardized measurement, extensive use of self-reports) and research designs (i.e., case studies, cross-sectional correlational designs) limit the interpretation of causation and the role of organizational characteristics over time.

REFERENCES

Altman, D. G. (1995). Sustaining interventions in community systems: On the relationship between researchers and communities. *Health Psychology, 14*, 526–536.

Amodeo, M., & Gal, C. (1997). Strategies for ensuring use of needs assessment findings: Experiences of a community substance abuse prevention program. *Journal of Primary Prevention, 18*, 227–242.

Barnette, J. E., & Clendenen, F. (1996). The quality journey in a comprehensive mental health center: A case study. *The Joint Commission Journal on Quality Improvement, 22*, 8–17.

Becker, H., Dumas, S., Houser, A., & Seay, P. (2000). How organizational factors contribute to innovations in service delivery. *Mental Retardation, 38*, 385–394.

Bedell, J. R., Ward, Jr., J. C., Archer, R. P., & Stokes, M. K. (1985). An empirical evaluation of a model of knowledge utilization. *Evaluation Review, 9*, 109–126.

Boehm, A., & Litwin, H. (1997). The influence of organizational and personal characteristics on community planning activity. *Administration in Social Work, 21*, 31–48.

Bossert, T. J. (1990). Can they get along without us? Sustainability of donor-supported health projects in Central America and Africa. *Social Science Medicine, 30*, 1015–1023.

Bracht, N., Finnegan, J. R., Jr., Rissel, C., Weisbrod, R., Gleason, J., Corbett, J., & Veblen-Mortenson, S. (1994). Community ownership and program continuation following a health demonstration project. *Health Education Research, 9*, 243–255.

Bratt, J. H., Foreit, J., & de Vargas, T. (1998). Three strategies to promote sustainability of CEMOPLAF clinics in Ecuador. *Studies in Family Planning, 29*, 58–68.

Campbell, R., Baker, C. K., & Mazurek, T. L. (1998). Remaining radical? Organizational predictors of rape crisis centers' social change initiatives. *American Journal of Community Psychology, 26*, 457–483.

Chinman, M., Imm, P., & Wandersman, A. (2004). *Getting to Outcomes 2004: Promoting accountability through methods and tools for planning, implementation, and evaluation* (TR-TR101). Santa Monica, CA: RAND. Available online at *http://www.rand.org/publications/TR/TR101/*.

Clark, C., Teague, G. B., & Henry, R. M. (1999). Prevention homelessness in Florida. *Alcoholism Treatment Quarterly, 17*, 73–91.

Cooke, M. (2000). The dissemination of a smoking cessation program: Predictors of program awareness, adoption, and maintenance. *Health Promotion International, 15*, 113–124.

Dearing, J. W., Larson, R. S., Randall, L. M., & Pope, R. S. (1998). Local reinvention of the CDC HIV Prevention Community Planning Initiative. *Journal of Community Health, 23*, 113–126.

DiFranceisco, W., Kelly, J. A., Otto-Salaj, L., McAuliffe, T. L., Somlai, A. M., Hackl, K., Heckman, T. G., Holtgrave, D. R., & Rompa, D. J. (1999). Factors influencing attitudes within AIDS service organizations toward the use of research-based HIV prevention interventions. *AIDS Education and Prevention, 11*, 72–86.

Dohlie, M. B., Mielke, E., Mumba, F. K., Wambwa, G. E., Rukonge, A., & Mongo, W. (1999). Using practical quality improvement approaches and tools in reproductive health services in east Africa. *The Joint Commission Journal on Quality Improvement, 25*, 574–587.

Dooley, K. (2002). Organizational complexity. In M. Warner (Ed.), *International encyclopedia of business and management* (pp. 5013–5022). London: Thompson Learning.

Elder, J. P., Campbell, N. R., Candelaria, J. I., Talavera, G. A., Mayer, J. A., Moreno, C., Medel. Y. R., & Lyons, G. K. (1998). Project Salsa: Development and institutionalization of a nutritional health promotion project in a Latino community. *American Journal of Health Promotion, 12*, 391–400.

Ethier, K. A., Fox-Tierney, R., Nicholas, W. C., Salisbury, K. M., & Ickovics, J. R. (2000). Organizational predictors of prenatal HIV counseling and testing. *American Journal of Public Health, 90*, 1448–1451.

Florin, P., Chavis, D., Wandersman, A., & Rich, R. (1992). A systems approach to understanding and enhancing grassroots community organizations: The Block Booster Project. In R. Levine & H. Fitzgerald (Eds.), *Analysis of dynamic psychological systems*. New York: Plenum.

Friedman, A. S., Glickman, N. W., & Kovach, J. A. (1986). The relationship of drug program environmental variables to treatment outcome. *American Journal of Alcohol Abuse, 12*, 53–69.

Friedmann, P. D., Alexander, J. A., & D'Aunno, T. A. (1999a). Organizational correlates of access to primary care and mental health services in drug abuse treatment units. *Journal of Substance Abuse Treatment, 16*, 71–80.

Friedmann, P. D., Alexander, J. A., Jin, L., & D'Aunno, T. A. (1999b). On-site primary care and mental health services in outpatient drug abuse treatment units. *The Journal of Behavioral Health Services and Research, 26*, 80–94.

Gilman, S. C., & Lammers, J. C. (1995). Tool use and team success in continuous quality improvement: Are all tools created equal? *Quality Management in Health Care, 4*, 56–61.

Glisson, C., & Hemmelgarn, A. (1998). The effects of organizational climate and interorganizational coordination on the quality and outcomes of children's service systems. *Child Abuse and Neglect, 22,* 401–421.

Goodman, R. M., & Steckler, A. B. (1987). The life and death of a health promotion program: An insititutionalization case study. *International Quarterly of Community Health Education, 8,* 5–21.

Goodman, R. M., & Wandersman, A. (1994). FORECAST: A formative approach to evaluating community coalitions and community-based initiatives. *Journal of Community Psychology* (CSAP special issue), 6–25.

Handler, A., Geller, S., & Kennelly, J. (1999). Effective MCH epidemiology in state health agencies: Lessons from an evaluation of the Maternal and Child Health Epidemiology Program (MCHEP). *Maternal and Child Health Journal, 4,* 217–224.

Hanlon, P., Murie, J., Gregan, J., McEwen, J., Moir, D., & Russell, E. (1998). A study to determine how needs assessment is being used to improve health. *Public Health, 112,* 343–346.

Healton, C., Messeri, P., Abramson, D., Howard, J., Sorin, M. D., & Bayer, R. (1996). A balancing act: The tension between case-finding and primary prevention strategies in New York State's voluntary HIV counseling and testing program in women's health care settings. *American Journal of Preventive Medicine, 12,* 53–60.

Hermann, R. C., Regner, J. L., Erickson, P., & Yang, D. (2000). Developing a Quality Management system for behavioral health care: The Cambridge Health Alliance Experience. *Harvard Review of Psychiatry, 8,* 251–260.

Hilderbrandt, E. (1994). A model for community involvement in health (CIH) program development. *Social Science Medicine, 39,* 247–254.

Hodges, S. P., & Hernandez, M. (1999). How organizational culture influences outcome information utilization. *Evaluation and Program Planning, 22,* 183–197.

Humphris, D., Littlejohns, P., Victor, C., O'Halloran, P., & Peacock, J. (2000). Implementing evidence-based practice: Factors that influence the use of research evidence by occupational therapists. *British Journal of Occupational Therapy, 63,* 516–522.

Johnson, K. W. (1985). Research influence in decision making to control and prevent violence. *Knowledge: Creation, Diffusion, Utilization, 7,* 161–189.

Johnson, K. W. (1989). Knowledge utilization and planned change: An empirical assessment of the A VICTORY model. *Knowledge in Society: The International Journal of Knowledge Transfer, 2,* 57–79.

Johnson, K. W. (1990). Impact of a university-government partnership in criminal justice: A linkage model for the 1990s. *Journal of Criminal Justice Education, 1,* 167–194.

Johnson, K. W. (1999). Structural Equation Modeling in practice: Testing a theory for research use. *Journal of Social Service Research, 24,* 131–171.

Kaluzny, A. D., & Veney, J. E. (1973). Attributes of health services as factors in program implementation. *Journal of Health and Social Behavior, 14,* 124–133.

Kieler, B. W., Rundall, T. G., Saporta, I., Sussman, P. C., Keilch, R., Warren, N., Black, S., Brinkley, B., & Barney, L. (1996). Challenges faced by the HIV health services planning council in Oakland, California, 1991–1994. *American Journal of Preventive Medicine, 12,* 26–32.

Kim, C.-Y., & Cho, S.-H. (2000). Institutionalization of quality improvement programs in Korean hospitals. *International Journal for Quality in Health Care, 12,* 419–423.

Korr, W. S., & Joseph, A. (1996). Effects of local conditions on program outcomes: analysis of contradictory findings from two programs for homeless mentally ill. *Journal of Health and Social Policy, 8,* 41–53.

Loue, S., Lloyd, L. S., & Phoombour, E. (1996). Organizing Asian Pacific Islanders in an urban community to reduce HIV risk: A case study. *AIDS Education and Prevention, 8,* 381–393.

Maciak, B. J., Guzman, R., Santiago, A., Villalobos, G., & Israel, B. A. (1999). Establishing LA VIDA: A community-based partnership to prevent intimate violence against Latina women. *Health Education and Behavior, 26,* 821–840.

McGrew, J. H., & Bond, G. R. (1997). The association between program characteristics and service delivery in assertive community treatment. *Administration and Policy in Mental Health, 25,* 175–189.

Miller, R. L. (2001). Innovation in HIV prevention: Organizational and intervention characteristics affecting program adoption. *American Journal of Community Psychology, 4,* 621–647.

Moss, N. (1983). An organization–environment framework for assessing program implementation. *Evaluation and Program Planning, 6,* 153–164.

O'Loughlin, J., Renaud, L, Richard, L., Sanchez Gomez, L., & Paradis, G. (1998). Correlates of the sustainability of community-based heart health promotion interventions. *Preventive Medicine, 27,* 702–712.

Poor NASA management a factor in shuttle disaster. (2003, July 27). *The State,* p. A8.

Redman, B. K., Levine, D., & Howard, D. (1987). Organizational resources in support of patient education programs: Relationship to reported delivery of instruction. *Patient Education and Counseling, 9,* 177–197.

Riley, B. L., Taylor, S. M., & Elliott, S. J. (2001). Determinants of implementing heart health promotion activities in Ontario public health units: A social ecological perspective. *Health Education Research, 16,* 425–441.

Robins, B. (1982). Local response to planning mandates: The prevalence and utilization of needs assessment by human service agencies. *Evaluation and Program Planning, 5,* 199–208.

Scheid, T. L., & Greenley, J. R. (1997). Evaluations of organizational effectiveness in mental health programs. *Journal of Health and Social Behavior, 38,* 403–426.

Shediac-Rizkallah, M. C., & Bone, L. R. (1998). Planning for the sustainability of community-based health programs: Conceptual frameworks and future directions for research, practice, and policy. *Health Education Research, 13,* 87–108.

Shortell, S. M., O'Brien, J. L., Carman, J. M., Foster, R. W., Hughes, E. F. X., Boerstler, H., & O'Connor, E. J. (1995). Assessing the impact of continuous quality improvement/total quality management: Concept versus implementation. *Health Services Research, 30,* 377–401.

Smith, L. S. (1998). Cultural competence for nurses: Canonical Correlation of two culture scales. *Journal of Cultural Diversity, 5,* 120–126.

Sormanti, M., Pereira, L., El-Bassel, N., Witte, S., & Gilbert, L. (2001). The role of community consultants in designing an HIV prevention intervention. *AIDS Education and Prevention, 13,* 311–328.

Sosin, M. R. (2001). Service intensity and organizational attributes: A preliminary inquiry. *Administration and Policy in Mental Health, 28,* 371–392.

Stanton, A., Kennedy, M., Spingarn, R., & Rotheram-Borus, M. J. (2000). Developing services for substance-abusing HIV-positive youth with mental health disorders. *The Journal of Behavioral Health Services and Research, 27,* 380–389.

Streefland, P. H. (1995). Enhancing coverage and sustainability of vaccination programs: An explanatory framework with special reference to India. *Social Science Medicine, 41,* 647–656.

Tiamiyu, M. F., & Bailey, L. (2001). Human services for the elderly and the role of university–community collaboration: Perceptions of human service agency workers. *Educational Gerontology, 27,* 479–492.

Tyden, T. (1996). The contribution of longitudinal studies for understanding science communication and research utilization. *Science Communication, 18,* 29–48.

Wandersman, A. (2003). Community Science: Bridging the gap between science and practice with community-centered models. *American Journal of Community Psychology, 31,* 227–242.

Wandersman, A., Imm, P., Chinman, M., & Kaftarian, S. (2000). Getting to Outcomes: A results-based approach to accountability. *Evaluation and Program Planning, 23,* 389–395.

Williams, O. J., & Becker, R. L. (1994). Domestic partner abuse treatment programs and cultural competence: The results of a national survey. *Violence and Victims, 9,* 287–296.

CHAPTER 7

Empowerment Evaluation and Organizational Learning

A CASE STUDY OF A COMMUNITY COALITION DESIGNED TO PREVENT CHILD ABUSE AND NEGLECT

Barry E. Lentz, Pamela S. Imm, Janice B. Yost, Noreen P. Johnson, Christine Barron, Margie Simone Lindberg, and Joanne Treistman

An organization undergoing the empowerment evaluation process must be or become a learning organization. . . .
—WORTHINGTON (1999, p. 13)

CONTEXT AND USE OF EMPOWERMENT EVALUATION

Empowerment evaluation is deeply rooted in community psychology, action anthropology, and participatory evaluation. It shares their aim of developing concepts, tools, and techniques to help self-determining groups build the capacity to achieve their goals and increase their control over the direction of their lives (Fetterman, 1996). When choosing an evaluation approach, the fundamental nature of empowerment evaluation as an ongoing process that fosters program improvement should serve as the beginning point for any discussion about the utility of empowerment evaluation and its fit with an organization's capacity and culture. This is crucial because the successful implementation of empowerment evaluation requires a working commitment within an organization to openness, information sharing, experimentation, shared decision making, systems thinking, and knowledge creation (Austin et al., 1982; Usher, 1995; Worthington, 1999). This chapter is a case study of how empowerment evaluation is used to foster organizational learning during the pilot project phase in the development of the central Massachusetts Child Abuse Prevention and Protection Collaborative (the Collaborative).

Fetterman (1996, p. 4) defines empowerment evaluation as "the use of evaluation concepts, techniques, and findings to foster improvement and self-determination." Wandersman built on this definition by emphasizing that empowerment evaluation is an approach that helps increase the probability of achieving results by providing practitioners with tools for assessing the planning, implementation and evaluation of their programs (Wandersman, 1999; Wandersman, Imm, Chinman, & Kaftarian, 1999, 2000). In this chapter, we continue to develop the definition of empowerment evaluation by discussing the use of cycles of reflection and action (Fetterman & Eiler, 2001; Fetterman, 2003), and knowledge creation to foster the development of the Collaborative as a learning organization with the capacity to use empowerment evaluation to inform the planning, implementation and improvement of its initiatives.

WHY EMPOWERMENT EVALUATION?: IMPROVEMENT, CAPACITY BUILDING, ORGANIZATIONAL LEARNING, AND ACCOUNTABILITY

This chapter presents the implementation of empowerment evaluation during the pilot project phase of a multiyear project funded by The Health Foundation of central Massachusetts, Inc. (the Foundation) under its "Health Care and Health Promotion Synergy Initiative." The Synergy Initiative provides funding for projects that address significant anomalies in the health status of vulnerable populations in central Massachusetts by implementing integrated, comprehensive strategies designed to enhance systemic access to care and to promote healthier lifestyles. The Collaborative was established to create an infrastructure for providing a continuum of care for the victims of child abuse and neglect and to foster effective community-based prevention.

In accord with the systems change focus of its Synergy Initiative, the Foundation utilizes a results-oriented approach to grantmaking that views accountability as the shared responsibility of all partners (including the funder) working collaboratively to achieve project goals. An empowerment evaluation approach was chosen for the pilot project because the

Foundation wanted to build the capacity of the Collaborative to conduct self-evaluation as an ongoing activity that is integrated into planning and that informs program improvement. To achieve these goals, the evaluators emphasized that the Collaborative would have to become a learning organization committed to building participation among stakeholders that is based on sharing information and power, flexibility among members in roles, and significant participation of stakeholders in decision making. Table 7.1 was used by the evaluators to help stakeholders understand the principles and practices of empowerment evaluation and as a guide to implementation of evaluation activities.[1]

A DYNAMIC COMMUNITY OF LEARNERS

Organizational learning refers to organizations that provide the structures and encouragement for members to actively acquire knowledge, communicate and share that knowledge, and create new knowledge to resolve novel problems. This is achieved by finding innovative solutions that involve discovery, invention, and synthesis. Organizational learning entails inquiring into the systemic consequences of actions rather than settling for short-term solutions that address symptoms but fail to address underlying problems (Argyris & Schön, 1978; Nonaka & Takeuchi, 1995; Argyris, 1999).

When organizational learning becomes an overarching philosophy that is structurally embedded in an organization's policies and practices and is carried out through a working commitment of its members to continuous learning and knowledge creation, then an organization is said to be a learning organization (Senge, 1990; Jenlick, 1994; Kofman & Senge, 1995; Sveiby, 1997). Empowerment evaluation is a process that facilitates organizational learning, and organizational learning is necessary for the effective implementation of empowerment evaluation (Usher, 1995; Worthington, 1999). When operating within a learning organization, the evaluator is required to become a participant in the change process by combining the roles of organizational developer, consultant, and evaluator (Preskill, 1994).

Fetterman describes empowerment evaluation as a process that is "fundamentally democratic in the sense that it invites (if not demands) participation" in examining issues important to the community and determining how to best address those issues (Fetterman, 1996, p. 5; see also Fetterman, 2001). Becoming a learning organization and conducting empowerment evaluation requires stakeholders, including evaluators, to actively participate as members of a "dynamic community of learners" (Fetterman, 1996, p. 25; see also Fetterman, 2001). In a community of learners, participants are encouraged to experiment and take both risks

TABLE 7.1. Empowerment Evaluation Principles and Practices

Overarching aim: to increase the probability of achieving program success by fostering empowerment, organizational learning, and the continuous improvement of practice and programs.

Core principles	Core evaluator practices	Core community practices
1. Improvement		
1.1. A high value is placed on the improvement of people, practices, programs, organizations, and communities.	1.4. Be flexible and responsive to the community's current capacity for conducting evaluation and using evaluation results.	1.7. Make a working commitment to the improvement of people, practices, programs, organizations, and communities.
1.2. Practice and program improvement is seen as a means to achieving sustainable results.	1.5. Adopt a developmental approach in helping the organization integrate evaluation into program planning and implementation.	1.8. Identify and implement evaluation activities that provide the data necessary to determine program effectiveness.
1.3. A developmental perspective must guide decision making about implementation of strategies and assessing results.	1.6. Emphasize the implications of evaluation results for practice and program improvement.	1.9. Use evaluation results to guide practice and program improvement.
2. Community ownership		
2.1. The Community has the right to make decisions about actions that affect its members' lives.	2.4. Make explicit the differences between EE and other forms of evaluation, and clearly identify the costs and benefits of EE.	2.7. Make an informed choice to use EE based on community conditions.
2.2. Implementation of evaluation activities will be determined by the local context and the decisions of stakeholders.	2.5. Facilitate community ownership of the evaluation processes by helping participants (program staff and other stakeholders) articulate goals, indicators of progress, and outcomes and by helping them write their own reports, etc.	2.8. Assume ownership of the evaluation process and make decisions after careful consideration of the EE consultant's recommendations.
2.3. Evaluation is most likely to lead to program improvement when the community is empowered to exercise its legitimate authority to make decisions that direct the evaluation process.	2.6. Work to understand the history and context of program implementation.	2.9. Take part in evaluation activities, as warranted by the development of skills, knowledge, and capacity.

3. Inclusion

3.1. Inclusion of diverse perspectives and knowledge in the evaluation process is valued.

3.2. Direct participation by key stakeholders in decision making is used whenever possible.

3.3. Evaluation is most likely to lead to program improvement when inclusive decision making is integrated into planning and practice.

3.4. Help the community understand the value of inclusive fact finding and decision making in establishing and implementing an evaluation plan.

3.5. Work to foster opportunities for all stakeholders to have a voice and join in the decision making process.

3.6. Work to include diverse perspectives, skills, and knowledge in conducting evaluation activities.

3.7. Whenever possible, provide the necessary conditions for all to contribute, learn, and benefit from communicating and collaborating with others in shared decision making.

3.8. Ensure that all relevant constituencies have appropriate representation and access to relevant information in a timely manner.

3.9. Make sure that all decisions made, their justification, and actions to be taken are clearly communicated to all stakeholders in a timely manner.

4. Democratic participation

4.1. Active participation by all in shared decision making is valued.

4.2. Democracy is seen as a personal way of life based on belief in the capacity of all for intelligent judgment and action when supplied with the right conditions.

4.3. EE is a fundamentally democratic process based on deliberation, communicative action, and authentic collaboration.

4.4. Help the community understand the value of democratic participation in creating and implementing an evaluation plan.

4.5. Listen to community stakeholders to understand the context of the issues(s) being addressed.

4.6. Work with the community to provide opportunities for ongoing deliberation about goals, interventions, outcomes, and use of evaluation results.

4.7. Make a clear commitment to participatory democracy in decision making.

4.8. Identify and communicate the needs and resources of the community and the context of the issues(s) being addressed.

4.9. Support the provision of opportunities for ongoing deliberation about goals, interventions, outcomes, and the use of evaluation results.

(continued)

TABLE 7.1. *(continued)*

Core principles	Core evaluator practices	Core community practices
5. Social justice		
5.1. EE places a high value on addressing the larger social good of practices and programs.	5.4. Make clear the relationship between EE and social justice.	5.7. Understand the relationship between EE and its commitment to fostering the conditions that enable all individuals to develop their capacity for intelligent judgment and action as a means to achieving a more just society.
5.2. EE is committed to fostering the conditions that enable all individuals to develop their capacity for intelligent judgment and action as a means to achieving a more just society.	5.5. Create opportunities to deliberate about the implication of strategies and interventions for the greater social good.	5.8. Address the larger social good of practices and programs, and Implement intervention strategies that advance the larger social good.
5.3. EE is viewed as a means to help people address inequities in their lives by developing their capacity to implement and sustain programs that achieve results.	5.6. Help the community understand the value of using EE to foster the conditions that help all individuals develop their capacity for intelligent judgment and action as a means to achieving a more just society.	5.9. Enable people to take control of their lives by providing the resources and cultural support necessary for all people to develop their capacity for intelligent judgment and action.
6. Community knowledge		
6.1. Community-based knowledge and wisdom is valued and utilized.	6.4. Work to make explicit the tacit knowledge of the community, and provide opportunities for individuals to combine their tacit knowledge with others to create knowledge.	6.7. Provide opportunities for individuals to mobilize their skills and knowledge.
6.2. Identifying and sharing tacit knowledge within a community of learners to create new knowledge is viewed as essential for implementing EE.	6.5. Work to establish a culture of trust and mutual support so that opinions, ideas, and knowledge will be freely shared.	6.8. Utilize the skills and knowledge of stakeholders.
6.3. The experience of the community is seen as an essential resource for making		6.9. Be open and willing to listen, share, and learn as active participants in a community of learners engaged in the process of creating new knowledge to

decisions about evaluation activities, contextualizing evidence-based strategies, and interpreting evaluation results.

7. Evidence-based strategies

7.1. A high value is placed on providing logical and empirical justification for action.

7.2. The collective inquiry of scholars, researchers, and practitioners engaged in identifying and developing evidence-based strategies is highly valued.

7.3. Evidence-based strategies should be used to guide decision making about the implementation of strategies and activities.

8. Capacity building

8.1. A high value is placed on building the capacity of individuals and organizations to evaluate their own programs.

8.2. EE is based on a belief that all individuals and organizations are capable of conducting evaluation when provided with the necessary tools and conditions.

8.3. EE requires individual changes in thinking and behavior, and program changes in practices, procedures, and culture.

resolve novel problems.

6.6. Incorporate local expertise into suggestions regarding interventions and the choice of evaluation practices.

7.4. Give reasons based on logical and empirical justification for all assertions.

7.5. Guide program staff and other stakeholders in choosing and implementing evidence-based strategies, practices, and programs.

7.6. Help the program staff and other stakeholders choose consultants (if needed) in the implementation of evidence-based strategies.

8.4. Demystify (simplify. evaluation for community members, including staff and other stakeholders.

8.5. Teach members of the community (staff and stakeholders) the skills and knowledge required to implement evaluation activities.

8.6. Guide and encourage program staff and other stakeholders in building and using their evaluation tool kit.

7.7. Commit the resources necessary to identify and choose evidence-based strategies that are a good fit with community conditions.

7.8. Implement evidence-based strategies and model programs with appropriate attention to fidelity.

7.9. Work to implement practices that adhere to accepted evaluation standards.

8.7. Commit the time and resources required for training and other means of learning about evaluation.

8.8. Recognize and reward the efforts of individuals to acquire new skills and knowledge.

8.9. Make the necessary changes in practices, procedures, programs, and culture that are required to build the capacity to conduct EE as an ongoing activity that informs planning and implementation.

(continued)

TABLE 7.1. (continued)

Core principles	Core evaluator practices	Core community practices
9. Organizational learning		
9.1. A higher value is placed on improvement, innovation, and systems change than on maintaining the status quo.	9.4. Work with the community to create an environment conducive to experimentation, learning, sharing, and reflective action.	9.7. Be open to change and willing to modify existing practices to support the activities required for conducting ongoing evaluation.
9.2. The use of evaluation results to guide improvement is seen as an essential activity of successful organizations.	9.5. Foster open inquiry into the systemic causes of problems and the systemic consequences of action.	9.8. Commit to building participation, institutionalizing cycles of reflection and action, and fostering knowledge creation.
9.3. Full implementation of EE requires an organization to be or to become a learning organization.	9.6. Be a critical friend who advocates for improvement through organizational learning.	9.9. Commit to integrating evaluation results into planning, implementation, and development.
10. Accountability		
10.1. Empirical evidence is valued when determining the worth of interventions.	10.4. Establish working relationships based on trust so that the community is receptive to evaluation findings instead of being threatened by them.	10.7. Work collaboratively with funders and other external agents when developing goals, timelines, and measures of success.
10.2. A commitment to results-based interventions is essential for honest, accurate evaluation.	10.5. Highlight the importance of accountability in holding one another responsible for accomplishing tasks and objectives.	10.8. Use reliable and valid methods and tools for assessing results.
10.3. The greatest probability for the sustained achievement of results occurs when evaluation is employed in the spirit of continuous improvement.	10.6. Promote professional standards of implementation for all evaluation activities.	10.9. Be willing to honestly examine evaluation data, including negative results, and discern the implications.

and responsibility for their actions. This involves creating an honest, self-critical, trusting, and supportive atmosphere conducive to sharing both success and failures and that fosters personal growth and transformative learning.

A key to fostering this kind of transformative learning lies in understanding how learning organizations convert tacit knowledge (often referred to as "know-how") into explicit knowledge (formal presentations of information) that is shared through communicative action and synthesized to create new knowledge (Argyris & Schön, 1974; Schön, 1982; Argyris, Putnam, & Smith, 1985; Argyris, 1999; Nonaka & Takeuchi, 1995; Sveiby, 1997). Building local capacity to conduct empowerment evaluation is an instance of combining explicit knowledge (literature about the theory and use of evaluation), and the tacit knowledge of the professional evaluator, with the tacit knowledge within the local community of learners to create new knowledge. This artful transformation is required to actually conduct empowerment evaluation with proficiency and to use results to guide continuous practice and program improvement.

The transformative learning and knowledge creation process that occurs within a community of learners is akin to the form of participatory democracy that John Dewey characterized as a "way of personal life controlled, not merely by faith in human nature in general, but by faith in the capacity of human beings for intelligent judgment and action if proper conditions are furnished" (Dewey, 1940, p. 224). In characterizing democracy as a way of personal life, Dewey had in mind a form of authentic communicative action in which participants, engaged in the give-and-take of daily life, work together as co-inquirers learning how to resolve problems. In light of Dewey's vision of democracy, empowerment evaluation can be seen as a transformative process that aims to supply concepts, tools, and techniques to help individuals develop their capacity for intelligent judgment and action within the context of a dynamic community of learners.[2] The following summary of the context of implementation for this case study provides a background for discussing empowerment evaluation as a transformative learning process that fosters development of the Collaborative as a learning organization.

THE CONTEXT OF IMPLEMENTATION

The Problem of Child Maltreatment in Central Massachusetts

Child maltreatment is a recognized national problem. From 1986 to 1997, the number of abused and neglected children jumped nationwide from 1.4 million to 3 million—an increase more than eight times greater than the increase in children's population (Wang & Daro, 1998). In the decade from 1987 to 1997, Massachusetts saw a 98% increase in the number of children reported for abuse or neglect. Based on the latest data, roughly 46 of every 1,000 children in the state are involved each year in a child abuse or neglect report (Massachusetts Citizens for Children, 2001).

In April 2001, Massachusetts Citizens for Children, in collaboration with a wide range of policymakers and advocates, issued the *State Call to Action: Working to End Child Abuse and Neglect in Massachusetts. A State Call to Action* is a "consensus for change" motivated by the belief that the current systems in place for child protection and family support are inadequate. In central Massachusetts, a Child Abuse Task Force identified the problem of child abuse and neglect as a community priority. The University of Massachusetts Memorial Children's Medical Center, the largest pediatric medical provider in central Massachusetts, responded to this problem by initiating a Child Protection Program (CPP) in July 2000. The CPP is a comprehensive, hospital-based child protection program to resolve child abuse identification and child protection and prevention issues by providing (1) inpatient services, (2) outpatient clinic, (3) community services, (4) prevention services, (5) civic services, and (6) education services.

THE PLANNING AND PILOT PROJECT PHASE

This pilot project is the second phase of a multiyear project that began in January 2001 with a planning grant award from the Foundation to the University of Massachusetts Memorial Children's Medical Center to support the development of the CPP. The intent of the planning grant was to establish working collaborative relationships with all community agencies that deal with child maltreatment in central Massachusetts. The pilot project began in November 2002 and included two relatively well-defined initiatives, the Family Outreach Network (FON) and the Shaken Baby Syndrome Prevention Campaign (SBSPC). The pilot project also included less well defined goals involving ongoing community prevention education and the development of legislative and administrative initiatives to advocate for a more systemic approach to prevention and treatment.

Overview of the Family Outreach Network

The FON was planned as a group of service providers who would meet weekly to identify and refer families with a high level of risk for child maltreatment that do not meet the legal "threshold of abuse" for mandated protective services intervention by the Department of Social Services (DSS) but who are clearly in need of assistance because of problems such as substance abuse, mental health issues, and lack of parenting skills. The plan called for family advocates to work closely with enrolled families through home visitation for a 3-month period to help them access services that meet their needs and thereby decrease the likelihood of later DSS involvement.

The FON had not been organized prior to the beginning of the pilot project. The development of processes for the referral and enrollment of families as well as the development of assessment and evaluation tools required significant work. These tasks occupied the FON, with considerable involvement by the evaluators, for the first 4 months of the pilot project. While this enabled the evaluators to be integrally involved in the planning process, which is a fundamental aspect of empowerment evaluation, it also presented challenges that will be discussed in depth in the section titled "FON: It's Not What the Evaluators Want!"

Overview of the Shaken Baby Syndrome Prevention Campaign

This initiative is an extension of the work of central Massachusetts SBS Prevention Campaign, a grassroots community coalition organized to respond to a series of six infant deaths attributable to SBS in 2001. The SBS Prevention Campaign involves strategies to integrate information about the prevention of SBS and healthy parenting skills within settings such as hospitals, child care agencies, community centers, after-school programs, and other environments where caregivers and service providers congregate. The campaign has two major components: (1) the delivery of an in-hospital prevention education program based on a promising prevention initiative pioneered in western New York and Utah; and (2) a community training outreach component based on the work of the nationally recognized director of SBS Prevention Plus.

Upon award of the pilot project grant, members of the SBS Committee were eager to begin implementing both components of the campaign. They were especially enthusiastic to begin implementation of the in-hospital prevention education program in six local hospitals. The committee was contacting local hospitals to participate, identifying nurses to lead the hospital program, and reviewing potential materials (e.g., brochures, flyers, etc.) for wide dissemination within the community. However, it soon became evident that more research and planning would be required to develop an adequate protocol for implementation and evaluation of the in-hospital initiative. As with the FON, this provided an opportunity for the evaluators to become involved in the planning of the initiative, but it also presented a challenge for full implementation of the in-hospital initiative. Resolution of this issue will be discussed in the section titled "Starting a Conversation about Evidence-Based Interventions."

The Role of The Health Foundation of Central Massachusetts

With the growing demand for philanthropic dollars far exceeding the ability of foundations to meet this demand, foundations are showing increasing interest in evaluations that help achieve results. However, few foundations act on this interest to the extent of The Health Foundation of Central Massachusetts (THFCM), which has made a strong commitment to helping organizations develop the capacity to conduct evaluation as an integral part of their grant making. This commitment includes employing the results-oriented grantmaking/grant-implementation (ROGG) process as an empowerment evaluation based approach to grantmaking and implementation that brings the funder, the grantee, and the evaluator together as partners with a shared interest in achieving program results (Yost & Wandersman, 1998; Crusto & Wandersman, 2004). This partnership relies on shared decision making that draws on the strengths of each partner in setting objectives, monitoring progress toward fulfilling objectives, and using evaluation results to guide program improvement.

In this case, the Foundation's commitment to evaluation involved both financial support on the order of 15% of the pilot project's operating budget for evaluation and active participation in committee work. In addition, a representative of the Foundation serves on the Collaborative's Steering Committee, Planning Committee, Public Policy and Resource Development Committee, and the Grant Management Team (GMT). The nature of the Foundation's participation in the GMT provides a good example of its commitment to active participation in an empowerment evaluation process that facilitates improvement, capacity building, organizational learning, and accountability.

The primary purpose of the GMT is to ensure that evaluation informs the development of the pilot project by institutionalizing a systematic process of cyclical planning, action, and reflection to guide program improvement. This involves creating a context to foster the development of a community of learners, as discussed earlier. To facilitate the development of a self-critical, trusting, and supportive atmosphere conducive to personal growth and transformative learning, the GMT functions as a "leadership coalition" (McDaniel, 1997) that provides direction through communicative action to engage people in working toward achieving the common goals of the Collaborative.

In fostering the development of a dynamic community of learners with a funder as an active participant, it is critical that the funder not be perceived to be present only to promote its own interests. Establishing trust in the good-faith commitment of all to a shared decision-making process is essential for organizational learning. To monitor how the Foundation's participation was being perceived relative to this objective, the evaluators had candid discussions with stakeholders about the advantages and disadvantages of the Foundation's involvement. Stakeholders at times expressed concerns about the Foundation exercising undue influence over program decisions. However, the consensus is that the advantages of the Foundation's participation far outweigh any of the perceived disadvantages. While empowerment evaluation presents certain challenges for the funder, evaluator, and project staff, broad participation by key stakeholders in the development and implementation of an evaluation plan is an essential element of successful empowerment evaluation.

ENGAGING THE COMMUNITY

Fostering Community Ownership and Democratic Participation

As discussed earlier, empowerment evaluation is a process based on democratic participation in examining issues important to the community and determining how to best address those issues. A critical aspect of fostering democratic participation and community ownership of evaluation is ensuring that clients (e.g., the funder, project director, other stakeholders) are clear about what is required of all parties when they contract with an evaluator to conduct empowerment evaluation. To facilitate this, the evaluators began by reviewing the grant application and other supporting documents to construct the conceptual map of the pilot project presented in Figure 7.1. This conceptual map was repeatedly revised with input from the Foundation, the project director, and other key stakeholders. It took about 3 months to arrive at a consensus about the conceptual map. Building this consensus required a series of detailed conversations about how pilot project strategies "fit together," the timeline for development of strategies, and the level of flexibility for implementation and evaluation.

A similar process was used in developing the evaluation plan for the pilot project. In general, the approach of the evaluators was to emphasize that the evaluation plan had to be flexible. Specific activities, products, and timelines would be adjusted in light of project operations. The plan was contingent upon development of a clear commitment to evaluation and tracking of activities and outcomes. The goal of the evaluators during this initial phase was to establish clear expectations and to lay the foundation of a well-defined empowerment evaluation process based on community ownership, the use of a democratic process involving deliberation and communicative action, and utilization of community knowledge. This foundation would be used, as the project advanced, for the productive use of empowerment evaluation in fostering organizational learning.

To obtain specific information about the context of implementation, the evaluators conducted in-depth qualitative interviews with representatives from the eight collaborating agencies named in the pilot project

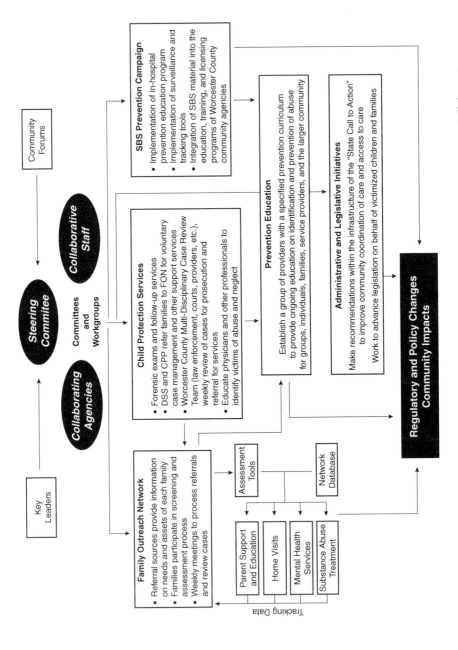

FIGURE 7.1. Central Massachusetts Comprehensive Child Abuse Prevention/Protection Collaborative.

application. The purpose of these interviews included relationship building and discussion of empowerment evaluation, obtaining information about specific evaluation skills and other knowledge that could be utilized in the evaluation process, and beginning the process of engaging participants in an evidence-based conversation about the goals, strategies, and projected outcomes of the pilot project. Through these interviews and attendance at committee meetings, it became evident to the evaluators that the Collaborative was committed to using evidence-based strategies. However, few members of the Collaborative had any real experience with implementing evidence-based approaches.

Starting a Conversation about Evidence-Based Strategies

The lack of experience with evidence-based approaches became clear when the evaluators began asking probing questions about the protocol for the in-hospital SBS prevention program. The SBS Committee was uncertain about the specific strategies associated with replicating the program, as well as the results that could be expected. After long discussion, the evaluators agreed to contact the original program developer to obtain answers to specific questions about the protocol, critical components of the intervention, and results achieved. Discussions with the program developer revealed a picture of the program that differed substantially from the description held by the committee. The target rate for decreasing SBS that the committee was using to promote the program was not based on a scientific analysis as reported in peer-reviewed journals. Instead, it was gleaned from various newspaper articles about the effectiveness of the program in its first year of implementation.

In fact, the program developer reported that he was in the process of analyzing 4 years of data and was already anticipating a rate of reduction that was far less than the commonly reported 75%. Additionally, he was suggesting varying rates based on different settings and discussed specific adaptations that certain states (e.g., Utah) had made when delivering the program. Not only was the data analysis incomplete and not subject to peer review, but there was no detailed protocol for delivery of the program that identified critical components and materials to be used.

The evaluators reported these findings to the SBS Committee to help its members "think through" the issues that needed to be addressed before full implementation would begin. Worth noting was the difficulty the committee had in determining what reduction in percentage of cases could reasonably be expected, given the uncertain nature of the research. Consequently, it was decided by the committee that the commonly reported 75% reduction rate was not realistic and should not be projected as an expected result of the Worcester County program.

In meetings between the evaluators and several key members of the SBS Committee, it became clear that the necessary planning activities for full implementation had not occurred. The committee expected to begin implementation in six different community hospitals without an implementation protocol or strategies for evaluation and follow-up. However, the review of the best-practices literature enabled the evaluators to work with key stakeholders to "slow down" the pace of development and complete the steps required to ensure quality implementation and evaluation.

Fortunately, the SBS Committee had several members who had experience with research interventions and the documentation of outcomes. They were able to speak about how and why research and evaluation standards should be followed. The Foundation expressed support for a more deliberate planning approach that would ensure quality implementation while at the same time developing mechanisms to track outcomes. In this case, the evaluators, the Foundation representative, the project director, and a few other key stakeholders acted together as a leadership coalition to promote additional planning steps. This included the suggestion to conduct focus groups to test the effectiveness of the educational materials and the protocol that the nurses would follow during implementation. Other members on the committee were less inclined to delay full implementation of the program and asserted, "If our program prevents one case of SBS, then it is worth it."

The tension between the "planners" and "doers" was acknowledged, and a compromise was reached that supported the distribution of education materials while engaging in further planning before full implementation. As a result, the committee decided to conduct several focus groups with new and expecting parents within the various communities to ensure that the program materials (e.g., video, brochure, etc.) were understandable, readable, and culturally relevant to the population's needs. A particular set of concerns involved the high concentration of Spanish-speaking parents in the communities, the mixed level of education and reading levels, and the relevance of a video to the variety of new parents likely to give birth in the hospitals within the targeted communities.

Members of the SBS Committee worked with the evaluators to develop a focus group protocol, recruit the focus group participants, and conduct six focus groups. They also analyzed the data and wrote a report that included suggestions for improvements to the materials and protocol. While none of the data suggested the need for major revisions, there was a renewed emphasis on getting the materials translated properly into the Spanish language and ensuring that the directions for the nurses who would deliver the program were clear and conveyed the intended message. This required reframing the original message that was focused on "not shaking your baby." The message was broadened to emphasize strategies for dealing with crying infants and other stressors that are part of the universal parenting experience.

As a result of data collected from the focus groups and an increased commitment to tracking implementation and program outcomes, the SBS Committee decided to begin implementation in two hospitals (instead of six) and "work out the kinks" before moving to a larger-scale implementation. Within 4 months of beginning implementation of empowerment evaluation, participants in the SBS Prevention Campaign assumed significant responsibility for conducting specific evaluation activities. In addition to the activities described above (e.g., conducting focus groups, report writing, etc.), this also involves having the nursing staff conduct a telephone survey with parents of newborns after they leave the hospital to help determine the effectiveness of the in-hospital program. Hence, the SBS Prevention Campaign is well on its way toward institutionalizing evaluation practices.

CAPACITY BUILDING AND LEADERSHIP IN A LEARNING ORGANIZATION

Establishing Cycles of Reflection and Action

Building the capacity of an organization to conduct evaluation and integrate the results into planning requires transformative learning. This learning must result in personal behavior changes and changes in the organization's practices, procedures, and culture (Patton, 1997). As previously discussed, this requires the organization to become (in whole or in parts) a community of learners. Participants in a community of learners are encouraged to experiment and to take both risks and responsibility for their actions that foster personal growth and transformative learning. This dynamic is evident in the example of the SBS Committee's struggle to come to terms with issues involving implementation of the in-hospital prevention education program.

To foster the development of this dynamic, the evaluators provided examples of how this process can help each committee develop into a community of learners. The best example of a functioning community of learners is the Grant Management Team. As discussed earlier, the GMT was specifically convened to ensure that evaluation informs the development of the pilot project by institutionalizing a systematic process of cyclical planning, action, and reflection to guide program improvement.

Learning organizations conduct evaluation as an ongoing collective form of inquiry through iterative cycles of reflection and action as a means to achieving continuous improvement of practices, programs, and products (Argyris, Putnam, & Smith, 1985; Reason, 1994; Heron & Reason, 2001). Empowerment evaluation is grounded in knowledge creation in which participants become co-researchers (and co-subjects) who work through cycles of reflection and action in which:

- Problems are formulated and goals are set.
- Resolutions to problems are proposed and interventions planned.
- Actions and interventions are conducted, and data are collected.
- The meaning of the data is reflectively examined.
- Problems and goals are modified (if necessary), and interventions are adjusted.

The process by which the evaluators developed the conceptual map presented in Figure 7.1, with ongoing input and refinement, established a pattern for how cycles of reflection and action could be used to inform planning and improvement. As described earlier, the conceptual map evoked a great deal of discussion among key stakeholders that culminated in a reflective process and related actions (e.g., priority setting, review of staffing and resource needs). A second example of this modeling process is provided in Figures 7.2 and 7.3, which present the FON General Logic Model and a flowchart of the FON screening and referral process, respectively. The evaluators and members of the FON developed these items in successive cycles of reflection and action that coincided with regular FON meetings.

Another method for integrating cycles of reflection and action is the use of FORECAST charts to assist with the planning of key activities, setting realistic timelines, and defining indicators of success (Goodman & Wandersman, 1994; Goodman, Wandersman, Chinman, Imm, & Morrissey, 1996). A major use of the FORECAST system is to ensure that a proposed project develops according to a clear plan, and if adjustments are necessary, they are made intentionally after a review of various types of data. Typical measures in the FORECAST system include key activities, anticipated timelines, meeting minutes, indictors of success, and other program documentation. The evaluators have also incorporated an action/planning document as part of the FORECAST system that represents an enhancement over the original process.

In order to facilitate the use of the FORECAST system and associated action plans, the evaluators developed an initial draft FORECAST chart for the Steering Committee and presented it at their meeting. The presentation included the purpose and uses of the FORECAST system and directions for use of the tools. One reason for this was to obtain "buy-in" from the Steering Committee, as we planned to propose this system for all of the committees of the Collaborative. Over the course of the year, the FORECAST system has been instrumental in helping the committees clearly articulate what tasks needed to be accomplished and provided

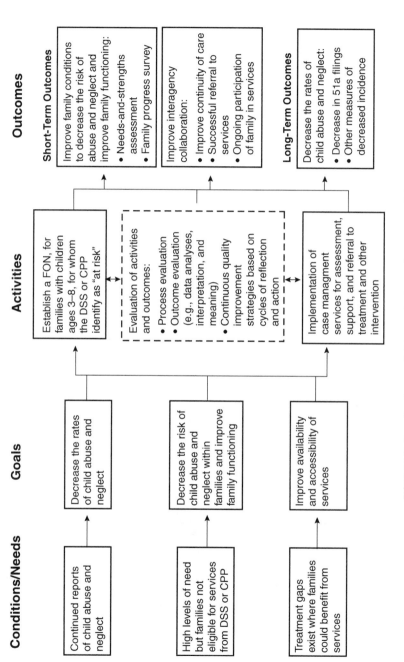

FIGURE 7.2. Family Outreach Network General Logic Model.

173

174

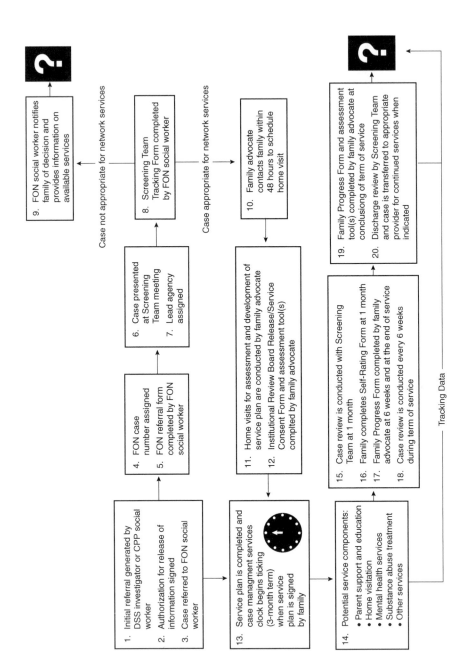

FIGURE 7.3. Family Outreach Network screening and referral process.

opportunities to reflect on initial timelines that were unrealistic. The FORECAST system established a developmental process by which the evaluators helped key stakeholders determine appropriate indicators of success. Using the FORECAST system to plan, monitor, and review information for improvement of project operations is the responsibility of each committee. The evaluators act as "coaches" in this process and meet with the committees when asked to highlight evidence necessary for promoting the cycles of reflection and action.

FON: "It's Not What the Evaluators Want!"

As described earlier, the FON is a prevention initiative that consists of a group of service providers in Worcester County (MA) who work collaboratively to identify and refer families whose level of risk for child maltreatment is not "high enough" to warrant mandated protective services intervention by the Department of Social Services, yet the families clearly need services. The FON began meeting weekly to develop the structure, procedures, and tools needed to prepare for referrals from the DSS and CPP. Agency representatives worked collaboratively to clarify and define the criteria for referral, develop a referral process and related forms, and define agency roles.

The evaluators met with the FON members to facilitate discussions regarding outcomes, data collection procedures, and the need to document implementation variables associated with their service delivery system (e.g., attendance, compliance, satisfaction, etc). These discussions helped the FON clarify the necessary planning steps required to enroll families into the system. In addition, the evaluators worked with the FON to develop an outline of a FORECAST chart to help identify the key activities, target dates, and potential measures for success and the logic model and flowchart presented in Figures 7.2 and 7.3. Members of the FON were focused on providing services to families and were eager to begin enrolling families. Hence, they initially perceived the evaluation process as something that was mandated by the funder and "outside" of their purview. They wanted the evaluators to tell them what they had to do to comply with the expectations so they could begin enrolling families into the FON.

In an effort to clarify the significance of empowerment evaluation, the evaluators asserted that it was not their position to "tell them" what needed to be done in order to satisfy particular evaluation standards or funder mandates, but rather to work with them to decide what outcomes they wanted to be accountable for and how they were going to measure them. Data collection procedures would be developed collaboratively to accomplish these evaluation tasks. The evaluators worked intensively with the FON over a 4-month period in order to address specific issues about

the policies and procedures that needed to be developed and the evaluation questions that they were interested in addressing.

As anticipated, some members were frustrated with this "excessive"
planning and the subsequent delay in enrolling families into the FON. In
addition, the development of assessment tools further slowed down the
process of implementation and led to increased levels of frustration. This
situation was complicated by the fact that the University of Massachusetts
Medical School determined that it was necessary to obtain Institutional
Review Board (IRB) approval for the pilot project as a requirement for
referring CPP families.

To address this issue, the project director and the foundation's representative, in consultation with the evaluators, functioned as a leadership
coalition in discussing the IRB process with the FON. The project director
emphasized the importance of obtaining IRB approval, including the need
to collect data, document achievements, and disseminate the results as a
way of strengthening the evaluative process. She also explained that the
IRB process protects families by ensuring that they officially register their
proper informed consent to participate in the program and that they know
the purpose of the research. The Foundation's representative discussed the
importance of gathering empirical data to inform development of the project and demonstrate positive results for sustainability of the initiative. The
Foundation also presented information about a similar program that had
successfully utilized the IRB process to systematically document the processes and outcomes of the work.

The group discussed the empowerment evaluation process and the
need for the FON members to articulate the critical research questions and
the outcomes desired as a way of ensuring that adequate documentation
would be gathered. Through this discussion, members of the FON developed a better understanding of the value of evaluation. A key question was
"What does this initiative want to be held accountable for?" The answer to
this question prompted FON participants to realize that their initial 3-
month contact with the family was probably not going to make significant
behavioral changes for most of the families. In fact, it made more sense for
the FON to be viewed as a short-term referral system that could possibly
begin some formal intervention but more likely than not would function
as an identification and referral system for the "at-risk" families.

Answering the question "What are you willing to be accountable for?"
required the FON participants to examine what they could realistically
expect to accomplish within a 3-month service period and what they
needed to do to increase the probability of success. While they remained
eager to enroll families, there was an increased recognition of the value of
proceeding in a deliberative manner that involved inquiry into how the
best-practices literature can inform their decision-making process. The

FON General Logic Model (see Figure 7.3) highlights the importance of being realistic in expectations for the programs as well as identifying specific activities and short-term outcomes that can be tracked and measured over time.

Obtaining the "buy-in" and support for a more thoughtful planning process and "ownership" of the evaluation process occurred when FON members came to understand the value of clearly identifying what they were willing to be held accountable for and what was required to lay the foundation for quality implementation and positive results. Members of the FON came to understand that they needed to "slow down" the process of implementation in order to clearly understand their service delivery processes and the measurements necessary to evaluate their efforts. It is also significant to note that the FON caseworker responsible for presenting new cases to the FON and tracking subsequent progress took the initiative in developing and implementing a tracking system to monitor the collection of data. The caseworker also developed a "reminder email system" to inform staff members about when their data collection tools were due. As with the SBS Prevention Campaign, participants in the FON have assumed significant responsibility for conducting specific evaluation activities. Consequently both the FON and SBS Committee are well on their way toward institutionalizing evaluation practices.

Leadership in Learning Organizations

Leadership within a learning organization cannot depend on a single leader. It depends on the leadership of many people throughout the organization functioning as leadership coalitions to collectively articulate compelling ideas that provide direction and attract people into giving their time and energy to achieve a common goal. Empowerment evaluation is a process that is well suited to the task of facilitating the development of leadership coalitions. In fact, it can be argued that the principles of empowerment evaluation embody the concept of a leadership coalition.

The discussion of how the SBS Committee and the FON both came to see the value of empowerment evaluation also showed how a leadership coalition functions. In each example, leadership is provided by the behavior of a group of people who come to collectively articulate the idea of empowerment evaluation as a means of helping them achieve their goals. The following anecdote provides another example of the behavior of a leadership coalition, in this case the Steering Committee, as it chose a new lead agency.

In July 2003 the project director informed the Collaborative that her excessive workload would prevent her from continuing to serve as the project director beyond the pilot project phase and that the University of Massachusetts Medical Center would not be able to continue as the lead agency. This occurred 6 weeks before the grant application deadline for first-year funding of an anticipated 3-year implementation phase. The foundation was encouraged by the progress during the first 9 months of the pilot project and the potential for systems change by the Collaborative, but the implementation grant application could not go forward without a lead agency. Members of the Collaborative quickly developed a list of potential lead agencies. Discussions between the Foundation, the project director, and potential lead agencies resulted in the identification of two strong candidates from the proposed list, and lead agency candidates were invited to present proposals at the August Steering Committee meeting.

Each potential lead agency was scheduled to make a presentation at the Steering Committee meeting. The presentations were to be followed by open deliberation, and the Steering Committee would choose a lead agency from among the candidates. To help guide the decision-making process, the GMT asked the evaluators to help the Steering Committee summarize the qualities of a lead agency that had been established during previous discussions. After the two presentations, the evaluators would facilitate the discussion by helping the group compare the presentation to the established criteria.

During the Steering Committee discussion, the group quickly identified the importance of such qualities as adequate fiscal management and administrative capacity, and "mission match." A more in-depth conversation followed in which the group affirmed the importance of a lead agency that was committed to the "consensus-based, democratic decision-making process" that had become the operating style of the Collaborative. As one member put it, "I want a lead agency that will be a partner rather than an owner." This comment proved prophetic. During the course of the presentations and the following discussion, a pronounced consensus emerged that one agency clearly personified a collaborative partnership style in its presentation, while the other agency projected the image of an "owner." Both agencies were considered evenly matched with respect to their fiscal and administrative capacity, so the Steering Committee was easily able to choose the agency that presented itself more like a partner than an owner.

During this decision-making process that unfolded over a period of 6 weeks, the Steering Committee functioned as a leadership coalition and came to a deeper understanding of its organizing principles and purpose. The experience of the Steering Committee members with empowerment evaluation during the preceding 10 months played a significant role in developing their capacity to behave as a leadership coalition in choosing a new lead agency. The new lead agency submitted a grant application to the Foundation that, in turn, awarded the Collaborative funding for the first year of an anticipated 3-year implementation phase.

CONCLUSION AND NEXT STEPS

Improvements in planning and implementation of Collaborative initiatives resulted from an effective partnership among the funder, evaluators, lead agency, and other stakeholders working together to achieve results. The two committees implementing the Family Outreach Network and the Shaken Baby Syndrome Prevention Campaign have both begun to incorporate empowerment evaluation practices into their operations. Both are also showing signs of becoming learning organizations. Accountability has been established through several overlapping leadership coalitions that are working to use evaluation results to inform planning and implementation.

The continued development of the Collaborative as a learning organization requires the continuous monitoring and improvement of strategies that are working and those that remain a challenge. Successes fostered by the implementation of empowerment evaluation include:

- The commitment to evaluation and the active role necessary to accomplish tasks.
- The development of evaluation tools/processes for the FON and SBSPC.
- Accepting responsibility for collecting and analyzing data and writing reports by members of the FON and SBSPC.
- Revisions of goals and strategies based on review of best-practices literatures.
- Use of FORECAST charts, conceptual maps, and logic models to facilitate planning through cycles of reflection and action and promote accountability.
- Demonstrating accountability through an active leadership coalition with THFCM, the lead agency, evaluators, and other stakeholders working together to achieve results.
- Successful negotiation of a change in the lead agency.
- Receiving funding for the first year of a 3-year implementation grant.

Challenges that remain for members of the Collaborative as they transition into the implementation phase and continue to develop their capacity to implement and institutionalize empowerment evaluation include:

- Completing the transition to a new lead agency.
- A more extensive and methodological use of the FORECAST system, including the development of long-term action plans.
- Continued development of the capacity of the FON and SBS Committee to conduct an evaluation and eventual transfer of all evaluation activities to staff and stakeholders.

- Continued progress toward all committees becoming a dynamic community of learners.
- Establishing a public policy agenda for systems change and a resource development plan to sustain the Collaborative beyond the anticipated 3-year implementation phase funded by THFCM and the continuation of successful initiatives.

Substantial progress in the implementation of empowerment evaluation during the pilot project phase of the Collaborative has been achieved. While most of this activity to date falls in the category of process evaluation, outcome data are now being collected with staff and other stakeholders already assuming responsibility for some evaluation activities. A solid foundation has been established for the Collaborative to continue becoming a learning organization that uses evaluation results to increase the probability of program success. With a strong commitment to implementing empowerment evaluation, and funding for the first year of a 3-year implementation phase already secured, the Collaborative appears to be well on its way toward institutionalization of an empowerment evaluation system.

NOTES

1. Table 7.1 presents the full set of empowerment evaluation principles introduced in Chapter 2 of this book along with the associated practices for the evaluator and the community. This table is used by Lentz and Imm, Action Research Associates, to help clients understand the core principles and practices of empowerment evaluation and to monitor their implementation.
2. Viewed in this light, empowerment evaluation can also be seen as a movement in the historical development of American pragmatism. American pragmatism is an intellectual tradition that is embedded in the country's heritage of working-class rebelliousness. It consists of a future-oriented instrumentalism, with the moral aim of expanding democracy by using ideas as tools that enable individuals to engage in more effective action (West, 1989).

REFERENCES

Argyris, C. (1999). *On organizational learning*. Malden, MA: Blackwell Business.

Argyris, C., Putnam, R., & Smith, D. M. (1985). *Action science*. San Francisco: Jossey-Bass.

Argyris, C., & Schön, D. (1974). *Theory in practice: Increasing professional effectiveness*. San Francisco: Jossey-Bass.

Argyris, C., & Schön, D. (1978). *Organizational learning*. Reading, MA: Addison-Wesley.

Austin, M. J., Cox, G., Gottlieb, N., Hawkins, J. D., Kruzich, J. M., & Rauch, R. (1982). *Evaluating your agency's programs*. Thousand Oaks, CA: Sage.

Crusto, C. A., & Wandersman, A. (2004). Setting the stage for accountability and program evaluation in community-based grantmaking. In A. Roberts & K. Yeager (Eds.), *Desk reference of evidence-based research in health care and human services*. New York: Oxford University Press.

Dewey, J. (1940). Creative democracy—the task before us. In. S. Ratner (Ed.), *The philosopher of the common man: Essays in honor of John Dewey to celebrate his eightieth birthday* (pp. 220–228). New York: Greenwood Press

Fetterman, D. M. (1996). Empowerment evaluation: An introduction to theory and practice. In D. M. Fetterman, S. J. Kaftarian, & A. Wandersman, *Empowerment evaluation: Knowledge and tools for self-assessment and accountability*. Thousand Oaks, CA: Sage.

Fetterman, D. M. (2001). *Foundations of empowerment evaluation*. Thousand Oaks, CA: Sage.

Fetterman, D. M. (2003). Fetterman-House: A process use distinction and a theory. In C. A. Christie (Ed.), *The practice-theory relationship in evaluation: New Directions for Evaluation* (No. 97, pp. 47–52). San Francisco: Jossey-Bass.

Fetterman, D. M., & Eiler, M. (2001). *Empowerment evaluation and organizational learning: A path toward mainstreaming evaluation*. St. Louis, MO: American Evaluation Association.

Goodman, R., & Wandersman, A. (1994). FORECAST: A formative approach to evaluating community coalitions and community-based initiatives. In S. Kaftarian & W. Hansen (Eds.), Improving methodologies for evaluating community-based coalitions for preventing alcohol, tobacco, and other drug use. *Journal of Community Psychology* (CSAP Special Issue), 6–25.

Goodman, R., Wandersman, A., Chinman, M., Imm, P., & Morrissey, E. (1996). An ecological assessment of community-based interventions for prevention and health promotion: Approaches to measuring community coalitions. *American Journal of Community Psychology, 24*(1), 33–61.

Heron, J., & Reason, P. (2001). The practice of co-operative inquiry: Research "with" rather than "on" people. In P. Reason & H. Bradbury (Eds.), *Handbook of action research* (pp. 179–188). Thousand Oaks, CA: Sage.

Jenlick, P. (1994). Using evaluation to understand the learning architecture of an organization. *Evaluation and Program Planning, 17*(3), 315–325.

Kofman, F., & Senge, P. (1995). Communities of commitment: The heart of the learning organization. In S. Chawla & J. Rensch (Eds.), *Learning organizations: Developing cultures for tomorrow's workplace* (pp. 15–43). Portland, OR: Productivity Press.

Massachusetts Citizens for Children. (2001). *A state call for action: Working to end child abuse and neglect in Massachusetts*. Boston: Author. Available online at *www.masskids.org*.

McDaniel, R. (1997). A leader? No. Many leaders! *Journal of the Organization Development Network, 29*(4) 35–38.

Nonaka, I., & Takeuchi, K. (1995). *The knowledge creating company*. NewYork: Oxford University Press.

Patton, M. Q. (1997). *Utilization-focused evaluation* (3rd ed.). Thousand Oaks, CA: Sage.

Preskill, H. (1994). Evaluation's role in facilitating organizational learning: A model for practice. *Evaluation and Program Planning, 17*(3), 291–298.

Reason, P. (1994). Human inquiry as discipline and practice. In P. Reason (Ed.), *Participation in human inquiry* (pp. 50–56). Thousand Oaks, CA: Sage.

Schön, D. (1982). *The reflective practitioner: How professionals think in action.* New York: Basic Books.

Senge, P. (1990). *The fifth discipline: The art and practice of organizational learning.* New York: Doubleday.

Sveiby, K. E. (1997). *The new organizational wealth: Managing and measuring knowledge-based assets.* San Francisco: Berrett-Koehler.

Usher, C. L. (1995). Improving evaluation through self-evaluation. *Evaluation Practice, 16,* 59–68.

Wandersman, A. (1999). Framing the evaluation of health and human service programs in community settings: Assessing progress. *New Directions for Evaluation,* No. 83, 95–102.

Wandersman, A., Imm, P., Chinman, M., & Kaftarian, S. (1999). *Getting to outcomes: Methods and tools for planning, self-evaluation and accountability.* Rockville, MD: Center for Substance Abuse Prevention.

Wandersman, A., Imm, P., Chinman, M., & Kaftarian, S. (2000). Getting to outcomes: A results-based approach to accountability. *Evaluation and Program Planning, 23*(3), 389–395.

Wang, C., & Daro, D. (1998). *Current trends in child abuse reporting and fatalities: The results of the 1997 annual fifty-state survey.* Chicago: National Center on Child Abuse Prevention Research, National Committee to Prevent Child Abuse.

West, C. (1989). *The American evasion of philosophy: A genealogy of pragmatism.* Madison: University of Wisconsin Press.

Worthington, C. (1999). Empowerment evaluation: Understanding the theory behind the framework. *The Canadian Journal of Program Evaluation, 14*(1), 1–28.

Yost, J., & Wandersman, A. (1998). *Results-oriented grantmaking/grant-implementation: Mary Black Foundation.* Presented at the annual meeting of the American Evaluation Association.

CHAPTER 8

Will the Real Empowerment Evaluation Please Stand Up?

A CRITICAL FRIEND PERSPECTIVE

J. Bradley Cousins

There exists considerable confusion in the literature concerning conceptual differentiation among collaborative, participatory, and empowerment approaches to evaluation. It is important to differentiate these approaches in order to minimize talking across purposes at all levels of abstraction: evaluation theory, research on evaluation and evaluation practice. Conceptual clarity will help to extend knowledge about the circumstances and conditions under which particular approaches are likely to be effective, meaningful and appropriate. At the invitation of Abe Wandersman and David Fetterman, my purpose in the present chapter is to critically examine current practice and theory on empowerment evaluation by applying a conceptual framework originally developed by Cousins and Whitmore (1998) and subsequently extended by Weaver and Cousins (2003). This analysis is intended to help further understanding of empowerment evaluation and how it might be situated among other forms of collaborative inquiry.

In a 2002 session at the annual meeting of the American Evaluation Association, Patton suggested that the challenge of differentiating collaborative, participatory, and empowerment evaluation may not be a productive exercise. It is not so important, he argued, to label the approach as it is to tailor the evaluation to the needs of the program community. While I concur with his tailoring sentiment, I tend to disagree with his basic point on the grounds that conceptual clarity is essential to making informed evaluation choices. Without it, terms such as participatory and empowerment evaluation become confused and meaningless and may be relegated to the status of buzzwords or code words, the use of which imply that the speaker is "in the know." As a case in point, a student at the University of Ottawa recently completed a master's thesis examining several donor-funded "participatory" research studies in the education sector in sub-Saharan Africa (Meier, 1999). Of the dozen or so studies examined, he found little evidence of anything resembling participation of program staff and other non-research-based stakeholders. Yet, participatory research was noted to be a central element in donor agency proposal requirements (part of his criteria for selecting the studies in the first place).

Taking up the editors' challenge, I decided to approach the project from the point of view of a critical friend for at least two reasons. First, I consider myself a friend of empowerment evaluation because it links in very direct ways to evaluation approaches in which I have been involved as both an evaluation practitioner and researcher/theorist. Specifically, much of our own work centers on "participatory evaluation" as a general approach (see Cousins, 2003; Cousins & Whitmore, 1998). Despite my perception of the enigmatic character of empowerment evaluation, I know that the approach is aligned with my own value stance in many ways. Second, the critical friend perspective, as I understand it, is central to the role of the empowerment evaluation evaluator. As Fetterman puts it:

> The primary role of the evaluator is to serve as a coach, facilitator, and critical evaluative friend. . . . The evaluator must also be analytical and critical, asking or prompting participants to clarify, document, and evaluate what they are doing to ensure that specific goals are achieved. (2001, pp. 30–31)

I think this is a suitable role for me; maybe it could even be labeled "metacritical friend." I might be able to help empowerment evaluation proponents to clarify, document, and evaluate empowerment evaluation to ensure that it is achieving its goals. My challenge, as such, is to address coherently the following questions:

1. What are the goals or interests of empowerment evaluation? What is it trying to accomplish?
2. What form does empowerment evaluation take? What processes differentiate it from other approaches?
3. How good is good enough? How can we tell a good empowerment evaluation from a bad one?

In taking up the challenge, it is important for me to make my own basis for reflection and analysis clear. There are three important points for consideration. First, as I mentioned above, much of our work centers on participatory evaluation. But I refer specifically to a particular form of participatory evaluation, one that is practical in orientation and intends to foster program decision making and problem solving and the use of evaluation findings and processes. This is a stream of participatory evaluation that Whitmore and I differentiated from another major stream that is more political and transforming in intent. We called the former Practical Participatory Evaluation (P-PE) and the latter Transformative Participatory Evaluation (T-PE; Cousins & Whitmore, 1998). Second, much of my work, dating way back to my graduate student days, has been grounded in theories and principles of evaluation utilization. This program of inquiry led quite naturally into my interest in P-PE. Finally, as I tried to self-portray in a chapter in Alkin's recent book (Cousins, 2004), I consider myself to be an empiricist with primary and considered emphasis on bridging the gap between evaluation theory and practice. As a consequence, I am prone to think in operational terms when it comes to abstract psychosocial constructs, typically asking such questions as "How would we measure that?" and "How would we know?"

THE GOALS AND INTERESTS OF EMPOWERMENT EVALUATION

In our chapter on PE streams (Cousins & Whitmore, 1998), Whitmore and I framed the term "collaborative inquiry" as a generic umbrella term under which many different approaches and species might be located. Essential to a definition of collaborative inquiry is the notion that members of the stakeholder, program practitioner community, or community of practice are in some way involved in the inquiry. Empowerment evaluation fits the bill.

We identified three primary justifications for collaborative inquiry. First, we talked about *pragmatic* justifications. Inquiry guided mostly by this justification tends to have a distinct problem-solving or instrumental focus. Utilization-oriented approaches such as P-PE and Patton's utilization-focused evaluation (1997) would fall into this category. Support for program and organizational decision making and learning are central to this category. Next we identified a category of approaches that would be more normative in form and function and *political* in orientation. Various genres of participatory action research (McTaggert, 1991) and participatory evaluation (Brunner & Guzman, 1989) would fit into this category. Finally, we talked about *philosophic* justifications, an appropriate consideration when the researcher is most interested in using collaborative inquiry to deepen understanding and enhance the meaning of the phenomena under study. Stake's responsive evaluation, as I expressed recently (Cousins, 2004), would fall into this category, since his argument centers on being responsive to context and ensuring that localness is represented in meaning. The pragmatic, the political, and the philosophic, then, are the three P's of justification for collaborative inquiry. I do not mean to imply that a given approach is necessarily exclusively associated with one of the P's. It is more a question of emphasis and balance. I personally have never seen or participated in a P-PE that was not, to some extent, empowering for program practitioners. Likewise, I have not seen or read about a T-PE that did not lead to practical consequences.

What are the goals or interests of empowerment evaluation? What is it trying to accomplish? On the face of it, even at the level of its name, empowerment evaluation is about empowerment and self-determination. One would naturally conclude that it best fits in the political category. Support for this conclusion is abundant. To be sure, the language of empowerment evaluation is teeming with the vocabulary of empowerment, using terms like liberation, emancipation, advocacy, self-determination, enlightenment, to name a few (Fetterman, Kaftarian, & Wandersman, 1996; Fetterman, 2001; Wandersman et al., Chap. 2 of this volume). Yet, looking closer, such a conclusion about empowerment evaluation interests may be hasty. Let's listen to the principal definitions and goal statements of the term:

> . . . the use of evaluation concepts, techniques and findings to foster improvement and self-determination. (Fetterman, 2001, p. 3)

> . . . providing program developers with tools for assessing the planning, implementation, and evaluation of programs, program practitioners have the opportunity to improve planning, implement with quality, evaluate outcomes, and develop a continuous quality improvement system, thereby increasing the probability of achieving results. (Wandersman, 1999, p. 96)

The agreed-upon definition of empowerment evaluation for the purposes of this volume is

> An evaluation approach that aims to increase the probability of achieving program success by (1) providing program stakeholders with tools for assessing the planning, implementation, and self-evaluation of their program, and (2) mainstreaming evaluation as part of the planning and management of the program/organization. (Wandersman et al., Chapter 2, p. 28)

We hear elements of the transformative rhetoric in these definitions and the lingo of self-determination, but even more pronounced, I would assert, are pragmatic considerations. Terms such as "foster improvement," "achieving program success," "continuous quality improvement," and "planning and management of the program/organization" are completely aligned with the pragmatic problem-solving justification for collaborative inquiry. Is empowerment evaluation more about evaluation utilization than about self-determination? Let's push further on that.

Fetterman is also a contributor to Alkin's recent book (Fetterman, 2004). In the book Alkin and Christie (2004) developed a theory tree, which consists of evaluation roots (arising from social sciences research theory) and three primary branches of evaluation theory: use, method, and valuing. They then located a selected (nonexhaustive) list of contributors to evaluation theory within one of the three branches, and asked each contributor to prepare, in the form of a short chapter, a reaction to this decision and a summary of self-contributions. Despite the language of transformation associated with empowerment evaluation (and despite Fetterman's contributions to qualitative methods in evaluation and educational research), Alkin and Christie chose to locate Fetterman on the use branch, focusing primarily on his contributions to empowerment evaluation. This independent assessment, and Fetterman's own reaction (2004), supports the claim that empowerment evaluation is not so much about the political or transformative agenda but rather it is really an approach to fostering organizational and program decision making and problem solving. In Fetterman's own words (p. 14):

> Empowerment evaluation is fundamentally about process use as exemplified by Patton's utilization-focused evaluation (1997). However, methods matter. It is the methods used in empowerment evaluation that facilitate involvement, engagement, and buy-in concerning the evaluation findings and recommendations.

Further, in the same piece and now as an integral principle of empowerment evaluation (see Chapter 2 of this volume), the editors draw on Argyris and Schön's work on organizational learning as theoretical underpinnings of empowerment evaluation. They cite determining the alignment of theory of action (espoused program theory) and theory of use (actual program theory) as being a central contribution of empowerment evaluation. Much has been made of the links between evaluation and organizational learning theory of late (e.g., Cousins & Earl, 1995; Preskill & Torres, 1999; Owen & Lambert, 1996; Patton, 1997), and most of it from the standpoint of evaluation utilization scholars (see Alkin & Christie's theory tree, 2004) and linked to the concept of process use.

And so, do we conclude that the goals and interests of empowerment evaluation are practical problem solving and support for decision making? The weight of the foregoing arguments would suggest so. Yet, even earlier in the same piece quoted above, Fetterman harkens back to empowerment theory as being conceptually fundamental to empowerment evaluation:

> *Self-determination* is one of the foundational concepts underlying empowerment theory and it helps to detail specific mechanisms or behaviors that enable the actualization of empowerment. (Fetterman, 2004, p. 306, emphasis in original)

Similar spanning of justification categories is inherent in the statement of empowerment evaluation principles (Wandersman et al., Chapter 2 of this volume). The improvement of program quality and capacity building and organizational learning are juxtaposed with democracy and participation, and responsibility for decision making. Add to this the valuing of local community knowledge, and the complete spectrum of pragmatic, political, and philosophic justifications for collaborative inquiry is covered.

As a critical friend I would suggest that conceptual clarity is called for regarding the depiction of empowerment evaluation goals and interests and what it is trying to accomplish. This is not to say, as I have stated above, that there cannot be overlap among justifications for the approach. I am saying, however, that it is my belief that empowerment evaluation cannot be all things to all interest positions, and those choices and emphases should be made clear. Fetterman recently communicated to me that he envisages empowerment evaluation as having two streams, much the same as those we identified in connection with participatory evaluation. He also suggested "that organizational and program decision-making improvements can be (but do not need to be) stepping-stones to transformation" (personal communication, April 30, 2004). Cousins and Whitmore (1998) developed their conclusions about two streams of participatory evaluation not to imply that participatory evaluation can be comprehensive and all-encompassing when it comes to collaborative inquiry but to show that fundamental differences in goals and interests exist and need to be taken into account in any discussion and framing of or, especially, planning and implementation of participatory evaluation. Such choices have direct implications for how one goes about doing participatory evaluation. My current impression is that empowerment evaluation does try to be all things to all interest positions regarding collaborative inquiry, and I think that weakens its quest for a unique identity among the menu options available. If indeed there are two streams of empowerment evaluation, this line of reasoning is not very evident in this volume and needs to be developed considerably. How, for example, would the 10 principles of empowerment evaluation apply differently to an empowerment evaluation project with a primary intention of practical program problem solving and decision making versus one designed to primarily foster self-determination and empower stakeholders within the program community? I would encourage proponents of empowerment evaluation to push their thinking in this regard.

EMPOWERMENT EVALUATION FORM AND PROCESSES

Getting a sense of what empowerment evaluation looks like in practice is another route to understanding its essence. Thankfully, enthusiasts have been very busy in this regard. There exists a considerable and commendable effort to document empowerment evaluation in practice and to use case examples to illustrate key characteristics, the operatonalization of principles, and the like. Chapters in this volume by Keener et al. (Chapter 4), Fetterman (Chapter 5), and Lentz et al. (Chapter 7) are excellent examples, although more and more case examples are appearing in the evaluation literature as well (e.g., Barrington, 1999; Lee, 1999; Schnoes, Murphy-Berman, & Chambers, 2000).

In our effort to differentiate streams of participatory evaluation Whitmore and I developed a conceptual framework for inquiry processes that attended to three dimensions of process that we believed to be fundamental. These are:

- Control of technical decision making (evaluator vs. nonevaluator stakeholder)
- Stakeholder selection for participation (primary users vs. all legitimate nonevaluator stakeholder groups)
- Depth of participation (involved in all aspects of inquiry vs. involved as a source for consultation)

We boldly claimed that any collaborative inquiry project could be described and located along each of these continua and that the dimensions were orthogonal (i.e., the location on one dimension did not imply the location on another).

Putting the framework to the test in the context of teaching a graduate course, I subsequently came to understand that the three-dimensional process framework was inadequate, as one of the dimensions—stakeholder selection—was confounded and required further unpacking. Lynda Weaver and I proceeded to do just that and developed a revised version of the framework this time with five dimensions (Weaver & Cousins, 2003) (*italicized dimensions* representing the changes):

- Control of technical decision making (evaluator vs. nonevaluator stakeholder)
- *Diversity of nonevaluator stakeholders selected for participation (limited vs. diverse)*
- *Power relations among nonevaluator stakeholders (neutral vs. conflicting)*
- *Manageability of the evaluation implementation (manageable vs. unwieldy)*
- Depth of participation (involved as a source for consultation vs. involved in all aspects of the inquiry)

Using the revised version in a "radargram," we showed hypothetical differences in form among conventional stakeholder-based evaluations, P-PE, and P-TE. The result of that analysis is represented in Figure 8.1.[1]

Starting at the top of the figure, we can see that P-PE and T-PE can involve balanced control in technical decision making but that they differ quite considerably in diversity, owing to principles of inclusivity associated with T-PE and a utilization orientation with P-PE. Power relations are likely to be somewhat conflicting in the case of T-PE, since voice is given to those who have normally been marginalized from such opportunities. In P-PE one might expect relative conflict neutrality, particularly in the case of a formative evaluation on which primary users were in agreement as to

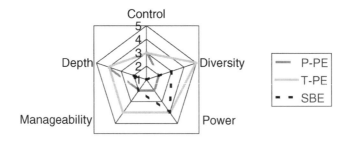

FIGURE 8.1. Hypothetical dimensions of form in collaborative inquiry. Adapted from Weaver and Cousins (2003).

program goals, objectives, and important questions and variables for consideration. This being the case, P-PE is likely to be much more feasible than is T-PE, in the norm. Finally, both of these collaborative approaches to evaluation subscribe to principles of involvement and participation by nonevaluator stakeholders in as many technical aspects of the evaluation as is possible and reasonable. SBE is a third collaborative approach that is differentiated in the hypothetical example. We can see that in SBE, in its conventional form, the evaluator maintains control of evaluation decision making and responsibility for implementing the project from start to finish. There may be a diverse range of interests represented by the non-researcher stakeholder groups that the evaluator chooses to approach, and it may be the case that value positions vary quite substantially over groups. SBE is sometimes recommended as an appropriate and responsive approach when there is little agreement about the object of evaluation or questions and variables of interest in the evaluation. In contrast to T-PE, we might expect SBE to be relatively easy to manage, given that the evaluator is fully in control of the process and able to integrate and synthesize findings in fairly short order. Finally, typically it is the case that nonevaluator stakeholders would be called upon to help plan and scope out the evaluation and later to provide interpretations of the findings presented by the evaluator. Their role would be more consultative than directly participatory.

What form does empowerment evaluation take? What processes differentiate it from other approaches? To answer the question I refer to the delineation of the empowerment evaluation approach outlined in the several case applications described in this volume: Keener et al. (Chapter 4), Fetterman (Chapter 5), and Lentz et al. (Chapter 7). The case examples are characterized by a variety of approaches including Fetterman's three-step process (Fetterman, 2001) and the "Getting to Outcomes" (GTO) approach developed by Wandersman and colleagues (Wandersman, Imm, Chinman, & Kaftarian, 2000). Let's begin with Fetterman's three-step process.

Fetterman (2001) describes at length the three steps of empowerment evaluation: mission, taking stock, and planning for the future. In the process an empowerment evaluation team works in a facilitating capacity with nonevaluator program stakeholders (usually program personnel and in some cases intended program beneficiaries) to help them "brainstorm" the mission of the program, which is subsequently refined and developed into a concise statement that everybody "can live with." In the next step, important program activities are brainstormed by the same group and then prioritized in terms of "which are the most important activities meriting evaluation at this time" (p. 25). Having completed this, the phase of "taking stock" commences; the group rates the rank-ordered list of activities in terms of "how well they are doing." The participants are asked to provide written justifications for their ratings. The ratings from 1 to 10 are recorded on a master sheet for all to see. This information serves as a stimulus for discussion for the third step, which is planning for the future. In that step participants set goals for program implementation and change. They identify strategies for goal implementation and indicators or evidence that would yield information about goal attainment. The empowerment evaluation process unfolds as an ongoing cyclical process, with the initial taking-stock record serving as baseline data and subsequent exercises leading to continual change. What is not really made clear in the Fetterman (2001) book is whether the nonevaluator stakeholder participants actually develop instruments, gather data, process and analyze data, and bring their interpretations back to the process when the next taking-stock exercise occurs. Fetterman assures me that this is the case (personal communication, April 30, 2004).

The GTO approach is a bit different. Wandersman et al. (2000) describe it as a user-friendly tool that can be used in the context of empowerment evaluation. The GTO framework is actually a 10-step approach to program planning, development, implementation, and evaluation based on a set of accountability questions associated with: (1) needs and resources; (2) goals, target population, desired outcomes; (3) incorporation of best practices, defined in scientific terms; (4) fit with other programs; (5) required capabilities for implementation; (6) planning; (7) implementation evaluation; (8) outcome and impact evaluation; (9) continuous quality improvement; and (10) sustainability and institutionalization. Empowerment evaluation activities are related to some but not all of these elements, but it is understood that empowerment evaluation is implemented within this comprehensive framework. For example, members of the program stakeholder community would be involved with needs assessment, process evaluation, and impact evaluation aspects as well as ongoing improvement and development toward sustainability.

As is clarified in Chapter 1 of this volume, empowerment evaluation is not about particular methods or approaches; it is "first and foremost about principles, theories, ideas, and values" (Chapter 1, p. 2). The 10 principles of empowerment evaluation outlined in Chapter 1 and expanded upon in subsequent chapters speak not only to what empowerment evaluation is trying to accomplish but how it is trying to go about accomplishing its goals. Nevertheless, it is of interest to see how the case examples (Keener et al., Chapter 4; Fetterman, Chapter 5; Lentz et al., Chapter 7) provided in this volume stack up on the five-point process framework described above. Of particular interest is the extent to which there is uniformity or variation across these fundamental process dimensions. For convenience I take the case examples chapter by chapter, noting that in each of these chapters two case examples of empowerment evaluation are described.

Keener et al. (Chapter 4) Case Examples

The authors describe empowerment evaluation in the context of two programs funded by the same foundation but suggest that one of the examples was probably more appropriately thought of as participatory evaluation, while the other was a better example of empowerment evaluation. The case in point was located at the Middle Tyger Community Center (MTCC), an educational support program for adolescent mothers and their children that also was involved in interagency collaboration. The evaluation team took a strong role in implementing the evaluation, relying on local program personnel for input to shape planning and implementation. The evaluation report was ultimately prepared by the evaluators, and feedback from program participants was integrated within it.

The second example was the Foundation for the Future (FFF), a collaborative program that was designed to provide services to families of Boys and Girls Club members in the interest of ameliorating multiple risk factors associated with such youth. According to Keener et al., the FFF evaluation was much more aligned with the principles of empowerment evaluation. The evaluation team served as facilitators, while FFF staff were active in deciding data collection methods and strategies and in gathering and analyzing or interpreting data and reporting findings. I now turn to an analysis of the case examples according to the five process dimensions described above (see Figure 8.2).

- *Control of technical decision making (evaluator [1] vs. nonevaluator stakeholder [5])*. The MTCC evaluation was heavily guided by the empowerment evaluation team, as the authors noted. To be sure, program practitioners were routinely consulted about key aspects of the evaluation plan-

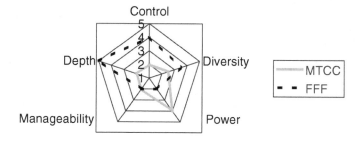

FIGURE 8.2. Dimensions of form of Keener et al. (Chapter 4) case examples.

ning, implementation, and ultimately interpretation, and their input was seriously considered and integrated by the evaluation team. For the FFF project, the empowerment evaluation team took a much less directive role and served as critical friends to the program practitioner team that ultimately carried out the evaluation. In this context, the evaluators provided advice that helped to direct the decision making of the program personnel, but control of evaluation technical decision making rested in the hands of the staff.

• *Diversity of nonevaluator stakeholders selected for participation (limited [1] vs. diverse [5])*. In each case personnel fairly directly involved with program implementation were involved in the evaluation. In neither case were intended program beneficiaries participating. For MTCC, included were program staff, the executive director, and even a member of the funding organization at one point. Program staff, the collaboration manager, and members of the participating partner organizations took part in the FFF evaluation. All in all, moderate levels of diversity were evident.

• *Power relations among nonevaluator stakeholders (neutral [1] vs. conflicting [5])*. Given the observed diversity of involvement, some notable differences in power relations among participants were evident. In MTCC, the empowerment evaluation team adopted the role of expert regarding best practices in the substantive domain of programming. The executive director, though collaborative and willing to engage in open dialogue, tended to represent the practitioner voice, while the staff was somewhat less vocal, owing perhaps to the heavy workload and the lack of time for reflection and input. Some conflict was observed concerning report content. Ultimately, this was resolved by the empowerment evaluation team's choice to involve a member of the funding agency to get its perspective on the matter at hand. The FFF evaluation was somewhat more balanced in terms of power differentials. The evaluator/collaboration manager position was created within the host organization, but members from the partner agencies were more or less on an equal footing and conflict on the project was minimal.

• *Manageability of the evaluation implementation (manageable [1] vs. unwieldy [5])*. Both projects were quite manageable from the standpoint of focus and time intensitivity and thus could be located on the manageable end of the continuum.

• *Depth of participation (involved as a source for consultation [1] vs. involved in all aspects of the inquiry [5])*. For MTCC, staff participation in the evaluation, with the exception of the executive director, was limited to consultation and some involvement with data collection and data entry. These people typically participated in a mode of following instructions. By contrast, the FFF team was actively involved in all facets of the evaluation from planning to data collection and analysis to reporting. This was clearly a deep level of participation.

Fetterman (Chapter 5) Case Examples

Fetterman describes two case examples in Chapter 5. The first was associated with a $15-million investment by Hewlett-Packard in a program designed to help disadvantaged communities cross the "digital divide" in terms of their access to and use of contemporary information technology. Although the program was located in three sites, each characterized by disadvantaged communities, the case example is largely restricted to the description of activities in California involving 18 Native American tribes, referred to as the Tribal Digital Village. The projects all involved the distribution of laptop computers in schools, aid to community centers, aid to small businesses, and an effort to help the district's development of Web-based tools to enhance community access to local resources. The second case example was in a disadvantaged rural school districts in Arkansas that had been labeled as being at risk or in "academic distress" for several years by the State Department of Education, over 40% of the students having scored at or below the 25th percentile on the annual state education assessments. The Arkansas State Department of Education provided resources for capacity building at the individual, program, and district levels in order to establish a foundation for future improvement.

In both cases, empowerment evaluation was employed, using Fetterman's (2001) three-step approach. In the chapter the author describes the process of identifying and developing the mission, taking stock, and planning for the future in advance of providing details about the specific cases. He then proceeds to examine each of the cases through the lens of empowerment evaluation principles laid out in Chapter 2. These choices limit the amount of information available from which to assess the individual case examples in terms of the process dimensions from the aforementioned framework. Nevertheless, I provide below my best guess as to the dimensions of form operating within each case example. The result is represented in Figure 8.3.

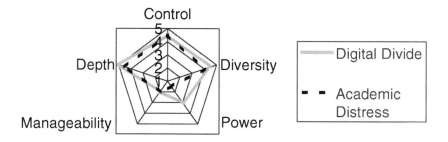

FIGURE 8.3. Dimensions of form of Fetterman (Chapter 5) case examples.

• *Control of technical decision making (evaluator [1] vs. nonevaluator stakeholder [5]).* From the outset both cases involved the evaluator or empowerment evaluation team in the role of facilitator or coach, with local program stakeholders taking the lead role in decision making about evaluation questions, data collection and analysis, and ultimately use. The three-step process involves initial exercises led by the facilitator for developing understanding of the group's mission and then taking stock or establishing a baseline of performance on important identified dimensions. The stakeholder participants provide input in the form of perception data and then engage in interpretive discussions. It is at the third step, planning for the future, where the local groups play a key role in planning and implementing evaluative inquiry. The groups not only plan appropriate activities to help improve the situation regarding the identified focal areas but also develop credible lines of evidence that will be used as a systematic way to monitor performance and improvement on these dimensions. Ongoing monitoring and formalized taking-stock exercises help the group to systematically and cyclically check improvement and adjust activities to enhance improvement over time. Given the active role played by the local stakeholder groups in deciding lines of evidence, gathering data, and interpreting and using data, I scored both the Digital Divide and Academic Distress projects as being nonevaluator stakeholder controlled (see Figure 8.3).

• *Diversity of nonevaluator stakeholders selected for participation (limited [1] vs. diverse [5]).* I scored the projects as involving diverse groups of nonevaluator stakeholders. In the Digital Divide project, community executives, program directors, faculty, students, and parents participated in the collection of baseline data, the development and administration of surveys, and the use of information arising from data collection for decision making. The Academic Distress project was similarly inclusive and involved a broad range of nonevaluator stakeholders. Here school district teachers, administrators, staff members, and community members were involved with the evaluative activities. I scored this project as being slightly lower in diversity than the Digital Divide group because students in the Arkansas school district did not appear to be involved with the evaluative activities in a capacity other than as sources of data (e.g., academic test scores, interviews).

• *Power relations among nonevaluator stakeholders (neutral [1] vs. conflicting [5]).* With such a wide spectrum of interests represented in both case examples, it is natural that some conflict would emerge. My reading of the case descriptions suggests that such conflict was fairly limited, however. In the Digital Divide project, mild conflict emerged when an important housing advocacy group was inadvertently not invited to an evaluation workshop. Also, in the taking-stock exercise, concern about the overrepresentation of special interest groups was raised, given the disproportionate numbers of people in attendance. These concerns were relatively easily handled in the project. Despite the contentious nature of the focus for evaluation (academic distress), and the involvement of such a wide range of interest groups in the project and its evaluation, the author's description of the Academic Distress case example was virtually devoid of signs of conflict. According to the narrative, the project appears to have unfolded in a very harmonious way. For this reason, I rated the Academic Distress project as being relatively conflict-neutral.

• *Manageability of the evaluation implementation (manageable [1] vs. unwieldy [5]).* The case example description for both the Digital Divide and Academic Distress projects provides little in the way of detail about actual project functioning and management. Both included activities that involved diverse groups of stakeholders participating together to develop understanding and decide on courses of action. No mention was made of difficulties and challenges arising in logistically pulling together these meetings or about the efficiencies associated with data gathering, processing, analysis, and reporting. As such, I rated both projects as being highly manageable, although I recognize that the rating may be an artifact of information missing from the case description.

• *Depth of participation (involved as a source for consultation [1] vs. involved in all aspects of the inquiry [5]).* Fetterman's three-step process, as a matter of design, engages nonevaluator stakeholders in all aspects of the evaluative inquiry, including planning, instrument development, data collection, analysis and interpretation, and reporting and follow-up with the findings. In the Digital Divide case, participants developed with the assistance of the evaluators their own pre- and posttests for training workshops, some of these including online surveys. They also conducted interviews and observation of training sessions. The participants also used the information collected to inform ongoing decision making about project activities. A similar scenario developed in the case of the Academic Distress project. Participants tested students to document change over time and conducted their own assessments of critical aspects of the school, including academic performance and discipline. In the case report there is mention of students giving video camera interviews about school, truancy, and discipline issues and these being shared via email with the evaluators. It is unclear in the description who conducted the interviews and what the evaluators' role was once the data were received. Nevertheless, I rated both projects high in terms of the depth of participation of nonevaluator stakeholders in the evaluative inquiry.

Lentz et al. (Chapter 7) Case Examples

The case examples provided by Lentz et al. in Chapter 7 both pertain to the same pilot project initiative funded by The Health Foundation of Central Massachusetts (the Foundation). The initiative was developed in response to the growing problem of child maltreatment in central Massachusetts. The lead agency in the project was the University of Massachusetts Memorial Children's Medical Center. The two case examples were actually separate initiatives under the Medical Center's Child Protection Program. One was the Shaken Baby Syndrome Prevention Campaign (SBSPC), a grassroots community coalition organized to develop strategies to integrate information about the prevention of shaken baby syndrome in hospitals, child care agencies, community centers, after-school programs, and other related settings. It had two main components, the delivery of in-hospital prevention education programs and a community training outreach component.

The second initiative was the Family Outreach Network (FON), a collection of service providers who would meet regularly and refer families to a regime of home visitation to help them access services to meet their needs. The families for referral were in need of assistance because of problems such as substance abuse, mental health issues, and limited parenting skills but did not meet the criteria for mandated protective services by the Department of Social Services.

A single evaluation team was contracted by the Foundation to implement empowerment evaluation within both initiatives because the Foundation was very much interested in fostering the development of self-evaluative skills and capacity among the service providers. Based on the case examples described by Lentz et al. in Chapter 7, my analysis of dimensions of form of collaborative inquiry is reflected in Figure 8.4. I now turn to an explication of these analyses.

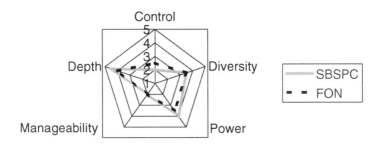

FIGURE 8.4. Dimensions of form of Lentz et al. (Chapter 7) case example.

• *Control of technical decision making (evaluator [1] vs. nonevaluator stakeholder [5])*. In both cases, I found the empowerment evaluation team to take a fairly directive initial role in terms of technical decision making regarding the evaluation activities. The evaluators began by developing a concept map of the various Child Prevention Program initiatives as a way to help nonevaluator stakeholders situate their initiatives within the larger pilot project. This map was developed on an iterative basis through consultation with the Foundation and others. The evaluators then conducted in-depth qualitative interviews with representatives from the collaborating agencies within the pilot project exploring the purpose of relationship building, assessing the available evaluative skills and competencies, and warming the nonevaluator stakeholders up to empowerment evaluation principles. Data from these initial interviews helped to shape implementation planning for the SBSPC and the development of a leadership coalition to promote additional planning steps. Members of the SBSPC committee subsequently worked with the evaluators to plan and implement focus groups and took a more directive role in the inquiry. Members of the FON worked with the evaluators to clarify initial planning steps, develop a chart to help identify activities, and target dates and potential success measures in a logic model. FON members initially perceived the evaluation to be a compliance-oriented activity, although over time they developed a deeper appreciation for evaluation and the benefits to which it could lead.

• *Diversity of nonevaluator stakeholders selected for participation (limited [1] vs. diverse [5])*. Both of the initiatives involved diverse groups of nonevaluator stakeholders in the evaluation process, but typically these were limited to primary stakeholders, including service providers, directors, foundation representatives, and others. In neither case were the intended beneficiaries of the services, the families or the parents needing services, involved in the evaluation activities in any capacity other than in providing data—through, for example, participation in focus groups.

• *Power relations among nonevaluator stakeholders (neutral [1] vs. conflicting [5])*. Conflict was seen to emerge in each of the two initiatives but was handled through deliberation, dialogue, and compromise. In the case of SBSPC, initial plans to implement in-hospital educational services full-scale in six hospitals came into question as a result of early information gathering by the evaluation team. The evaluation team effectively engaged the SBSPC Committee in discussions about readiness for implementation, and eventually a compromise was reached in which more elaborated evidence-based planning was coupled with a decision to begin with two hospitals instead of six. In the FON context, service providers were eager to implement the planned referral system and were frustrated by perceived excessive planning and demands to develop data collection instruments and strategies. Adding to their concern were requirements to obtain Institutional Review Board approval. The evaluators worked with the project director and the Foundation representative to function as a leadership coalition to deal with the issue. Through ongoing discussions members of the FOB developed their appreciation for the value of evaluation. The key question "What does this initiative want to be held accountable for?" served to trigger in-depth reflection and the development of an appreciation of the value of evaluative inquiry.

• *Manageability of the evaluation implementation (manageable [1] vs. unwieldy [5]).* No major concerns about the manageability of the empowerment evaluation process in either of the two initiatives were reported by Lentz et al. My sense is that the management of the evaluation went fairly smoothly despite the wide range of stakeholder interests involved, but this may be an artifact of information missing in the chapter.

• *Depth of participation (involved as a source for consultation [1] vs. involved in all aspects of the inquiry [5]).* Despite an evident early leadership role played by the evaluators, eventually evaluation capacity was developed within each of the two sites, and nonevaluator stakeholders were very much involved in all phases of the inquiry and related activities. In the SBSPC initiative, participants developed focus group protocols, implemented six focus groups, and developed a report that outlined suggested improvements. The nursing staff also conducted a telephone survey with parents of newborns concerning the effectiveness of the in-hospital program. As mentioned above, FON members came to understand the need to take a more deliberative pace and to clearly understand their service delivery processes and the measurements necessary to evaluate success. A tracking system was also developed by an FON caseworker to monitor data collection.

I conducted the foregoing analysis of authentic case examples of empowerment evaluation to look for identifiable patterns of implementation according to key dimensions of form in collaborative inquiry and to get a sense of what differentiates this approach from other forms of collaborative evaluation. My analysis is based only on the information available in the case example descriptions and is therefore limited because the authors obviously did not write the chapters with my analytical framework in mind. Despite these limitations, I think it is safe to say that there exists a great deal of variation in the implementation of empowerment evaluation. As the editors have argued in the first few chapters, empowerment evaluation is not about particular paths or methods but rather about adherence to the principles and values that have been made explicit in this volume. Principles will be given differential weighting depending on the contextual exigencies of the specific empowerment evaluation project.

That is all fine, but as we see in Figures 8.2 through 8.4, variation across the six case examples is apparent on virtually each of the five dimensions of form. Typically, control of technical evaluation decision making is largely in the hands of the participants, but this varied. In some instances my ratings correspond mostly to early control by the evaluators, who were ultimately working toward developing evaluation capacity, as was the situation with the Lentz et al. case examples (SBSPC and FON). Usually, the case examples involved considerable diverse inclusion of nonevaluator stakeholder groups. This did not necessarily imply, however, that all groups were included. In a few instances, intended beneficiaries of the programs in question operated only as sources of data and did not participate as part of the inquiry process in any other capacity. Sometimes direct participation in the inquiry was limited to primary stakeholders such as program developers, implementers, and funders. Generally, conflict was evident—as one might expect when wide ranges of interests come together—but this was not always the case. I was surprised by the relative absence of conflict surfacing in the Fetterman case examples (Digital Divide and Academic Distress). I found very little comment in the respective chapters about issues of the manageability of the project, and I was somewhat surprised by this. In my own experience, which is largely with small groups of primary users, manageability can sometimes be an issue. When a project is openly inclusive one would expect the logistics of implementation (scheduling meetings, timing data collection, interpreting data in a timely fashion) to present challenges. The chapters were silent on this issue either because the projects were logistically smooth or because reporting on that aspect was not central to the authors. Finally, in most cases, nonevaluator stakeholders were involved in a wide range of activities associated with the inquiry process. This was fairly consistent across at least five of the case examples.

And so, how does empowerment evaluation differ from other forms of collaborative inquiry? My current understanding is that this will depend on the particular empowerment evaluation approach one chooses to implement, which may in turn depend on which combination of principles are most important, given the needs of the local context and the impetus for the empowerment evaluation in the first place. Such flexibility is fine, I think, and it is admirable that empowerment evaluation enthusiasts are guided by a set of principles that help them to structure their interrelations with members of the nonevaluator stakeholder community. But on another level more needs to be known about when one approach might be superior to another. Most of Fetterman's practical experiences with empowerment evaluation that I have read about center on the three-step approach. Is that because he developed that approach and is most familiar and comfortable with it? Or is it because it is the most sensible approach given the kinds of evaluation and program development contexts that he encounters and the questions that are asked? Wandersman and colleagues (in Chapter 2) are somewhat guided by steps in the GTO program development, implementation, and evaluation framework. Why is that the case? It struck me that the approach taken by Lentz et al. was very much grounded in the needs of the local context, although I sensed some implicit similarities to the GTO model. I think this is a redeeming feature of any approach to evaluation. I personally have never actually implemented an evaluation on the basis of the dictates of a particular model or approach. It is the exigencies of the local context that must remain paramount. Yet, I know that when I set out to undertake a participatory evaluation in the context of providing needed information to inform program planning and problem solving and program improvement, the approach that I will take will be quite distinct from that invoked by a colleague working on a community development project in an underdeveloped country where self-determination and mobilization for planned social action are the driving forces behind the evaluation. Those differences will chiefly manifest in who is involved in the evaluation from the nonevaluator stakeholder community, what sorts of conflict might arise and how that will be handled, and how feasible or manageable the project will be. I think more needs to be known about what kinds of empowerment evaluation approaches should be followed under what sorts of circumstances.

HOW GOOD IS GOOD ENOUGH?

Demonstrating how empowerment evaluation adheres to its basic principles, as has been the primary motivation of the case examples presented in this collection, is certainly one route to identifying quality. It must be understood, however, as empowerment evaluation proponents have made clear, that different principles will come into play in different situations. From my point of view, however, the answer to the question of quality resides in the extent to which authors can provide persuasive evidence that the empowerment evaluation approach fulfills the claims that it makes. This, of course, will come as no surprise to empowerment evaluation enthusiasts. Fetterman (2004, p. 306) quotes Zimmerman on the matter: "The process is empowering if it helps people develop skills so that they can become independent problem solvers and decision makers." Fetterman himself remarks, "When specified outcomes are achieved, it is possible to retrace steps to determine which processes were most effective" (2004, p. 307). That being said, it is important that empowerment evaluation outcomes be operationalized, measured, observed, and analyzed. Achieving all that, however, is not an easy undertaking.

Over the years through our work on evaluation utilization and P-PE, we have developed a conceptual framework for thinking about the nature, conditions for, and consequences of participatory evaluation (Cousins, 2003). In that framework consequences are conceptualized according to conventional evaluation utilization constructs such as instrumental, conceptual, and symbolic use of findings. Use of process is another component, conceived at the individual, group, and organizational levels. Such concepts form the basis of the links made between P-PE and organizational learning. Beyond thinking about evaluation utilization are the more amorphous and temporally distant knowledge utilization constructs. These include such concepts as enlightenment, empowerment, liberation, emancipation, and self-determination.

All things considered, it is comparatively easy to operationalize evaluation utilization concepts as consequences. It would be of interest for empowerment evaluation evaluators to conceptualize outcomes of empowerment evaluation in this way and to demonstrate the links to its processes. As an example, in the FFF case in the Keener et al. chapter (Chapter 4), such evidence is available concerning the notion of institutionalizing evaluation within the organization. Through training and experience with empowerment evaluation the evaluation/collaboration manager developed significant evaluation skills and then moved on. It was relatively easy for the organization to train someone to take the place of the original manager. This might be thought of as an example of process use at the organizational level. In my view, it would be advantageous for empowerment evaluation proponents to consciously and systematically capture such utilization effects of empowerment evaluation, thereby documenting the potency of the approach in producing them. Documenting effects such as liberation, emancipation, self-determination, I think, would be much more difficult to do. Nevertheless, it is important for empowerment evaluation proponents to capture more concrete expressions of impact.

But at some level that is what this volume is about. The principles of empowerment evaluation are developed and then case examples are provided to illustrate how these principles manifest themselves in practice. You will notice that I consistently use the phrase "case example," as opposed to "case study." I would argue that a case study is the product of intensive systematic inquiry that involves systematic data gathering, processing, analysis, and interpretation, be those data qualitative observations, interviews, document reviews, or quantitative outputs from field surveys using questionnaires, or a mix of the two. The selected mode of inquiry utilized in the current collection is not unlike much of that which appears in the evaluation literature of late. I would choose to refer to these glimpses into evaluation practice as reflective narratives or essays grounded in observations and experiences of the narrator(s). These are entirely rich and vivid ways of knowing about practical phenomena and, in my view, have considerable value in uncovering the subtle nuances and complex interrelationships among variables. They are limited, however, in that they tell a story from a particular point of view and they are directly a function of the story telling capabilities of the narrator. To the extent that multiple authors from multiple stakeholder perspectives participate in the telling of the story, the narrative becomes even more enriched. This I believe to be the case with the Keener et al. chapter (Chapter 4) and that by Lentz et al. (Chapter 7). Regardless, there exist deeper and more powerful and penetrating ways to understand the nature, causes, and consequences of complex phenomena in practice.

My challenge to empowerment evaluation enthusiasts is to invest heavily in the prospect of empirical inquiry into empowerment evaluation by engaging in established modes of research that have explicit cannons for determining the trustworthiness, validity, and reliability of interpretations arising from the data. Qualitative research designs involving dependable comparative methods, comparative case studies, and longitudinal single-case studies are options for consideration. Quantitative field surveys of practices and effects would assist greatly in learning more about empowerment evaluation implementation and the consequences that it helps bring about. Mixed-method designs have enormous potential for laying bare observed relationships and interrelationships and corroborating their existence. For each of these a clear specification of methods of inquiry used and steps taken to ensure trustworthiness of the data would serve to strengthen claims that would arise from the research.

OTHER MUSINGS FROM A CRITICAL FRIEND

This exercise has been very helpful for me in clarifying many aspects of empowerment evaluation that were previously enigmatic. I conclude the chapter with some final thoughts about the approach and suggestions for consideration.

Defining "Evaluation" in Empowerment Evaluation

I am struck that in this volume the term "evaluation" is never really addressed in the definition of empowerment evaluation. Most would tend to agree that evaluation is the formulation of judgments about the merit, worth, or significance of a program on the basis of systematic inquiry. When we make a judgment, we make a comparison between observations of program implementation and effects against something. That something can be another program or set of programs, some external standard of program performance, or it can even be a comparison against itself at an earlier point in time.

Empowerment evaluation has strong links to program development, and this is clearly acknowledged among the case examples, I think. But such ties leaves empowerment evaluation open to the claim that it is not truly evaluation but some sort of "change agentry" with strong development and implementation interests integrated with a regime of evidence-based inquiry. If program development and implementation are indeed key elements of the approach, as would seem to be the case according to the current definition of empowerment evaluation stipulated above, why not reflect that in the nomenclature (e.g., using the term EDIE, Empowerment Development, Implementation, and Evaluation)? Personally, I think that empowerment evaluation identity would benefit from a more concerted attempt to integrate "evaluation" into its basic definition than is presently the case.

Self-Evaluation As the Root of All Goodness

The most powerful aspect of empowerment evaluation for me is its obvious commitment to and power in developing among members of the program community the capacity for self-evaluation. This I see as process use, as opposed to the more distant and amorphous term "empowerment." In any case, it has become clear to me that the more we can involve program practitioners as the judges of their own programs, the more potent will be the evaluation in bringing about program improvement. This is a strength, I think, of all forms of collaborative inquiry, but one that is particularly central to the empowerment evaluation approach.

Diversity of Method

Empowerment evaluation as described by Fetterman (2001) was a bit vague about methods of systematic inquiry but clear about methods for mission development, stock taking, and planning for the future. It struck me that some methodological choices might be very appropriate for at least some aspects of this process. For example, concept mapping (e.g., Trochim, 1989) would provide an excellent approach to mission development. Such an approach would be creative and potentially effective in tapping into everyone's input on a risk-free basis. Given espoused adherence to the principle of inclusion, depending on power relations, some participants might be highly reserved about sharing their true value positions with superiors or others with access to more power or privilege.

The Powers That Be

I think empowerment evaluation should be much more explicit about how differences among participants in terms of power relations and conflict are handled. Apart from the general principle of inclusion, I found little comment on just how program practitioners are selected for participation, why, and by whom. If the empowerment evaluation evaluator is operating in the role of critical friend, would it be appropriate for him or her to intervene in the case of dominant personalities or persons in positions of added responsibility and power intruding on the democratic process? How is this handled? I think this issue is central to successful empowerment evaluation. There were some anecdotes that touch on the issue among the case examples, but generally I see this point worthy of further inquiry.

Accountability Issues

As a final note, Fetterman and colleagues have made the case that empowerment evaluation represents an evaluation choice and in no way try to convey that it should replace more traditional forms of evaluation. I would agree. I have always maintained that the optimal use for P-PE would be within the improvement-oriented context. Sometimes, however, evaluation needs extend well beyond improvement into the summative domain. In such circumstances, where "hard-nosed" decisions and judgments about program funding, continuation, termination, expansion, and the like are needed, it is my view that collaborative evaluation approaches, with an inherent tendency toward self-serving bias, are less than adequate and inappropriate. Empowerment evaluation proponents cast the approach as a means for establishing accountability (Fetterman, 2001; Fetterman et al., 1996; Wandersman et al., Chapter 2). My sense is that they are referring to the situation where program practitioners need to be accountable to funders by demonstrating their commitment to self-reflection and improvement of services. I see empowerment evaluation as being particularly well positioned in this regard. But in the context of the tough-minded evaluation questions—Has the program met its stated objectives? Should program funding be continued? Should the program and all of its commitments to the gainful employment of managers and implementers be terminated?—I would argue that the approach should not be used.

A FINAL REMARK

Well, having completed my rather lengthy analytical critical-friend journey, I am a little bit uncertain whether I have provided the kinds of insight that Wandersman and Fetterman sought from me when they invited me to contribute to this volume. I know they were interested in challenges and questions that I might have, and I trust that I have delivered on that score. But I think also they wanted to know how I would differentiate empowerment evaluation from other forms of collaborative and participatory evaluation. While I believe I have a better idea about that now, the concept still remains a little bit fuzzy. I do see empowerment evaluation as being more intimately and explicitly connected with the interests of program development and implementation than other forms of collaborative evaluation familiar to me. While, for example, I see practical participatory evaluation as a viable and effective means of fostering program improvement and development, I am not of the view that strong program development skills would be essential to an evaluator's wanting to bring that about. I am less certain that this would be the case with regard to the empowerment evaluation aficionado. In any case, I do see empowerment evaluation as a powerful stimulus to self-evaluation within the program community—and that is a principle that I hold in high esteem—and I remain committed to monitoring its continued evolution over the years to come.

ACKNOWLEDGMENT

A previous version of this chapter was presented at the annual meeting of the American Evaluation Association in Reno, Nevada in November 2003.

NOTE

1. The figure and ensuing description are adapted from Weaver and Cousins (2003).

REFERENCES

Alkin, M. C., & Christie, C. A. (2004). An evaluation theory tree. In M. C. Alkin (Ed.), *Evaluation roots: Tracing theorists' views and influences* (pp. 12–65). Thousand Oaks, CA: Sage.

Barrington, G. V. (1999). Empowerment goes large scale: The Canada Prenatal Nutrition Experience. *Canadian Journal of Program Evaluation* (Special Issue), 179–192.

Brunner, I., & Guzman, A. (1989). Participatory evaluation: A tool to assess projects and empower people. In R. F. Connor & M. H. Hendricks (Eds.), *International innovations in evaluation methodology: New directions for program evaluation* (No. 42, pp. 9–17). San Francisco: Jossey-Bass.

Cousins, J. B. (2003). Utilization effects of participatory evaluation. In T. Kellaghan, D. L. Stufflebeam, & L. A. Wingate (Eds.), *International handbook of educational evaluation* (pp. 245–265). Boston: Kluwer.

Cousins, J. B. (2004). Crossing the bridge: Toward understanding use through empirical inquiry. In M. C. Alkin (Ed.), *Evaluation roots: Tracing theorists' views and influences* (pp. 319–330). Thousand Oaks, CA: Sage.

Cousins, J. B., & Earl, L. M. (Eds.). (1995). *Participatory evaluation in education: Studies in evaluation use and organizational learning.* London: Falmer Press.

Cousins, J. B., & Whitmore, E. (1998). Framing participatory evaluation. In E. Whitmore (Ed.), *Participatory evaluation approaches: New directions in evaluation* (No. 81, pp. 5–23). San Francisco: Jossey-Bass.

Fetterman, D. M. (2001). *Foundations of empowerment evaluation.* Thousand Oaks CA: Sage.

Fetterman, D. M. (2004). Branching out or standing on a limb?: Looking at our roots for insight. In M. C. Alkin (Ed.), *Evaluation roots: Tracing theorists' views and influences* (pp. 304–318). Thousand Oaks, CA: Sage.

Fetterman, D. M., Kaftarian, S., & Wandersman, A. (Eds). (1996). *Empowerment evaluation: Knowledge and tools for self assessment and accountability* Thousand Oaks, CA: Sage.

Lee, L. (1999). Building capacity for school improvement through evaluation: Experiences of the Manitoba School Improvement Program Inc. *Canadian Journal of Program Evaluation, 14*(2), 155–178.

McTaggart, R. (1991). Principles for participatory action research. *Adult Education Quarterly, 41*(3), 168–187.

Meier, W. (1999). *In search of indigenous participation in education sector studies in sub-Saharan Africa.* Unpublished master's thesis, University of Ottawa.

Owen, J. M., & Lambert, F. C. (1995). Roles for evaluation in learning organizations. *Evaluation, 1*(2), 237–250.

Patton, M. Q. (1997b). *Utilization-focused evaluation: The new century text* (3rd ed.). Newbury Park, CA: Sage.

Preskill, H., & Torres, R. (1999). *Evaluative inquiry for organizational learning.* Twin Oaks, CA: Sage.

Schnoes, C. J., Murphy-Berman, V., & Chambers, J. M. (2000). Empowerment evaluation applied: Experiences, analysis, and recommendations from a case study. *American Journal of Evaluation, 21*(1), 53–64.

Trochim, W. (1989). An introduction to concept mapping. *Evaluation and Program Planning, 12,* 1–16.

Wandersman, A. (1999). Framing the evaluation of health and human service programs in community settings: Assessing progress. *New Directions for Evaluation, 83,* 95–102.

Wandersman, A., Imm, P., Chinman, M., & Kaftarian, S. (2000). Getting to outcomes: A results-based approach to accountability. *Evaluation and Program Planning, 23,* 389–395.

Weaver, L., & Cousins, J. B. (2003). *Unpacking the participatory process.* Unpublished manuscript, University of Ottawa (currently under review for publication).

CHAPTER 9

Conclusion

CONCEPTUALIZING EMPOWERMENT
IN TERMS OF SEQUENTIAL TIME AND SOCIAL SPACE

David M. Fetterman

This collection provided a group of seasoned empowerment evaluators
with a rare opportunity to share their common understandings about
the principles of empowerment evaluation in practice. The introduction provided a common language in which to communicate about the
principles in practice. The principles chapter made the values guiding
empowerment evaluation explicit. The practice and case example chapters
provided insights into the application of these principles in real-world settings, including organizational settings. The entire collection provided an
intellectual foundation for this concluding discussion about empowerment. It is conceptualized within the dimensions of time and space.

TIME

Time is one of the dimensions in which empowerment is conceived and
discussed. There is a logical sequence or timely order to the application of
empowerment evaluation principles. Although there is no absolute order
to the principles, and an alternative sequencing could be legitimately

argued, the reasoning behind our own selection used in this book is presented next, focusing on the logical sequence of the principles.

A brief discussion about one logical approach to the empowerment evaluation principles helps to elucidate the process and to guide practitioners in the field. The first principle, improvement, reflects the pragmatic and utilitarian nature of empowerment evaluation. The aim is to help people improve their programs and practice and succeed in accomplishing their objectives. Community ownership is required to make this happen in a meaningful and sustained manner. This is linked to process use. The more people take ownership of the evaluation, the more committed they are to using the evaluation findings and following through on the recommendations. Authentic community ownership requires inclusion. It cannot be a single elite group making all the decisions. People from all parts of the organization and/or community need to be included. Participation from many stakeholders, including those typically marginalized or excluded, is critical if the effort is to be credible and taken seriously. It is also more efficient to include major stakeholders at the beginning rather than having to revisit each of the issues every time a new group is invited to participate in the group.

Democratic participation follows logically from inclusion. While inclusion brings people together, democratic participation shapes the nature of the interaction. It enhances the quality of the endeavor. Everyone gets a vote or a voice in the decision-making process. This makes the process credible, fair, and transparent. It also creates an environment conductive to inquiry, debate, and action. Democratic participation is the intellectual caffeine of empowerment evaluation. It is also a training ground for group decision making in the future, since people have to make their case with evidence and listen to one another as they deliberate and sift through the data to make their decisions. It is a place for thoughtful inquiry, debate, and decisive action.

Social justice could be considered the first step as easily as the fifth. It is the guiding light that reminds us of the purpose of our efforts. Typically we are concerned about equity or, more specifically, inequity. It might be social, economic, or environmental in nature. Racial tolerance, educational equity, violence prevention, or peace keeping may all be themes shaping both the program and the evaluation. However, many programs do not make an explicit statement about social justice. It is often an implicit and subtle force in the community's life. A teenage pregnancy prevention program may not make a formal declaration about its role in improving the economic, educational, and social conditions of youths and/or minority youths, but the underlying social justice agenda is present and easily traced to the rationale for creating the program. Therefore, while a reasonable argument can be made for making social justice the first principle it is reasonable and realistic to view it as the next stage of consciousness after people have been engaged in a democratic form of participation. Democratic participation creates a structure for higher-level thinking about issues such as social justice.

Democratic participation and social justice are both principles and value statements. They focus on communities and their needs. Democratic participation and a social justice orientation create an environment that fosters an open exchange of views and positions. This is conductive to planning, problem solving, and taking action. The community knowledge principle is in alignment with these principles. It values the community's insights and understandings. It places the community at the center of the dialogue. This culturally contextualized setting sets the stage for a consideration of evidence-based strategies. The community knowledge needs to be the baseline or context in which to meaningfully interpret, adopt, or adapt evidence-based strategies. The community knowledge is required to determine what evidence-based strategies are appropriate for the community. Community-based knowledge is also needed to determine how to apply evidence-based strategies to community concerns appropriately. Ignoring community-based knowledge is not only insensitive and arrogant, it is wrong and inefficient.

The use of evidence-based strategies in conjunction or contextualized by community knowledge is one of the unique features of empowerment evaluation. Instead of starting with a tabula rasa each time and reinventing the wheel, evidence-based strategies provide communities with tools and programs that have proven to be effective in similar settings. They should not be adopted blindly and without adaptation to the local community. They should be used appropriately. However, appropriate use of evidence-based strategies can save time and resources and ensure more effective implementation.

Capacity building is the product of engaging in the evaluation as a community of learners with the aim of improving practice, valuing community knowledge, and experimenting with evidence-based strategies. Individuals and groups learn new skills. They learn how to conduct their own evaluations. The terms baseline, pre- and posttest, survey, interview, outcome, and impact become familiar to them. They also learn how to think in terms of an evaluative perspective, which includes a baseline, intervention or treatment, formative feedback, and outcomes. Evaluative capacity building often translates into program capacity building, since evaluation becomes part of program planning and management.

Organizational learning requires the development of an evaluative capacity. An evaluative capacity is the product of a synergistic interplay between community knowledge and evidence-based strategies, which promote sensitivity, relevance, rigor, and improvement. An inclusive learning organization characterized by democratic forms of participation also promotes organizational learning.

Accountability becomes meaningful when most of these principles are in force. These principles foster a sense of internal accountability, particularly when community ownership is operating and community knowledge is used to guide and temper evidence-based strategies. A social justice agenda also provides both an internal and external framework for accountability.

A discussion about the sequence or logical order of the principles is instructive. It organizes a host of ideas and concepts within a sequentially structured and linear dimension of time. It is not designed to be an absolute or restrictive way of conceptualizing empowerment evaluation. No two empowerment evaluations are (or should be) exactly the same. This time-oriented manner of conceptualizing empowerment evaluation is, however, a recipe or formula for action. A recipe provides some guidelines and a set of instructions that makes the end product identifiable as an empowerment evaluation.

Time is only one dimension. A step beyond this linear conceptualization is space. Empowerment evaluation and self-determination can also be conceived of in more fluid terms—specifically, the social space in which capacity building, self-determination, and empowerment take place.

SPACE

Empowerment evaluation rests on a foundation of participation from the community, the evaluator, and the funder. It is guided by the principles of empowerment evaluation, including improvement, community ownership, inclusion, democratic participation, social justice, community knowledge, evidence-based strategies, capacity building, organizational learning, and accountability. The quality and scope of a community's empowerment and self-determination are determined by (1) the level of engagement or participation in the evaluation and (2) the application of the principles of empowerment evaluation. The greater the degree of community, evaluator, and funder participation and the greater degree of use of empowerment evaluation principles in practice (in a systematic manner), the greater the resulting degree of empowerment and self-determination.

Empowerment and self-determination viewed as desired social outcomes can be visualized in terms of community capacity space. Empowerment and self-determination are fluid dimensions in a social container. The theory behind this process can be visualized as the volume of a three-dimensional cylinder. The quality and scope of empowerment in the community rises as more of the participants are engaged and more principles are applied to the engagement. Empowerment from this vantage point is a fluid form of social capital and capacity. It is depicted in Figure 9.1.

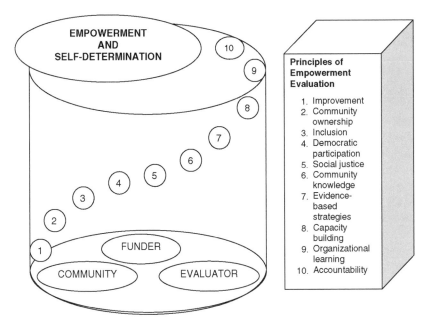

FIGURE 9.1. This is visual representation of the fluid capacity of empowerment and self-determination in a social container. The community, funder, and evaluator provide structural integrity for the container. They are also part of the mix. The 10 principles guide the collaboration. The interaction among the participants and the principles results in a rising level of empowerment and self-determination.

CONCLUSION

Empowerment evaluation is only a decade old. In this short period of time it has become a part of the intellectual landscape of evaluation. It helped launch the Collaborative, Participatory, and Empowerment Topical Interest Group in the American Evaluation Association. Empowerment evaluation is also an entry in social science and evaluation encyclopedias. It has been used throughout the globe, including the United Kingdom, Finland, South Africa, Brazil, the United States, and many other countries. Within the United States, Native Americas, African Americans, Latinos, Pacific Islanders, whites, and many other groups have used it in their communities to build capacity and get to outcomes. The types of programs applying this approach is equally enormous, including drug prevention and teenage pregnancy prevention programs, HIV prevention programs, battered women's shelters, tribal partnerships for substance abuse and technological development, and full-inclusion programs for children with disabilities. It has been used in K–12, higher education, hospitals, government, private industry, synagogues, and foundations. Empowerment evaluation is even used in the title of recent requests for proposals and grant submissions, such as the Center for Disease Control's "Empowerment Evaluation and Sexual Violence Prevention."

This widespread acceptance and use of empowerment evaluation is gratifying. It is part of a larger wave of change in which people want to take charge of their own lives and communities. This collection reflects empowerment evaluation at its current stage of development, and, as such, this third book devoted exclusively to the approach to date[1] must stand on its own merits. This product of a dedicated community of learners represents one more building block in the development of knowledge[2] in empowerment evaluation. This book represents an important social space to engage in the dialogue about empowerment evaluation and self-determination. It is our hope that, as we conclude our dialogue in this collection, we initiate a new one about empowerment evaluation in your community.

NOTES

1. The two earlier volumes (Fetterman, 2001; Fetterman, Kaftarian, & Wandersman, 1996) focus exclusively on empowerment evaluation. Suarez-Balcazar and Harper (2004) is an excellent collection with a combined focus on empowerment and participatory approaches.
2. See Chelimsky (1997) for a discussion of the multiple purposes of evaluation, including knowledge generation and development.

REFERENCES

Chelimsky, E. (1997). The political environment of evaluation and what it means for the development of the field. In E. Chelimsky & W. Shadish (Eds.), *Evaluation for the 21st century: A handbook*. Thousand Oaks, CA: Sage.

Fetterman, D. M. (2001). *Foundations of empowerment evaluation*. Thousand Oaks, CA: Sage.

Fetterman, D. M., Kaftarian, S., & Wandersman, A. (Eds.). (1996). *Empowerment evaluation: Knowledge and tools for self-assessment and accountability*. Thousand Oaks, CA: Sage.

Suarez-Balcazar, Y., & Harper, G. W. (Eds.). (2004). *Empowerment and participatory evaluation of community interventions: Multiple benefits*. New York: Haworth Press.

Author Index

Subject Index

About the Editors

David M. Fetterman (PhD, Stanford University) is President of Fetterman & Associates, an international consulting firm, and Consulting Professor of Education and a member of the accreditation team in the School of Medicine at Stanford University. Formerly he served as Director of Evaluation, Career Development, and Alumni Relations and as Director of the MA Policy Analysis and Evaluation Program, both in the School of Education at Stanford University. Dr. Fetterman is the past president of the American Anthropological Association's Council on Anthropology and Education and of the American Evaluation Association (AEA), and has received both the Paul Lazarsfeld Award for Outstanding Contributions to Evaluation Theory and the Myrdal Award for Cumulative Contributions to Evaluation Practice—the AEA's highest honors. He consults for organizations ranging from the U.S. Department of Education and the Centers for Disease Control and Prevention to the W. K. Kellogg Foundation, and provides consultations throughout the United States, the United Kingdom, Brazil, Japan, Finland, and South Africa. Dr. Fetterman has contributed to a variety of encyclopedias and is the author of numerous books in evaluation and in ethnography, including *Foundations of Empowerment Evaluation*; *Empowerment Evaluation: Knowledge and Tools for Self-Assessment and Accountability*; *Speaking the Language of Power: Communication, Collaboration, and Advocacy*; *Ethnography: Step by Step* (2nd edition); *Qualitative Approaches to Evaluation in Education: The Silent Scientific Revolution*; *Excellence and Equality: A Qualitatively Different Perspective on Gifted and Talented Education*; *Educational Evaluation: Ethnography in Theory, Practice, and Politics*; and *Ethnography in Educational Evaluation*.

Abraham Wandersman (PhD, Cornell University) is Professor of Psychology at the University of South Carolina–Columbia and was interim Co-Director of the Institute for Families in Society at the University of South Carolina. Dr. Wandersman performs research and program evaluation on citizen participation in community organizations and coalitions and on interagency collaboration. He is currently co-principal investigator on a participatory research study of an empowerment evaluation system, funded by the Centers for Disease Control and Prevention (CDC), and is working on a project for the program implementation and dissemination branch of the CDC center for injury prevention to facilitate a process and develop a framework on "how to bring what has been shown to work in child maltreatment prevention and youth violence prevention into more widespread practice." Dr. Wandersman is a coauthor of *Prevention Plus III* and a coeditor of *Empowerment Evaluation: Knowledge and Tools for Self-Assessment and Accountability,* among many other books and articles. In 1998, he received the Myrdal Award for Cumulative Contributions to Evaluation Practice from the American Evaluation Association. In 2000, he was elected President of Division 27 of the American Psychological Association (Community Psychology): The Society for Community Research and Action.

Contributors

Christine Barron (MD, State University of New York Health Science Center) is Clinic Director of the ChildSafe Child Protection Program, Department of Pediatrics, at Hasbro Children's Hospital (HCH), and Assistant Professor of Pediatrics at Brown University Medical School. She completed her pediatric residency at HCH in 1998. Dr. Barron held a fellowship in child abuse and neglect at HCH, where her clinical responsibilities included the evaluation of children for physical abuse, sexual abuse, neglect, failure to thrive, and factitious illness by proxy. She was recruited in July 2000 to establish the Child Protection Program at UMass Memorial Children's Medical Center and returned to Brown University in February 2004. As Clinic Director for the ChildSafe program, Dr. Barron oversees all its clinical aspects, including the training of fellows.

J. Bradley Cousins (PhD, University of Toronto) is Professor of Educational Administration at the Faculty of Education, University of Ottawa. His research program and graduate teaching reflect a strong commitment to educational field development. Dr. Cousins' main academic interests are participatory evaluation, evaluation use, and evaluation capacity building. In 1999 he received the prestigious Contributions to Evaluation in Canada award from the Canadian Evaluation Society in recognition of his research, practice, and development with students in the domain of evaluation. He is Editor of the *Canadian Journal of Program Evaluation* and the author of several articles and books, including *Participatory Evaluation in Education* (with Lorna M. Earl) and *Participatory Evaluation Up Close: An Integration of Research-Based Knowledge* (currently being completed).

David M. Fetterman (see "About the Editors").

Paul Flaspohler (PhD, University of South Carolina) is Assistant Professor of Psychology at Miami University. Before joining the faculty at Miami University, Dr. Flaspohler was a Peace Corps volunteer in West Africa and taught math, science, and English in Ghana and Liberia.

Pamela S. Imm (PhD, University of South Carolina) has extensive experience in the areas of program development, program evaluation, and applied research. Dr. Imm works with local community-based coalitions to help them integrate evaluation and research-based concepts into their work. She has published in the areas of alcohol and drug abuse prevention, evaluation research, and models of effective programming, and is coauthor of *Getting to Outcomes (GTO): Methods and Tools for Planning, Self-Assessment, and Accountability.* This empowerment evaluation manual, funded as a joint project of the Center for Substance Abuse Prevention and the National Center for the Advancement of Prevention, was awarded Best Self-Help Manual by the American Evaluation Association in 2001 and is now available in an updated edition (2004).

Noreen P. Johnson received her master's degree in public health from the University of Massachusetts in 1998. She is currently vice president for programs at The Health Foundation of Central Massachusetts and has served as director of the Massachusetts Prevention Center System for the Massachusetts Department of Public Health and as a professor of health education at the National Teacher's Training College in the Central African Republic. Ms. Johnson has extensive experience in program administration, prevention, coalition building, and program evaluation. Her commitment to public health includes current service as director of the Public Health Museum and previous service as director and treasurer of the Central Massachusetts HIV/AIDS Consortium, president of a local League of Women Voters, president of a parent–teacher organization, and member of a historical commission and numerous advisory boards.

Dana C. Keener is completing her doctorate in clinical–community psychology at the University of South Carolina. She is currently a psychology intern at the Center for Mental Health at the Reading Hospital and Medical Center in Reading, Pennsylvania, and has worked as an empowerment evaluator with family support and family literacy programs and programs for adolescent mothers. Ms. Keener is particularly interested in the process of collaboration and service integration between multiple service agencies.

Barry E. Lentz is an independent scholar and principal of Action Research Associates, a consulting firm that provides research, evaluation, planning, and development services for health and human service providers, educational institutions, community coalitions, and government agencies at the local, state, and national levels. He has extensive experience as a researcher and practitioner in the experimental analysis of behavior and applied learning theory, strategic narrative and educational storytelling, social reconstruction, organizational learning, knowledge creation, and community development. A recent focus of his work involves employing empowerment evaluation to foster the development of evidence-based prevention interventions that result in systems-wide change.

Melanie Livet is completing her doctorate in clinical–community psychology at the University of South Carolina. She is currently the Lead Evaluator for the Center for Public Health Preparedness at the University of South Carolina (USC-CPHP), which was created to prepare the nation's public health workforce to recognize and respond to acts of bioterrorism and other public health emergencies.

Prior to joining USC-CPHP, Ms. Livet worked as an evaluator and consultant with a number of community projects using both participatory and empowerment evaluation paradigms. She is particularly interested in the role of organizational characteristics in program planning, implementation, and evaluation, and in bridging the gap between the program evaluation and organizational development fields.

Margie Simone Lindberg received her master's degree in psychology from Assumption College in Worcester, Massachusetts. She has worked in the child welfare field for more than 20 years as a social worker, supervisor, and manager, and was the Program Director for the Central Massachusetts Child Abuse Prevention/ Protection Collaborative during the implementation phase. Currently employed as a consultant for the Commonwealth of Massachusetts Department of Social Services, Ms. Simone Lindberg has extensive experience in clinical case practice, program development, foster care, and adoption. For the past four years, she has directed "Team Fresh Start," a pilot foster care program for infants, and has published articles on the program's innovative approach.

Jessica Snell-Johns is completing her doctoral degree in clinical–community psychology at the University of South Carolina. Ms. Snell-Johns is a program evaluator and an individual and family therapist. Her publications have focused on a variety of topics, including the roles assumed by community coalitions when creating policy-level change; the application of change strategies in community settings; empowerment evaluation as a participatory research method; and evidence-based strategies for reaching underserved families. She is the coauthor of an evaluation manual entitled *Evaluation from the Start: An Evaluation Guidebook for Fatherhood Programs*.

Joanne Treistman received a master's degree in child development from Bryn Mawr College and a Master of Public Health degree from the University of Massachusetts School of Public Health. Ms. Treistman has worked as a research analyst and project coordinator with a health maintenance organization and community health center. She is Adjunct Professor in Child Study at Quinsigamond Community College and works with the March of Dimes and Shaken Baby Syndrome Prevention Campaign of Central Massachusetts.

Abraham Wandersman (see "About the Editors").

Janice B. Yost (PhD, University of Georgia) became the founding President of The Health Foundation of Central Massachusetts in 1999, a grantmaking organization resulting from the sale of a nonprofit, physician-initiated HMO. In 1998, Dr. Yost codeveloped with Dr. Abraham Wandersman a planning and evaluation system called Results-Oriented Grantmaking and Grant-Implementation. This system applies an empowerment evaluation orientation whereby program developers are provided with forms for facilitating the program planning, assessing the program implementation, and documenting the results of the program, with the funder and evaluator partners providing interactive support throughout the process. Dr. Yost has also been a college professor and an administrator, including serving as Associate Chancellor for University Relations at the University of South Carolina–Spartanburg campus.